Born in the United Kingd
Aluko LLB, B.L., MA (La
storytelling from her early teens, having been largely
influenced by her parents, who instilled in her the love
for reading and writing.

She began her law career in Nigeria, West Africa,
and progressed to complete her master's degree in
Migration and Law at the world-class research
institution, Queen Mary's University of London.

A writer by night, Olivia is the author of two
academic books: *Africans in the UK: Migration,
Integration and Significance* and *Globalisation, Human
Security and Social Inclusion*.

Olivia enjoys reading, travelling, dancing, and live
concerts, particularly old school music and jazz. *Life in
the Abrodi* is her debut novel, and she is currently
working on her second.

Thanks for your Support 11/09/2021. nay

Olivia Olajide Aluko

LIFE IN THE
ABRODI

OLIVIA OLAJIDE ALUKO

ABSOLUTE AUTHOR

Published by

Absolute Author Publishing House
1123 Williams Blvd, New Orleans, LA 70003

Absolute Author is an imprint of Absolute Author Publishing House

A CIP catalogue record for this book is available from the
British Library.

ISBN 978-1-64953-288-6

Cover design by Aisha
Edited and typeset by Tokunbo Emmanuel

Printed in the United Kingdom

To my sons, Isaac and Stephen, for your technical support with my laptop and patience as I devoted time to this book. Thanks for believing in your mum! I love you guys to the moon and back!

To my selfless mother, Mrs Ekundayo Aluko, the grammarian! You continue to inspire me. You are the best!

To all my readers. I hope you find reading this book as inspiring as I found writing it.

1

Home, sweet home. Akon meandered through the throng that swamped the baggage reclaim area. He was lucky his bags were one of the first set to come through the conveyor belt. *These same people were peaceful when boarding the plane back in London. Now they are a rowdy bunch!*

He had barely stepped out of the arrival lounge when he spotted Adebiyi running up to him. "Welcome, sir! Welcome, sir!" The effusive greetings in the local Yoruba language continued even as the man collected Akon's luggage. Akon reciprocated the greetings and was grateful for the help.

Mr. Adebiyi, Akon's driver, led the way to the car while Akon smiled at the warmth of the sun. Five weeks in the UK was a memorable experience, but

Akon preferred the blazing sun to the cloudy London weather.

Both men were a few metres from the car when Akon spotted his wife rushing to meet them. Akon wrapped his arms around her as she hugged him. Although surprised to see his wife, Akon was glad she came to meet him. He had not realised how much he missed his family.

"My darling husband!" Lara exclaimed in Yoruba. "Oh, I am so happy you are back. How are you? How was your flight? How was it over there? Did you have fun? How was the programme?"

"Lara, let's enter the car before you bombard me with a hundred questions," Akon said with a grin.

Lara blushed, stepped back, and entered the car, moving so that Akon could enter as well. Adebiyi finished loading the luggage into the boot, and soon they were on their way.

Akon turned to his wife. "How are you, my dear? You did not tell me you would meet me at the airport. What about Jabez?"

"I'm fine, dear. I decided to come at the last minute. I left Jabez at home with Maria. He missed you so much and wanted to come, but he was asleep when Adebiyi was about to leave. You know him, before you can wake him up..." Lara let the words trail off. Akon laughed, knowing exactly what his wife meant. Getting Jabez to wake up from sleep had always been a battle. Leaving him with their maid was surely the better option.

"Anyway, my flight was fine. The programme went well too." Akon's faux British accent amused Lara.

"Okay o, Mr Londoner. My husband is now a *Britico*."

Akon talked about his experiences in London. "It was pretty fun. I mean the programme and sightseeing, oh! Not the part where I had to learn how to prepare some dishes or do my laundry. The best discovery I made was the launderette close to where I stayed."

Lara chuckled. "I wish I had seen how my darling husband washed his clothes and cooked by himself."

"It wasn't easy, my dear. I cannot remember the last time I entered a bus in Nigeria, but I had to use trains to go almost everywhere. Of course, public transport was neater and less rowdy than what we have here, but it felt strange."

"Why didn't you just take taxis?"

"Ah, Lara, do you want me to go bankrupt?"

They laughed and continued chatting. Akon described the architecture and places he visited and could not help but remember his favourite place, the Soho Art Gallery. He remembered wishing that one day he would bring Lara to see it with him.

As they both got lost in thought, Akon remembered boarding the plane back to Nigeria. He had vowed that somehow, someday, he would move his family to the UK. He had even changed the lyrics of one of the songs he heard often in Nigeria: *"I've got my mind made up, and I'm not turning back. I'm going to live in London someday."*

He knew it would not be easy. In Nigeria, he belonged to the upper-middle class. Yet, he would only be a few steps above the poverty level in London. He would have to make sacrifices. He might have to leave Lara and Jabez in Nigeria until he secures a good job and a suitable place for them to live.

This was the reason why he had applied for the Highly Skilled Migrant Programme (HSMP). It would help him build highly needed skills in the UK and improve his job eligibility. But how would he tell his boss? The programme he had just completed was sponsored by the man, and Akon wondered how he would agree to take on the HSMP.

It was not likely, though, that his manager would agree, and Akon would have to refund the programme's fees. He will use some of his shares to pay off his boss's investment if he makes a fuss. *Where there is a will, there is a way.*

Akon would rather take his family to a better society where the police were helpful rather than connive with robbers to steal from ordinary citizens or collect bribes.

As if in agreement with his thoughts, the car slowed as a police officer flagged them down, stretching out his hand. Adebiyi quickly dipped his hand in the glove box and brought out a fifty naira note, which he handed to the officer.

Things will never change in this country, Akon thought, shaking his head. Then, he realised something. "Ade, where is the Peugeot? You know I don't like to drive the Lexus around except on special occasions."

"Ah, *oga*, I'm sorry. I thought since you were just coming from abroad, we should use the finer car."

Just as Akon prepared to reprimand him, Lara intervened. "I agree with him, dear. After all, you just returned from abroad and should do it in style." She winked at Akon, and he laughed. She added, "We took the other car back to the mechanic. They messed up the engine."

Mollified, Akon sat back and relaxed. He had not told Lara about the HSMP and had decided it was a conversation best had face-to-face. He hoped she would see its merit.

Akon was about to fall asleep when the car hit a pothole. He jumped up in confusion. "Sorry, sir," Adebiyi called out apologetically.

They moved slowly through the city's gridlock. The cars ahead were moving slowly. People around the world know how Lagos roads are often choked up like an overfed animal.

Throughout their journey, Akon observed, in horror, how drivers cut into different lanes like immortals, ignoring the traffic lights. Many cars should not be on the road. Some needed extensive bodywork. Drivers were swearing at one another and hooting their horns, narrowly missing the hawkers on the street, all of which were missing in London. It was cacophony here. Some of the vehicles were battered beyond operability.

Only in Nigeria would people dare drive without breaks and windscreens. In the gridlock, he saw two trailers blocking the road; the drivers hurled insults at each other.

"Bar wannan wurin, tafi," one driver screamed in Hausa, beads of sweat dripping from his body. The other driver yelled back. A vague sense of headache brewed as Akon watched the two men exchange insults.

Even at the airport, there were unnecessary checkpoints just to extort money from passengers. It was a nightmare, especially for foreigners. He chuckled as he replayed what happened to him while he was going through the customs checkpoint. Looking into the official's eyes, Akon had replied confidently, "Nothing dey, oga."

It was like morning stars turned to black cinders. They had lunged for his bags, putting them gently on the counter, trying every means to delay him.

"Ah, oga. I dey joke now. Take jare. Abeg, leave my bag oh," joked Akon, pulling out several naira notes from his coat pocket. They accepted the money and allowed him to go.

The gridlock eased a bit. Akon rubbed Lara's arm slowly. She did not push him away and did not look at him either, which amused Akon.

"I was asking what you liked most about London," Lara said. "Are you sure you are alright?" Akon nodded and smiled. Lara shook her head. "You haven't been here for six hours, and you look lost already."

"Well, the changes are enough to get me lost," Akon said.

"Changes? Lagos can never change. In this city, the colours are always the same—yellow with a touch of stress."

Akon laughed. He agreed. There was little change, and none of it was good. "It reminds me of London," He said. "I cannot but notice that I've just been to somewhere saner, a place where the noise doesn't make you feel like you are drowning."

"You make it sound so bad," Lara said, her brows coming together.

"It is bad," Akon replied. This was what he had missed most of all. Lara shook her head in disagreement. "You should have seen London, babe," Akon continued. "The roads are safe, no potholes, and the cities are beautiful. You get to watch matches live and jeez! You should taste their crunchy apples! Everything has an expiry date—the weather, food, music. It's like a fairy tale."

"Whoa! Calm down, hon," Lara said.

Akon sighed.

Their car was moving faster now. He watched Lara's face and wondered if she noticed what he was driving at. That would make his plan easier.

The city seemed better as they moved further into it. The lights made the streets colourful. He had been charmed by this city before, its burst of colours and the way it seemed to come alive. Akon remembered a time when he never wanted to leave. He could have sworn that he would spend the rest of his days in this city. He chuckled at the memory. *How naïve was he!*

Lagos was getting dry. It was late August, and the weather was being kind to the country after the heavy downpour of the previous months. Lara had complained about the many reports of floods.

They finally reached their residence. Adebiyi honked the horn as he approached the gate. Aminu, the gateman, ran to open the gate.

"Welcome, oga," he greeted happily in Yoruba as they drove in. He was grinning as if he was seeing Akon for the first time. Akon nodded weakly at the man. He was too tired to return the greeting in a similar enthusiastic manner. Aminu bowed and returned to his duty post. Adebiyi took Akon's luggage out of the car while the maid carried it inside the house. Akon thanked her as she took the bags.

Akon leaned on the sofa and smiled at Lara. *I'm blessed to have a woman like her*. Lara was a beautiful, slim woman, always well-behaved. Men gave him envious looks whenever he went out with her. She treated his family and friends with respect. She was also a prayerful and God-fearing woman. *But who knows? We have only been married for nine years; I guess it is too early to tell.*

Women can keep secrets. For all he knew, she may not be as innocent as she seemed. Sometimes, he wondered if she might be playing games behind that good girl facade. The thought of what happened to his best man, Taye, and how he ended up marrying a lady who wanted to use him as an opportunity to obtain a green card to the USA never left him.

Taye was his childhood friend, and the trauma of his broken marriage had destroyed him. He relocated to Canada and disconnected from everyone who knew him, even his mother and twin sister. Akon had vowed that he would never trust a woman again. He was still thinking about Taye when Lara said, "Akon in wonderland, why don't you freshen up and let's have dinner. Then you can tell me more about your experiences in London."

"I've missed you, beautiful," Akon said, winking as he gently drew her closer to him.

Lara blushed and said, "I will set the table then join you. Go ahead."

Akon went upstairs to freshen up in high spirits, whistling a love tune. Lara set the table hurriedly and went to their bedroom. She laid out a fresh change of clothes for him.

Akon stopped her, a smile on his face. "Hold on," he said.

Lara giggled. "It's two in the morning. Lower your voice, honey. You don't want to wake Jabez up."

Akon leaned over the side of the bed and opened his luggage. He brought out a black box and gave it to her. She opened it eagerly and gasped when she saw the silver necklace in the shape of the Tower of London.

"Oh my! It's so beautiful!" Lara exclaimed, tears brimming in her eyes.

"It is just my way of telling you I love you, Lara. And thank you, for staying with me all these years,"

Akon said before kissing her.

"I love you too," Lara replied as tears streamed down her cheeks.

Akon's tummy rumbled as he dashed towards the dining area. "That smells good," Akon said, perceiving the aroma of egusi soup. He sat at the table as Lara emerged with the food.

Akon opened one of the dishes, saw layers of Jollof and fried rice, and started whistling. "Iyan l'ounje' oka l'oogun," honey, please serve me pounded yam. Lara opened the second dish and served her husband before serving herself. They ate together, talked, and shared experiences.

"It seemed like you had been away for so long," Lara said.

"I missed you too," Akon replied, putting a fork of chicken into Lara's mouth.

"You must be so tired now," said Lara as Akon drank a glass of water. "Let us go upstairs." Lara called Maria to clear the table while they retired to their room.

The next day, Jabez bounded into their room, screaming in sheer delight.

"Daddy! I missed my daddy," Jabez screamed.

Akon sat up sleepily. "Hey, champ. How is my *son* doing?"

"Fine, daddy! I told mummy to wake me up

yesterday when you get home. She did not," Jabez huffed.

"Well, you needed a good night's rest, my prince."

"Where are my gifts, daddy? Did you get me any toys?" Jabez looked around with his big brown eyes.

"Yes, my boy. Come, I will show you." Akon took his hand and made to leave the room, careful not to wake Lara. Jabez pulled his hand back and gestured for him to bend down.

"You will never leave mummy and me alone, promise?" he sniffled.

"I will try my best, my prince," Akon hugged him. Sometimes it was hard to believe that Jabez was only five. He was so smart. *Well, that is the benefit of putting your child in an International quality school with an excellent educational curriculum paid for in dollars.*

"Now, let's get your toys."

*   *   *

"Don't worry, Adebiyi. We'll drive. You can take the day off," Lara told the driver. She and Akon had planned an afternoon outing. Jabez would not come along with them because he had to complete his homework.

Later that evening, Lara and Akon sat beside the pool at Lekki, the Beach Resort. Akon could not take his eyes off his wife as she laughed and sipped her drink. She had never looked more beautiful than she did now. He was having a hard time saying what he wanted to say. He did not want to hurt her.

"Hey, darling! Having a good time?" he asked, leaning over to kiss her. Lara blushed and smiled. She was not too comfortable with public displays of affection, even after being married for nine years. Akon loved to tease her and watch her blush.

"I have something to discuss with you, darling. I didn't want us to talk about it at home," Akon said, squeezing her hand gently.

Lara immediately became wary. "What is wrong, sweetie? I hope you're not planning to say something terrifying like there's another lady or something." Lara was pre-empting him.

"You know, before I left, I was so enchanted by the third mainland bridge. I liked how it looked like something imagined for a movie or a story. Then I went over there, and everything changed. I think it's because I saw something better," Akon explained.

"Like what?" Lara asked.

"In London, the nights are filled with lights, but they are ordered, unlike Lagos. There is no chaos there, so the neon lights show you just one thing—the brilliance of beauty," Akon continued.

"That sounds ordinary to me," Lara replied, and Akon laughed, shaking his head.

"It's not," he said. He would have to tell his wife about the plan, and he better do it quick. He had started it already, and it would not make sense for him to leave her out of it any longer.

Lara shrugged.

2

"At night, I walked the streets, flanked by neon lights. And after that, I went to galleries to view artwork and photographs. It was so new to me; it did not get old, even in the third week. It was..." He sighed and shook his head. Lara smiled. She was looking at him like she already knew where he was going. He grinned.

"We should move there," he said.

Lara shook her head. "I don't think it makes sense," she said. "I mean, we already have a life here." Akon nodded. He knew that was what she would say. "There is also the problem of time, love," Lara continued. "We don't know when Jabez and I would be able to join you. It could be three or five years. Would I have a husband at the end? Would Jabez have a father? Would you still be this enthusiastic about seeing me? I don't want to

21

lose what we have because of some uncertain greener pastures."

"Think about it though," Akon said, looking at her. The light on the balcony made her appear even more beautiful. "I wouldn't be going there to 'hustle' like other people, babe. I will be going through the Highly Skilled Migrant Programme. This will help me get the training and experience required. I will get a job, and in two years, you both can come when childcare isn't a problem anymore."

"Besides," he added, "I will be staying with Kay over there until I get a job and a place of my own."

"I don't think we have to move. We are comfortable here. If we travel abroad, things could turn out bad," Lara said. "Haven't we heard stories, dear?"

"Or don't you remember what happened to Peju? She was in the UK for almost a year, could not get a job and was eventually deported," Lara continued, with a concerned look on her face.

"Haba, Lara!" Akon responded. "Peju breached immigration rules. She went on a visiting visa and was caught working. That was why she was deported," he explained. "But I am not going illegally…"

"But what about Supo?" Lara cut in. "His wife went ahead and said she was going to send him an invitation to process their papers. What happened after two years?

Supo did not receive any invitation to join his wife. Instead, he received divorce papers!" Lara paused, wanting her point to sink in. "The wife met and married someone else in London. I can go on and on." Lara had become exasperated. She had a feeling her husband had already made up his mind.

"My dear," Lara persisted, "I don't want you, my husband, a whole manager of a prestigious company, to become a slave of anybody in the UK. I do not want you to join the bandwagon of people washing dead bodies in the mortuary to survive. These are stories we keep hearing about Nigerians living abroad. Think about it. To just throw all we have worked so hard for away in search of an uncertain future in a foreign land, sorry dear, I cannot see the sense in it. For holidays and for studies, yes. But to live there? I don't think it is worth the trouble. All that glitters is not really gold."

Akon moved closer to his wife and whispered in her ears, "Once we are out of the country, I would not be asked to take up the role of my father. I do not want to be a chief and practice fetish customs." He drew back and watched her reaction before continuing. "I want to live freely with my family and be myself, not what my extended family want me to be. Also, look at the pressure of corruption going on at work. You cannot even blow the whistle because almost everyone indulges in kickbacks."

Akon noticed the surprise on Lara's face. "Oh, you thought the directors sent me abroad for nothing or offered to transfer me to Port Harcourt to be a manager for nothing? It is all bribery, to dull my conscience and prevent me from exposing their financial misconducts. It is either I play ball, or they take me out, get me killed or something. It is that serious."

Akon drew Lara close to himself. "I agree we have built a good life here, but think about it, we are living in fear every day, always having to watch our backs. If it is not petty area boy thieves, it would be roadside police or armed robbers. Remember I was robbed at gunpoint last Christmas? If not for God, you may have become a widow and our son fatherless."

Lara took a deep sigh as Akon pulled away. "I understand, but I just don't want us to leave a life of certainty in our own country for uncertainty in a strange land," she said, slowly becoming convinced.

"It's a sacrifice worth making," Akon said. "Think about how much privacy we would have," Akon knew this part would interest Lara more. He knew how much she did not like his family's incessant requests and their rude attitude towards her. She never spoke about it, but he knew it was churning inside her. "We will never hear from anyone. It will just be you, Jabez, and me. No one else coming between us," he said. "I will have to resign from work when the application is approved, but you will see how easy things will be when we are settled over there. Babe, think about how good it will be for us financially if we stay abroad for just ten years and then move back after earning over there." Akon watched as his wife considered his proposition. He wondered if he should add the scary part.

"I've already sold some of my shares worth about a million naira for the application, honey," he confessed.

Lara's eyes widened in disbelief.

"But darling, just look at how insecure we are, living in fear every day. Is that a way to live? Remember how my dad was killed? Hired killers shot him dead and dumped his body in a forest. I'll never forget that night for as long as I live, Lara. The many times we have been robbed too. What if these same killers target me?"

"God forbid!" Lara softened visibly. "I'm sorry, darling," she said, drawing close to Akon. "I haven't thought about it that way. I understand your concerns. Fear of the unknown is my greatest worry." She sighed before asking her husband, "When are you planning to return?"

"In two months, when I hope to have finished tying up all loose ends."

"How would we break the news to Jabez? He made me promise that you would never go away again. He missed you so much, Akon. He'll be shattered."

"Don't worry. I'll tell Jabez." Akon promised.

"What if you are tempted to date other girls when you are lonely?" Lara asked tearfully. She feared those British ladies stealing her husband from her.

"I swear on my father's grave, darling. It will never happen. You are mine, and I am yours." Akon kissed her forehead. He recalled a conversation he had with Kay, his old school-friend who lived in London. Three days before he flew back to Lagos, the two had discussed Akon's plans to move to the city.

"So, what kind of man is your friend, Kay? Did you get on well?"

"Yes, we did. He was accommodating and generous. But perhaps he would have treated me differently if I had overstayed my welcome. London is different; you must ask for permission before you visit. You can't just burst into a conversation, and you have to learn to say, 'thank you' and 'sorry'. You cannot jump queues to enter the public transport. At the train station when you are fined for travelling without the right ticket, the ticket wardens remain polite. They still treat you with dignity; they are not like our *area boys*.

"However, I was unhappy when he prophesied doom for anyone trying to settle in London."

"Why?" Lara quizzed.

"He told me I was welcome to try, but it would be

an arduous journey."

"But hasn't he managed to settle there?"

"Yes, he has. What makes him think I can't handle the trouble if he can?"

"I've made up my mind, Kay. London is ready for Akon," Akon had said.

Kay had laughed. "London may be ready for Akon, but is Akon prepared for London? I know you've stayed here and enjoyed the city, Akon, but London is not Lagos. You need balls of steel to survive in London, my friend."

"But how have you survived here, Kay? Don't you want the same opportunities for me?"

Kay had sighed. "My friend, I have no time to tell you my story now, but I arrived in this country in 1999. Even though I was born a British national, it is different because I didn't grow up here. Every migrant has a story, but it is never a walk in the park. It is a journey of tears, struggles, hunger, and cold. It can wreak havoc on your ego, especially if you are a man. You are a manager in Lagos, aren't you? The UK doesn't give a damn about your African accolades, experience or status. You must leave them behind at the UK border. If you are not ready to swallow your pride and start from the bottom, you are not ready for London, Akon."

Akon had clenched his fists. "I will do everything in

my power to prove you wrong, Kay. I will succeed just the way you did. I know it won't be easy, but I come from a clan of fighters."

Kay had laughed at that. "So, all the others that came before you are not smart, right? We shall see." Akon had gone to bed, somewhat angry at Kay's attitude. *I'll show him what I'm made of. Does he think I cannot succeed? We shall see.*

"Kay offered me a piece of advice," Akon told his wife. "He said if I had made up my mind, then I'd better move there first and settle in before bringing my family over. He said it's easier that way."

"Okay, then. I agree," Lara said slowly.

"Thank you so much, darling. I promise you won't regret this," Akon said as he hugged her.

"I'll keep my fingers crossed," she replied, nodding uncertainly.

*   *   *

Four weeks had gone since Akon returned to Nigeria. It was a Tuesday but not an ordinary one. Akon had received a phone call from the British Embassy the previous day, inviting him to pick up his passport.

Waking up early, Akon felt a bit of anxiety. He wondered if the British embassy could decide to withdraw his application or deny him a visa.

Akon sneaked into the bathroom and did all he could not to wake Lara from sleep. He had told his driver, Adebiyi, that they would be going to the British embassy and he planned to get there in good time. Akon packed all his documents and dressed in a shirt and suit. He took one more look at the mirror, admiring his clean-shaven face before walking to the door.

"I thought we were going together," he heard Lara say.

"Not necessary babe. Remember you are going to work. I will tell you the good news on the phone and we can celebrate later at a restaurant." He managed mask the worry in his voice with a smile.

"Why are you counting your eggs before they are hatched?" Lara asked, smiling back at him.

"Am I? Are you not the one who preaches that we should have faith? O my wife of little faith!" Akon moved forward to plant a kiss on her forehead. A blush crept up on her the moment she felt Akon's lips and she pulled him closer and tried to kiss him.

Adebiyi's voice disrupted the love tangle.

"Good morning sir, good morning ma," he greeted with his head bowed. "Sir, I am ready when you are." Adebiyi turned and left them alone.

Akon kissed Lara and said his goodbye. He then stepped into the car where Adebiyi was waiting.

Within an hour, they arrived at the passport office, joining others who were already waiting for the door to be opened. Akon looked at the long line of people in the queue and shook his head. It was only 6:30 am and the embassy opened at 8:00 am.

Akon sat in the car listening to the radio, while his driver held the line for him, hoping to call for him when it was nearly his turn.

About thirty minutes later, Akon was next in line to enter the embassy. After all the security checks, he was ushered into a room.

"Please confirm your details again," the staff at the embassy said to Akon.

Akon felt some tightness in his stomach as he handed his drivers' license to prove his identity. The man at the embassy looked at his document and then stared at him with scrutiny, which made Akon's heart pound heavily.

"Congratulations mister Akete," the staff said before handing him his passport.

Akon was full of excitement as he raced to the parking lot.

"Yes babe, I got it! We got it!" Akon screamed into the phone as he broke the news to Lara. "Looking forward to seeing you soon so we can celebrate."

Akon could not stop himself from grinning ear to

ear as he made his way to the travel agency to pay for his travel ticket.

Later in the day, Akon picked up his wife and son and was more excited to break the news to Jabez, his son, after stopping at his favourite ice cream place.

"Dad, please do not leave me and mum alone, we would be scared." Jabez held Akon's hands tightly.

"Scared of what my prince?" he asked with mock concern.

"Armed robbers," Jabez said as his voice started to break.

Akon stroked Jabaz's head softly and tried to reassure him. "Jabez Olasubomi Akete, I will visit home every six months and within two years, you and your mum will join me," he said, trying to calm him down.

Akon had given Adebiyi the rest of the day off as he wanted to spend time with the family. He drove them back home from the ice cream place with tear-filled eyes, as he thought of how much he would miss them.

"Leave that to me, you know you can be a scatterbrain," Lara said to Akon. "I will prepare a list of everything you need to take along with you."

"I prefer to travel light," Akon said under his breath but Lara was not ready to listen. He had just a few days to tidy up before he left for the UK and she was not going to let him leave anything to chance.

"I was told I would not need many white shirts as their formal shirts in the corporate sector are mostly blue," Akon said to his wife, as he watched her pack his suitcase.

"Have you informed your boss?" Lara asked, ignoring his earlier comment.

"I plan to see him again tomorrow and finalise the discussion," he replied, while Lara continued to fix up his suitcase.

The following day Akon left for his workplace, arriving early as usual. He immediately made his way to the Director's office, wondering how he was going to take the news. He had previously sent an email but now he had to tell him in person.

"I am so sad to see you go. You have been an asset to the company," the director said. "We have invested a lot in you but will find someone else to replace you," he said with a weak smile. He knew it would be difficult.

"I will also pay up what I owe the company," Akon said quickly as he began to get emotional.

"Mr Akete, we cannot stop you from pursuing your dreams, even though we offered you the managerial position of our Port Harcourt office." The assistant to the director said to him with a stern look on his face, reminding him of the opportunities he had turned down.

Akon walked out of the building feeling sad to be leaving the company. At the same time, he was excited about the next chapter that lied ahead of him.

*   *   *

Akon checked his wristwatch. "We need to get going. It's almost half-past five. We should stop by at home to get Jabez. Mama will ask of her grandson."

"That's alright," Lara said.

Lara was always apprehensive whenever Akon suggested they visited his family. She could never please them. Right from the outset, Akon's family, especially his mother, had kicked against her relationship with their son. She has not yet accepted Lara as part of the family, even now that she is married to Akon. Whenever they visited, her mother-in-law never paid her any attention. She would not even acknowledge her greetings.

After Akon got married to Lara, his mum made it a habit to visit their house uninvited. She would make demands she knew Lara could not meet up with. One day, at about 1.00 am, she had woken Lara up and said, "I want to have pepper soup now; it helps me sleep."

"Pepper soup? But…" She did not allow Lara to finish her statement before throwing tantrums and hurling abuses at her. Lara was speechless as she fought back the tears that had formed in her eyes.

Akon was always caught in the middle. He knew he could not side with his mum because she was obviously wrong. He disliked how his mum treated his wife. Yet, he could not go against her because she would manipulate him and make him feel he was mistreating her. After all, her husband, his father, was dead. Akon's younger sister did not help matters either. She joined their mother to make Lara's life miserable. It got worse for Lara when she could not conceive after nine months of marriage. All hell was let loose on her.

On their way to visit Mama Akete, Lara recalled a particular visit her mother-in-law had paid them six years ago.

"Darling, Mama and Bose are coming over. Mama called me a few minutes ago," Akon informed his wife. They were seated at the kitchen table, and Lara wrote out a list of things that Maria, their maid, would buy at the market.

Lara winced when she heard the news. She dreaded her mother-in-law's visits. The woman never spared a chance to make her feel unloved.

"And Bose wants to stay with us for a few days," her husband added.

"Oh, you don't say?" Lara turned to face him. "And Bose is just informing us of this now?"

Akon glanced at his wife, feeling sorry for her. He

knew his sister openly antagonistic towards Lara, and that Lara always shied away from conflict. Akon, on his part, tried to protect Lara from the frequent tongue-lashings by his mother and sister as best as he could.

"I think it was an impromptu decision. She just decided today," Akon said.

Lara kept her anger in check. She knew Bose did not just decide. Bose had a nasty attitude, and Lara could not stand her. She wondered what she did wrong to get such terrible in-laws.

"What do you think they would like to eat?" Lara asked in a timid voice.

"Just make amala for Mama. She can eat it with the egusi soup you made. Add more of the goat meat you bought yesterday. For Bose, you can serve her the yam and fish stew we ate this morning," Akon suggested.

"That's good. What time are they coming?"

"They should be on their way," Akon said, glancing at his wristwatch.

Lara stood up; her cheerful attitude gone. She gave Maria the list and a wad of cash and went outside to instruct Adebiyi to take the maid to the market. Lara returned to the kitchen to prepare food. When she was done, she went upstairs to shower. The last thing she wanted to hear from her mother-in-law was that she smelled like smoke.

Before she had time to change into fresh clothes, she heard some chatter downstairs and Akon's laughter reverberating around the house. She dressed quickly in a simple but pretty Ankara gown and squared her shoulders, taking a deep breath as she exited the bedroom.

Mama Akete and Bose were already seated by the time Lara got downstairs. Bose's bag, a huge travelling box, was beside her. Lara sighed. It did not look like Bose was planning to stay for just a few days. Lara could only hope that her stay would be peaceful.

"Good afternoon, ma," Lara greeted in Yoruba, kneeling in front of her mother-in-law. "How was your trip down here?"

"Fine," Mama replied coldly. Lara's smile faltered a little, and she stood up. "E kaasan, Aunty Bose."

Bose snickered but did not say anything.

"I'll serve your food, Mama. Would you like to drink water or soft drinks, ma?"

"Anything is fine, Lara." Akon smiled at her.

After she had given Mama some water, she dished the food. "Your food is ready, Mama, Aunty Bose."

Bose skipped over to the table and opened the plates. She grimaced when she saw four wraps of amala in a Pyrex dish and egusi in another dish. There was a plate of yam and a bowl of fish stew for Bose.

"I'm not eating yam."

"What do you want to eat then?" Lara asked calmly. She knew this was going to happen. Bose ignored her question.

"Broda mi, I want to eat noodles with snails and dried shrimps."

Lara sighed in relief. Noodles were not difficult to cook and did not take up much time. She stood up to go to the kitchen when Bose's haughty voice stopped her.

"Make it spicy, with lots of crayfish. Dice snails on the side and add peppered fish with two boiled eggs."

"Shut up, Bose! Is Lara your maid?" Akon snapped, pushing her not so gently from where she was seated.

"Don't you dare shut my daughter up, Akon! Her brother's house is also her house. She has a right to eat anything she wants to eat, and she shouldn't have to cook it herself."

Bose nodded vigorously, pouting.

"And who told you I want amala? Eh, Madam Lara? How dare you give me this smelly thing? I know you bought it from dirty hawkers so you can kill me. If you think you can poison me, you need to think twice. Bose, let us leave this house before we are killed."

"I am sorry, Mama. I made this myself, ma. Akon said you wouldn't mind that..."

"Shut up!" Akon's mother said.

Lara turned to look at Akon with pain in her eyes.

"Mama, please stop it. Today is a beautiful day. Let us enjoy it without you throwing jabs or insults at my wife," Akon said in a firm voice. "I told Lara to prepare amala for you since there were no good yams at home. Just tell Lara what you want, and she'll prepare it for you."

"Make me some pounded yam, Lara. Not poundo yam o. And add ponmo to this egusi."

"The yams are not good for pounding, ma. They are new yams," Lara replied. "I can make you some eba. It will be soft and fluffy. You will like it, Mama."

Mama Akete nodded reluctantly. Lara left, carrying the tray of food with her while Bose laughed maliciously.

Akon went after her and hugged her from behind, rocking her from side to side.

"I'm sorry on her behalf, my love," he pleaded as he turned her around.

"What do you want from me, Akon? I have no problem catering to your mother's needs, but your sister is not a baby. I am a career woman for heaven's sake! Not her maid. I don't like this."

Lara moved towards the sink to wash the snails and boil some eggs for Bose's noodles. Akon sighed and moved closer to her.

"I'm sorry, babe. It's just for a few days. Please, just endure it for me," he pleaded. Lara nodded, and he left.

After a while, Lara came in with two trays of food. She set them on the dining table and took a deep breath.

"Mama, Aunty Bose, your food is ready."

Bose rushed to the dining and opened the plate. She snickered when she saw the content. She picked up her food and went to sit in front of the TV. Her favourite show was on.

Mama Akete sat at the dining table and nodded approvingly at the food. Lara was an elegant lady and an excellent cook. Too bad, she was an orphan and not from a wealthy family.

An hour later, Bose finished eating. She left her plate on the white sofa, saying she was going to take a shower. Lara shook her head, picked up the plates, and cleaned up the sitting room.

"The fact that I do not say anything does not mean I'm stupid, Akon. Look at how she messed up the sitting room, expecting me to clean up after her," Lara snapped. "I already told you; catering for your mum is one thing. But slaving over your sister, I cannot do."

"I'm sorry, my love. I will talk to her. Bose can be such a baby sometimes."

"She's not a baby; she's just a spoilt brat. She enjoys

making me feel miserable," Lara glared at him. "I'm a lot older than she is, and I won't tolerate this any longer, especially if she's staying here for more than a few days."

Akon rubbed his hands over his face.

3

Lara snapped out of her reverie when the car stopped. That was seven years ago. She wondered how Akon's family would treat her now that Akon was going to the UK for a while. She hoped everything would be okay, but she was much stronger now. She prayed she would be able to deal with any issues that surfaced.

"Adebiyi, why did you stop the car? We haven't gotten to Ikorodu," she said to the driver, who was peering out of the window.

"I spotted a friend of mine, so I told him to stop. Oh, here he comes," Akon said, waving to someone at the back. He got out of the car and leaned against it.

"How far, my man? How you dey?" Akon greeted in pidgin.

41

"O boy, I dey! E no easy sha! Na you be this?" his friend, Chidi Agu replied. "E don reach five years wey we see last o!"

"Time flies, man."

Chidi stuck his head through the window. "Good afternoon, madam. How are you?"

"I'm fine, thanks," Lara responded with a smile. Chidi nodded and straightened up to face Akon.

"See this nice car, bros. I've been hearing say na London you dey live permanently now."

Akon laughed. "Rumours travel fast in this area. I am not staying there permanently. I just went there to complete a course, and I am back, thankfully. But if everything works out well, I may go again." He did not want to give Chidi any reason to suspect that he would soon leave for the UK. His trip was to be kept a secret.

"You are still considering? If I get an opportunity to go, I will grab it fast. Life is too hard in this country. No electricity. Food is too expensive. Everyone is just surviving. Is your wife going with you?"

"Chidi, you are funny. Why would I leave my wife behind?" Akon laughed uneasily. He could not tell Chidi that he planned to leave Lara behind for now.

"Omo, you are a smart guy. Many would kill for the opportunity you have—a beautiful family, an above-average lifestyle. I wish you the best. Anyway, whatever you do, do not leave your wife alone with these horny Lagos wolves. They will devour her before you know it," Chidi advised. "She is beautiful and nice."

"Of course not! I would never try that. But I still don't see anything wrong with a couple being apart for a while."

Chidi guffawed. "You don't know these Chiefs, Alhajis, Chairmen, and young successful businessmen. They will try everything possible to fill the gap."

"Guy, you don't know my wife," Akon boasted. Even as he did, a feeling of uncertainty swept over him. *Would Lara be a faithful wife when I am seven thousand kilometres away?* "See you around," he said to his friend, waving as he climbed into the car.

They got to the Akete's house on the outskirts of Ikorodu. His mother ran a large grocery store where she sold vegetables and different seafoods like crabs, shrimps, and fish. The grocery was lavishly furnished with all types of sea animal paintings and backgrounds. Even the attendants and cashiers had gills on their uniforms. An ice cream shop was set apart from the rest of the large supermarket. Akon got Jabez some ice cream.

When Mama Akete saw Akon and his family, she handed over to her trusted assistant and led them inside the house. The house was about two metres from the beach, with a fantastic sea view. It was part of a new project, built for retired politicians. This was where Otunba Akete lived before he was killed.

"You look stressed out, Mama. What are these dark circles under your eyes? You should rest; instead, you keep working at the supermarket," Akon said.

"Rest?" she said with disbelief, as she jumped up to demonstrate how fit she looked. "Does this body look sick to you? I will work until I am ninety!"

Mama Akete was seventy-seven years old. Despite the occasional high blood pressure scare, she remained fit as a fiddle.

"Anyway, congratulations, olori ebi! I was overjoyed when you informed me last week that your visa for work in the UK has been approved," Mama Akete said. "Now, listen. The only thing I am concerned about is that you do not have a job over there yet. Why did you make up your mind to leave in such a hurry?"

Akon groaned. "Mama, come on."

"I'm just expressing my own opinion, son. I have no choice because the decision is yours to make. As long as your wife is okay with it, I'll keep praying that God should bless you and your journey."

"Mama, unless a man is ready to take the risk and climb a ladder, he will remain at the bottom. There is a limit to what I can achieve in Lagos. It is all about who you know, and you know that things have been rough since dad was killed."

"Indeed, my son. God will watch over you." His mother placed her hand on his shoulder. "Akanni Ibikunle Omo Akete o'je ki ẹmi baba rẹ ki o tẹle ọ. Ori a tele o, ooo! Eledumare a si ona fun ọ oo, wa ko ere oko dele o."

"Amen, Mama," Akon responded to his mother's prayers. "One more thing, under no circumstances should you discuss my plans with any of our relatives. If they ask about me, just tell them I travelled to Ghana. Don't even tell any of your women's association or church members."

"Never! Just do not forget your siblings and me," Mama Akete pleaded. "Send for them when you are comfortable in London. Look at your sister, Folu. Since she graduated from the university three years ago, she has not had a stable job. If she travels to London, she can sort herself out. Do not forget Ibukun either. She is working in a fashion institute but wants to travel abroad to gain more industry skills. Bose had just completed her secondary school, and she also wants to go to the university. Still, she could only get admission to Yaba Technology in Lagos. Please, allow her to follow you to Lagos so she can attend classes from your house. Don't forget to send me money regularly so I can use it to refurbish one of your dad's abandoned properties downtown."

Akon grunted. "Mother! Wait until I sort myself out. As for Bose, she can come over to our house until she secures an accommodation on campus."

"Thank you, my son. Now, listen to me. You have stood like a pillar and taken up many responsibilities as the first male, and I appreciate your generosity. But your wife Lara, are you sure it is safe to leave her alone? Again, please remember your sisters and me," Mama Akete said.

Then she called Akon aside. "Make sure you impregnate your wife before you travel. It will keep any man from talking to her while you are away."

"Stop this, Mama. I married Lara, not my mother! I have told you before that my wife is a conservative Christian. She does not flirt around. Stop putting ideas into my head," Akon said firmly.

"I am just saying my own o," Mama said before beckoning to one of her helpers to bring the foodstuff she had packed for Akon.

"Mama, thank you, but Lara has packed some too," Akon said.

"Food is never too much, my son. I got a lot of pepper packed in sachets for you. I have bottles of groundnut and garri. I also have fish, meat, and snails that I fried myself," Mama beamed.

"Thank you so much, Mama. As long as they do not

stop me from entering the UK with the foodstuff, I should be okay." Akon hugged her.

Akon and the family stayed with Mama until evening. When it was time for them to leave, Mama escorted them outside.

"Bose will be at your place first thing tomorrow morning," she announced. "Make sure you bring my grandson to visit me o," mama Akete said to Lara.

"Yes mama," Lara responded.

Jabez was fast asleep in the backseat by the time they left mama's house. Glancing at Lara, Akon noticed her countenance.

"You put me on the spot…" she stated angrily. "You did not tell me that Bose would come over when you travel abroad. You can be very inconsiderate sometimes," she said.

"Let's not mess up the joy of today, okay?" Akon pleaded.

"There is no joy," Lara murmured and looked the other way through the window.

"Haven't I had enough? You know how difficult it is to please your family members. But…"

"But you also welcomed her," Akon interjected, his hands gripping the steering firmly. "You said it was okay. You could have just said you were not okay with it at the time," he said with traces of anger.

"So, you are blaming me, right?" Lara asked, fuming as she tried to hold his gaze.

"Okay, I am sorry. You know mama is very manipulative. You know I do not want to handle her, all because of the respect I have for you," Akon stated apologetically as he stretched his hands over the gear to hold her palms.

*   *   *

A day before Akon was to travel, Bose arrived in Lagos. They had arranged for her to stay at Akon's house in her first year until she could move into the school hostel or somewhere nearer to school. Bose was infuriated that she was not invited to accompany Akon to the airport, but she kept her anger to herself. *That wretched Lara would be the one to suffer for it.*

On the day Akon was to travel, Lara had packed everything he would need, including his travel documents. They knelt to pray for a safe journey while Adebiyi moved the bags into the car. Jabez was sad and despondent because his dad was leaving without him. Lara felt like wailing. She wondered how life would be without Akon, her husband, best friend, lover, and brother. Tears streamed down her cheeks, but she wiped them away.

Akon hugged them. He knew things were going to

be quite hard, but he trusted Lara's capabilities. She was a strong woman.

"Babe, you will be with me before you know it," Akon assured her. He held her hand and squeezed it gently. She refused to let go throughout the journey from Gbagada to the MMA airport in Ikeja. It was a rainy night.

When they got to the airport, it was nearly time for his flight. He lifted Jabez and kissed him.

"Promise me that you'll be a good boy for mummy. Don't give her any problems."

"I cross my heart. Come back quickly, Daddy," Jabez said.

"I will champ." Akon wiped a tear from his face. He turned to Lara and kissed her, his lips lingering on hers.

"Take care of yourself, my babe. I love you. I will always call home."

"I love you. Bye for now," Lara replied, wiping her teary eyes. Akon hugged her a little longer before he released her. Adebiyi helped Akon with the suitcases, and they went towards the departure hall.

Lara sat in the car with Jabez and comforted Jabez as he cried. "I want my daddy. I want to go with my daddy."

* * *

The Royal Air Maroc plane landed at Gatwick Airport at 9.30 p.m. UK time. It was an exhausting journey; nevertheless, Akon was tired after waiting for his suitcases to emerge on the conveyor belt. He brought out his mobile phone to call Kay only to find out that he had no connection.

Akon knew what he had to do. This was not his first time here, but he still needed directions. He walked over to the BT payphone and inserted a coin to call his friend. Kay did not pick up at first. He cut off the call so that the BT payphone would not use up his credits.

Akon was a bit scared; he had heard stories of visitors who had been stranded at the airport when friends who had promised to assist them refused to turn up. Akon called Kay again. By the time his friend picked up the phone, Akon had spent almost £1.20. "Hey, my guy. The eagle has landed," Akon said cheerfully.

"Hello?" a voice echoed from the other side of the phone.

"Kay, it's me, Akon. How are you?"

"I'm alright. How about you? Have you landed?"

"Oh boy, I don land o," Akon said excitedly.

Kay was silent. After a pause, Akon asked, "Are you still on the phone?"

"Yes. Do you know how to get to my place?"

"No. Last time, a cab got me there, and if you remember, I stayed in the guest house before I came down to yours."

"Oh, yes, I remember. I do not live in that house anymore. I am still in Forest Hill, just two roads away from my former address. Did you get your luggage?"

"Yes, I'm outside the arrivals terminal."

"Good! You are in the right place. Look for the signals across the board for the train going to London Bridge. It is the one specifically for Gatwick express. Did you buy the ticket online as I told you?"

"No, I forgot."

"It's okay. Follow the direction to the ticket line and get one for the rest of the journey. I will wait for you outside my place. When you see an Asda supermarket and a dental practice, that's my area."

"Will do, thank you."

The number of people at the airport made Akon uneasy. He struggled with the luggage when he was switching trains and felt tired from the busy atmosphere. London might be bubbly and charming, but at the end of the day, it is full of individuals rushing through its diverse means of transport. He grabbed a map to get his bearings and continued the journey. The complicated intersections from each line made him cringe. But then, he realised they were separated by colours, and things became easier.

Eventually, Akon made it to his friend's house. It was a typical British home with red bricks and brown roofing. Akon would have missed it if Kay had not waved at him. They went inside, and Kay showed Akon where to put his luggage. Kay invited him into the living room for a cup of tea. It did not take long for him to notice his friend's bizarre mood. Kay seemed preoccupied from the moment he picked up the phone to the second he greeted Akon.

"Are you okay? You seem tense, my friend," Akon asked curiously, hoping he had not said anything to upset him.

"Yes, yes. How is Lagos?"

"Lagos is fine. Just as you remember it."

"Is the family doing alright? How are your wife and boy?"

"They are both great. They cannot wait to hear from me."

"Of course."

"What's that smell? Were you cooking?"

"Yes. Dinner is ready."

Akon sat at the table in front of a jacket potato, some baked beans and cheese. Kay joined him, looking nervous. They did not talk for some minutes while they munched on the food. Kay eventually broke the silence with a long sigh.

"Oh boy, life is not easy at all." Kay's voice was melancholic.

"What do you mean? What's going on?"

"Nothing. Just saying things are not exactly as planned. It gets tough, you know."

"I knew that something was bothering you. Why aren't you telling me? What's up?"

"It's complicated. Maybe another time."

"Are you sure? I don't mind talking about it."

"Yes, I'm fine."

"I see. I cannot force you to talk about it. Let's talk about something else then. Why did you move from the other place? I thought you liked it."

"I did, but it was too big for me," Kay said, cutting the topic short.

Akon understood it was a sensitive topic and dropped it. He looked around and noticed that this place had fewer furnishings than the last one. Kay did not even have a garden, which was weird because he loved sitting outside. Akon wanted to make the best out of it. He was humbled to have a roof over his head and a friend in a city that was totally unknown to him.

"This place is lovely anyway. It is cosy. You were telling me about your new lady. How is she?"

"She's good. She is at her place in North London. I visit her often."

"Glad to hear you are not lonely."

"Hmmm..."

"Where did you meet?"

"You know the usual. A friend of a friend."

Akon finished his dinner and looked through the window. It had started to rain, making every little pause uncomfortable.

Kay was in fact hiding something from Akon. He did not want to disclose that he had lost his job and was in so much debt. Life had changed for him since Akon's last visit to the UK. Kay's work contract was not renewed because his company had gone into administration. He had struggled to find a suitable job in the past twelve months. The workers dismissed, including him, and he was not even paid his last wages. It was a mess that came around with no warning. Shocked to see himself in this situation, he went through every platform and agency. Still, he could not land a full-time, permanent role. To have a means of income, Kay accepted temporary jobs in factories, as a kitchen porter, or anything else in between. However, it was never enough. Bills kept piling up, and he was missing one deadline after another. Not having a stable income also meant his wages were not enough to pay the rent, so he had to subsidise this with social benefits.

Receiving these benefits from the government came with stringent conditions. Kay must inform the benefit support services if he had a lodger because that would affect his benefits which, given the situation, was impossible to accept. If he disclosed this, his benefits would be reduced as it is assumed that the other adult would pay half the rent.

Akon was not a lodger in the real sense, neither was he a tenant. Hence the reason Kay was hesitant about Akon staying with him. He did not want to house Akon for more than two weeks; neither did he want Akon to know how irregular his income was. In fact, Kay did not tell Akon that he had lost his IT job and had to give up his previous two-bedroom maisonette because he could not afford to pay the rent. Kay had figured that, since his partner lives in North London, he would spend most of the day with her and return home late in the night. Akon would not discover that he was currently out of gainful employment. It was a compromise that gave them the needed privacy.

4

Kay had sourced agencies that Akon could register with when he arrived in London. He registered him with Ash House agency and Plan kitchen porter. After all, if Akon found a job, it would be easier for him to move out in two to four weeks so that no one would know he had lived there.

"Is it hard to find a job if you're new in the country?"

"A bit. London is a big city and there is a lot of competition, but I got you covered. If you are free next Tuesday, I will take you to two agencies. They are on the same street on Deptford High Street."

"Okay. What kind of jobs?"

Kay's face lit up. He was hopeful someone he knew would join him in the work he did. "It could be factory work, cleaning jobs, and so on. It depends on what you get. It is quick money. They pay around £6.50 per hour, and shift is possible. The rates go up on weekends— one-and-a-half hours for Saturday overtime and Sunday double pay."

"You must be kidding me! Is this a joke?" Akon snapped. He could not believe what his friend was saying. He had higher hopes. "You should have told me first! Why didn't you say anything before?"

"We all have to start from somewhere, and you have no experience working here. It is different. What did you expect?"

"A decent job!"

"It is. The employers would pay your wages. It is honest work, and you gain experience. You can upgrade later."

"Seriously? I will board the next flight out!"

"Fine. Return to your cloud cuckoo land. Did I not warn you not to come here if you are not ready to settle down permanently? You were bragging about your relocation and were so convinced."

"What do you think I am? A college drop-out?"

"You are so aggressive. Lower your voice. I am seeing another side of you. It has been a long journey.

You are here, and we shouldn't be arguing."

Akon sighed, gathered his thoughts, and sat next to Kay. It was terrifying to have to start your career from the scratch again.

"I am sorry, Kay, I appreciate all you have done for me. My annoyance is not about you. It just appears that the British labour market may be difficult to navigate, and that is what I am scared about. I have invested so much money into relocating to the UK. I had to give up my managerial position back home. I did not enter this country through the back door. My visa says HSMP. I'm a highly skilled professional! Doing manual jobs doesn't make sense when I can spend the same energy looking for jobs in my field."

"Humble yourself, my brother. You really cannot appreciate what I am saying. There's hardly anyone who comes and steps into a great job at the first instance. We all accepted whatever came first. It is normal.

"I know you mean well, and I appreciate you. Please, forgive my outburst; I did not mean to be rude. It's just that I have always believed life will not ordinarily give you what you want; you have fight for it. I want to apply for a more suitable role and take things from there, if that makes sense."

Kay shook his head.

Akon could not understand how hard it could be to find a professional role. Nevertheless, it was not the right moment to insist on something he knew little about.

"At the end of the day," Kay said, "it is your life, not mine. This is London, not Nigeria. Each man to himself."

Kay stood up and took his plate to the kitchen. Akon joined him.

"Now that you are here, we need to talk about the bills and how to share the chores."

"Sure, no problem, I am alright with that. You know I like to help."

Akon sounded disappointed. Kay felt bad. He did not want to let him down from the beginning. London is expensive, and Akon should know it.

"I just wanted you to have an open mind," Kay explained. "I do not want you to be frustrated when the reality of the system hits you. Do not rely on your work experience and achievements in Nigeria. Many foreigners continue to make that mistake, especially the men. Remember, we are all from a patriarchal society, and we have been trained to have the final say. This has gotten many people into trouble because they don't appreciate that this is a different society with varying rules and values."

"I get it. It is late though. I feel drained. Can you show me where I will sleep?"

"Sure."

Kay entered the bedroom and brought out a duvet and pillows. He laid it by the living room sofa, looking at Akon, who seemed a little puzzled.

"This is all yours, brother."

"You mean I will sleep on the sofa?"

"Yes, Akon. When you came last year, I gave up my room for you, but nowadays, I have some health issues. So, it is best for me to be in my room."

"Oh," said Akon. "Where do I change? What if you have visitors?"

"You can change in my room, and if there are visitors, just lie on the couch in my room."

"This is temporary, I hope?"

"You are like a brother to me, Akon. But it is time to face the real London life. You are not a visitor now; you are part of the system. Your mentality must change. There is no communal living in London. Each person has their own bills to take care of."

Akon nodded. *That's alright. I should get a job as soon as possible and move out,* He was shocked by the unwelcoming situation.

"I need to take a shower too."

"Do you have toiletries? Shampoo, toothpaste and so on?"

"Yes, but I forgot my toothbrush."

"It's okay. I will take you to the shops. There is a Lidl down the road. Marks and Spencer, Asda, and the One-pound shop too. I usually pick up a few groceries from Lidl because they are cheaper, and household things from the Pound shop."

"Alright, I do need some pounds. I only have dollars with me."

"Good idea. The utility bill for this month will come soon. It would be £20 for gas and £25 for electricity. I'll need £45 when we get there."

"Sure," Akon replied softly. He had not even unpacked, and he was already being charged. It was not pleasant to say the least.

As they headed toward the shops, Kay entered a cash and carry shop. He asked Akon to give him the £45. Akon sheepishly brought out the money he had with him. He only had £50, so he gave the note to the cashier, who ran it through a scanning machine, staring at Kay as he did so. Kay collected the £5 change and put it in his pocket. Akon did not understand why his friend did that, but Kay explained. "We will use the change for your Oyster top-up."

Kay entered another shop and Akon followed. In the back of his mind, he was still at home.

"See this sign? Anytime you see the oyster logo, it means you can top up your oyster card for bus and train rides."

Kay brought out the oyster card, topped up £5, and handed it to Akon, including the receipt, which he tucked in the oyster card wallet.

"Please, make sure you have this with you whenever you go out. The minimum top-up for bus rides is £5. If you are planning to take the underground, add at least £15 or £20."

Akon nodded, remembering how complicated the underground map looked.

"I might get lost a few times before I get used to it."

"Don't worry, Akon. I will take you around. It takes a while to get used to, but you will eventually learn everything. And if you are ever in doubt, you can always ask someone. The people working at the tube stations are more than happy to give a helping hand."

"What's the plan for tomorrow?"

"You need to open a bank account and register with the GP. I will take you to the Halifax bank on High Street tomorrow. Then, we will visit the GP surgery and make an appointment with one of the doctors so you can register there."

"But I am a generally healthy person, Kay. I do not need to register with the GP. I just need to burn my calories by working hard."

"Listen, Akon, I understand that you are fit, but it is important you register. Some of these recruiters may ask for your GP's name and address in case you have a medical condition that may impact on your ability to do your job. It is only through your GP records that they can assess this. It is more than that though. You will need proof of address. Because I have registered you with the agency and they have sent you letters, you can use them as proof of address."

"Well, I have you to thank for that."

Kay nodded as they walked back to his one-bedroom flat. They barely spoke afterwards; the atmosphere was thick like an iceberg. Akon was already missing home. He thought about how this city changed people and how the dynamics of friendship could easily descend into a landlord-tenant situation. But he had nowhere else to go and did not want to end up in the streets. He had to play along as Kay had said—each man for himself. Back home, his uncle, Bode, warned him about this. He told him, "Everyone is your friend when you go holidaying abroad. Wait until you move in permanently; it is then you will discover who your real friends are." If it were not for his relocation, Akon would not have known this side of Kay.

* * *

Time raced by. It had been three weeks since Akon moved into Kay's flat, and he was getting irritated. They kept fighting over bills. Kay nagged about living arrangements and costs. One day, Kay burst into his room, waving a BT telephone bill.

"Do you know what this is? You really do not care about bills, do you? You have been using the landline to call Nigeria and premium numbers. See, the phone bill is over £135! What is wrong with you? You did not even seek my permission. That is cruel. Now I understand why people do not allow Nigerians to stay with them; they would ruin you till the last penny. C'mon!"

"It's alright. Please, do not shout. I take responsibility, okay?" Akon dropped him three £50 crispy notes and said, "Sorted. Hope I can have peace now."

"I am sick of your attitude, Akon. I am trying to push you towards the right direction, but you take it personally and act aggressive. How am I supposed to sort things out with you?"

"Are you done?"

"I don't like how you are behaving. I used to help you and your family back home, and I have been here for you again. Doesn't that mean anything to you?"

"I cannot believe you are turning the past against me!"

"The past? Akon, I cannot afford these costs right now. It is not fair that you are making me go through this. Do you think that I do not like good things? I do! My wallet, however, cannot deal with it. I have been here longer than you. Trust me, you need to survive, not moan."

"Do you think that makes you important?" Akon raised his voice. "I am the son of a prominent man that has received so many praises in Nigeria."

"You were. We are nothing here."

* * *

The cold, merciless wind whipped Akon's face as he hurried to the bus station. He pulled his coat tighter around his body, hunching his shoulders. He needed to get home as soon as possible. He was sure he would freeze up on the pavement. Even though he was wearing a sweatshirt, a cardigan, a coat, a woollen scarf wrapped around his neck, and gloves, it was the coldest night he had ever witnessed in the three weeks he had spent in London. He got onto the bus and sat down, shivering like a leaf.

There were a few people on the night bus, and most of them were asleep. Akon removed his gloves and rubbed his hands together for warmth before putting them back on. He felt like bursting into tears. He felt helpless; he wished he could run back to Nigeria, bury his face in his wife's lap, and listen to her soft whispers of reassurance. His entire three-week stay in London had been disappointing to say the least. He was tired — mentally, physically, and emotionally. From the moment he left Nigeria, it was like everything started to fall apart. Barely five days after he left, robbers ransacked his mother's grocery shop, carting away goods worth thousands of naira. This led to his mother's cardiac arrest. His sisters had been ringing him nonstop, telling him to send money for his mother's treatment. He had spent so much money on his mother's treatment that he only had £5,000 out of the £8,000 he had initially brought to the UK.

Lara had tried as much as possible to help the family since no money was coming in from the shop. But she could only contribute little because he had taken all their savings, hoping to replenish the account when he started earning. He felt like a wounded eagle — powerful, but unable to fly. The bus stopped and the door opened, letting three more people in. Akon left the bus and started to walk the remaining distance home.

Home? Akon gave a short and bitter laugh. He had begun to feel like a stranger in Kay's apartment. Kay's silent treatment made him feel like he had overstayed his welcome. The bubbly and excitable Kay he had always known was no more.

Akon had considered getting a one-bedroom apartment but quickly discarded the idea when Kay told him he would need at least £1,200 to secure a flat, excluding bills. Kay advised him to look for a room in a house instead. There, he would only have to spend £400, including the bills. Akon frowned at the idea, but now he had no choice.

Is this the London of green pastures and fulfilment of dreams? The bitter taste of shame washed over him. Akon got home and groaned when he saw the lights on, signifying that Kay was home. He had hoped to avoid Kay tonight. His stomach rumbled as he recalled he had eaten only a bag of crisps all morning. He was managing his money as best as he could.

Akon sighed as he climbed up the dirty stairwell. He opened the door and stepped in. The house was blissfully warm.

"How far, my guy?" Akon greeted cheerfully, removing his coat and cardigan.

"I'm alright. How are you?" Kay replied formally. They used to speak Pidgin together, but it was now strictly formal English. However, Akon sometimes spoke Pidgin whenever he wanted to be playful.

Kay was seated on the sofa, eating a bowl of cereal. Akon sat down with a heavy sigh.

"How was the job hunt?" Kay asked. Just then,

Akon's mobile phone rang. He sighed when he saw it was Fola, his sister. He declined the call and called her back instead.

"Good evening, my brother," Fola greeted calmly in Yoruba.

"How are you?" He knew she would soon have an outburst. Hers was usually the calm before the storm.

"There is nothing okay here, egbon mi. Nothing at all, my brother," Fola continued, grumbling. "You are just there in London, making money and enjoying yourself. Please, remember us o."

"But I just sent money a few days ago, what is wrong with you people? Am I your ATM?" He moved into the other room for some privacy, even though Kay would not understand what he was saying in Yoruba.

A thought flashed through Kay's mind, making him suspicious. *Why is he always speaking his language to his people?* Kay mumbled his thoughts in his own Igbo language, "Na-asu bekee?" But Akon was too engrossed in the phone conversation to pay attention to Kay.

Kay stared into space for a while. His girlfriend, Monica, was pregnant. He planned for her to move in with him for the meantime before they executed their plan, as this would obligate the council to give Akon a bigger space. Since Akon had moved into his house, she could not visit him, so he had to visit her most of the time.

Akon hung up after Fola narrated the reason for her call.

"Sorry, my guy," Akon said, kissing his teeth. "It's my people again. Mama is sick and she has shut her shop. They want me to send this and that to them."

Kay looked up at Akon and pretended as if he did not hear him, the tension between them was deafening. "But Akon don't you think it is rude for you to speak in a foreign language when a non-speaker is present?"

Akon was left dumbfounded. "It's my mum we are talking about here." Nevertheless, Akon managed to offer a cursory apology. He was too scared to defend himself because he did not want Kay to throw him out.

Akon slung himself to the sofa where he had been sofa sleeping, not bothering to get his duvet from the other room. *This is worse than hell fire,* he thought.

Kay went into the room to get the duvet and Akon's pyjamas for him. He then switched off the light.

"Goodnight mate."

"Goodnight."

Akon lay on the sofa, weighing his options. They needed money back home, about £1,500. *Maybe I should just swallow my pride and do menial jobs like everyone else. Or perhaps I should give up and return to Nigeria.* He laughed bitterly. Returning to Nigeria was just as bad as being broke in the UK. *It would be a disgrace!*

Akon's boss had tried to persuade him to stay, offering to increase his salary and promote him. Instead, blinded by the allure, status, and glitter of being a *Londoner*, Akon had sold all his shares, emptied the family savings, and travelled abroad. He had nothing left in Nigeria except two plots of land that he and his wife had bought jointly, and a cocoa farmland he inherited from his dad. *With all the things happening in my family, if I return to Nigeria, people might think I was deported. They might even tag me a fraudster.*

Returning to Nigeria meant starting from scratch. He would have to go from company to company in search of a job. The elite lifestyle they once had was history. He would have to sell his cars and lands. They might even have to change Jabez's school to a less expensive one, and that alone would crush his son. *I 'will stay. For Lara and for my family, I would have to work things out.* Akon fell asleep, his hands fisted in determination.

5

The next day was a Saturday. Akon had a hot shower and recalled the previous day's events. He wondered if Kay was home as he walked into the small kitchen to have breakfast. He groaned under his breath when he saw Kay eating a bagel. He had hoped he would have the house to himself today.

"Hey, man! How you dey?" Kay greeted him, beaming.

Akon stopped in his tracks, stunned. Kay smiled even wider after seeing Akon's reaction. "Guy, I know I've been giving off cold vibes, but I had reasons. E no easy for me too. No vex abeg. We are still good friends."

"I'm not angry, man. I understand. But I want to

know what has been bothering you. Hollup, let me get breakfast," Akon patted his back.

He went to the kitchen, opened the cupboards, and sighed. There was nothing in the cabinets except cereal and fruits. He took a bowl, poured the cereal and milk, added a little water then took an apple. He sat down and faced Kay, who offered him a bagel. He accepted it graciously.

"So, guy, wetin dey happen?" Akon asked in between mouthfuls.

"Well, I will be honest with you," Kay said, "I lost my job. At the same time, there are some issues with this flat. The owner wants it back, for his son who has just graduated from university. The tenancy agreement prevents me from taking in any lodger, so you would have to consider getting your own place in fourteen days at the latest if you do not want your luggage out. I've started looking for another place, man,"

Akon's mouth hung open in shock.

Kay continued. "I am leaving South East London for Hertfordshire, to move in with my partner. We have been saving up for a three-bedroom apartment. Our baby will be here in six months."

"And you didn't tell me all of these before? That is not fair, man," Akon snarled. "You lost your job, you don't own this apartment, and you shouldn't take in anyone. No wonder you have been acting funny. You did not inform me about these developments—your partner, job, this property. At least, if you had told me, I would have planned better."

"I'm sorry, but at the same time, I told you not to come to the UK, but you didn't listen. Guy, I know this place more than you do. You were more than comfortable in Naija, honestly."

"Anyway, congratulations on your baby," Akon mumbled. His heart was heavy. He knew he was in trouble, serious trouble. He did not account for these things when he left Nigeria. He wished he had listened to Kay and stayed in Nigeria. He blamed himself for his stubbornness. He had been so blinded by his Londoner status that he had not weighed the pros and cons of relocating to the UK.

"The only thing I ask of you, man, is to please give me at least four weeks instead of two. I will register with as many agencies as I can so I can start working next week. As you know, I cannot convince any estate agent that I can afford the rent if I cannot produce a letter of employment," Akon pleaded.

"It's not something I can decide," Kay said, pausing in thought. "Okay, I can give you three weeks. That's all."

"Let's make a deal. I still have some money left. I

will pay you two more weeks rent instead of using it in a Bed and Breakfast," Akon suggested.

Kay's face lit up. "Good! Now you are talking, man. That will work. If you pay for three weeks, you can stay another five weeks. But guy, I still have to move my belongings out of here, including my furniture. I'll need them in my new house," Kay said.

"That's alright. I understand. I will be fine as long as I can pay for gas and electricity. Do you know how much a B&B costs?"

"Depends on the area, bro. Some are £25, £45, and above. You can get hostel accommodation for £5 per night. But most of them are mixed accommodation; they do not allow big suitcases. So, you are good with only your laptop bag and another small bag.

"I am sorry things turned out this way. I am under pressure. I have a lot of debts and, since I am unemployed, I had to apply for job seeker's allowance, and the Council pays the rent and council tax. The landlord could visit anytime, or a neighbour could report us, and we would both be in trouble," Kay said.

"It's okay. I understand. Congrats again. I would like to meet your partner before you leave."

"Thanks, man. I will bring her over perhaps for dinner one night or we can meet at a restaurant. So, how did your job hunting go yesterday?" Kay had recommended some agency jobs to him, but Akon had rejected them all. Instead, he went about with his CV in pursuit of managerial positions. However, because he had no work experience in the UK, no one was ready to give him a chance.

The money Akon brought would soon run out, and he was beginning to feel perturbed. He sighed and dropped his spoon. Kay already knew his answer. He patted Akon's shoulder.

"See my guy; I'm only trying to make you see things as they are. This is not Naija; this is not Lagos. I keep telling you this, but you never listen. It is different here. You need to drop this 'I have experience, I am a manager' business. Your managerial experience in Naija does not carry much weight here. You cannot avoid starting from the bottom, even if you were a professional back home. This society will clip your wings and prevent you from flying. As far as they are concerned, you are a bloody migrant, a slave. Nobody is going to take your bag from you; you carry your bag yourself. There is no maid or driver, and people will call you by your name, not Mr Lagbaja or Mrs Tamedu. London is a leveller, man."

Akon sighed. He remembered what Uncle Bode told him before he left Nigeria. "To survive in the abrodi, you need to forget the past, learn the culture and understand how the system works. It is about integration and knowing how to switch in between cultures. The UK is a great place; you get what you put in it. It is not a country for Africans to play the big man or lord it over their wives. It is an organised country, and the culture is different. You either flow with it or sink in it."

Akon stood outside the house, pondering these words. Perhaps Kay and Uncle Bode were right after all. He needed to drop his pride and start afresh, putting all his effort and strength into it. *How long would it take before I land a job? And what kind of job would it be? Is it worth bringing my wife and son to this place at all? Maybe I should forget I am a professional, and just do what every immigrant does — the dirty jobs the Brits would not do.* He went inside with a refreshed mind and vigour, whistling a song from Destiny Child: *"I am a survivor; I am not gonna give up. I am not gonna stop; I am gonna make it."*

Akon remembered he had promised Fola he would send money. He took his coat from the hanger and set out to the local money transfer outlet.

Akon spent the rest of the weekend planning his next move. He visited the mall on Sunday in search of job vacancies. He was glad it was the Christmas season, so there were quite a few openings. Akon eventually got his first job in a card and gift shop for just three hours per day. He was asked to report on Monday afternoon at 2.00 pm and provide a reference about his character.

Kay eventually gave him a reference through another contact. He was delighted to have a chance to work, and he reported to work smartly dressed and cheerful. It was a temporary job for six weeks, starting from the middle of November, and the mall was bustling. Akon determined to make the best of the opportunity.

On a sunny Friday afternoon, Akon had just finished his three-hour shift. He was hungry, so he planned to stop by a McDonald's restaurant to pick up a small bag of chips for 99p. Walking along the side road, he noticed some job vacancies displayed on the window of an office.

Akon looked through and saw a job placement for a customer service advisor. He stood by the entrance, and the door opened automatically. He was greeted by a female receptionist.

"How can I help you today?" the receptionist asked.

"Thanks, madam. I saw the vacancy, and I want to apply for the job," Akon said, straightening his shirt.

"I am not madam. My name is Regie. I'll get someone to assist you," the receptionist corrected and pointed to a seat. "Please sit down."

Akon sat nervously. If he got this job, it would be the best thing that ever happened to him in London. He was still deep in thought when the manager came in.

"I'm Paul Townsend. Are you here for the

interview?" He stretched out his hand for a handshake.

"I'm Akon, sir. I was just passing by, and saw the vacancy ad. So, I came in to apply," Akon said.

"Hi-Con. I'm only conducting interviews today, but I'll refer you to someone else to help you." He beckoned to Reggie and whispered something to her. She nodded and ushered Akon to another floor. He sat down and waited to be called. His palms became sweaty as he wondered if they would refer him to another person.

Akon waited for what seemed like hours, tapping his foot rhythmically on the marbled floor of the waiting room. He hoped he would strike lucky with this job and build himself as soon as possible. He was jolted from his thoughts when he heard someone call his name, asking him to come in. He went inside and was surprised to see an African behind the desk. He could bet his life that the man was either a Nigerian or Ghanaian. The man smiled and gestured to Akon to sit in front of him.

"My apologies, Mister. I didn't mean to keep you waiting; I've had a hectic day."

"There's no problem, sir." Akon forced a smile.

"Okay, down to business. I am the head of the security department in this agency. I assume you are applying for a security job. Am I right?" the man asked.

"Yes. No, sir." He scratched his head. "I mean yes, yes, sir."

The man looked at him for a while, making Akon squirm. The man had a piercing gaze as if he could see through you. Then he nodded.

"You are a Nigerian, aren't you?" the man asked.

Before Akon could respond, the man nodded again and continued to talk. "I knew you were a Nigerian from your accent. I am from the South-Western part of Nigeria too, proudly a Yoruba man. It's nice to meet you."

Akon broke into a broad smile and stretched out his hand for a handshake. "How are you, sir? The pleasure is mine."

"Very well, thank you. My name is Olu Johnson Ogunyinka, simply known as *Olu*." Akon was baffled by the way Olu pronounced his name. It sounded polished and anglicised.

"Welcome to London. I like to call it our little Lagos. As you can see, there are a lot of Nigerians in London. So, you will be seeing a lot of us here," Olu continued.

Akon's face brightened visibly. "I am Akon Akete, sir. Please, since we speak the same language, I hope you will understand my situation."

"Situation? What do you mean?" Olu asked.

"It is about my job situation, sir. Actually, I would

prefer a job as a manager or a customer service representative, but I can still manage the security job to keep body and soul together," Akon said.

"Call me Holuu, not sir. Is that alright?" Olu said in his anglicised accent, leaning back.

"Yes, sir. Sorry, Holuu," Akon stuttered. "I need a job. Any job. That's why I'm here."

Olu frowned. "Calm down. I understand your predicament, but there is little I can do. You have to go through the interview stage like everyone else looking for a job."

Akon's heart dropped in disappointment.

"Anyway, do you have your CV with you? And, most importantly, are you allowed to work in the UK?" Olu asked.

Akon brought out his CV folder from his briefcase.

"Yes, I have it with me, and I am allowed to work in the UK." Akon handed it over to Olu.

Olu took it from him and opened it. He perused it for a while before closing it.

"Five pages? I will be honest with you. One page will be enough for this kind of job. As a matter of fact, you are overqualified for the jobs available in this agency. None of the panel members would grant you an interview," Olu said.

"Ah! Please sir, is there anything you can do to get me interviewed? I really need a job, sir."

"That's the problem. You Nigerians come here, see a kinsman in a top position, and think it means you get automatic help. It does not work like that. I struggled to get to this position."

Akon was disappointed. He hoped Olu would help him as a fellow Yoruba man, but it seemed like wishful thinking.

"Okay, sir. What can I do to get an interview?"

"Change your CV completely; that's one thing. Think about transferable skills you can put on your CV. Visit the local libraries for tips on writing CVs and edit this one. Remove all your qualifications."

"But sir, if I remove all my qualifications, what will I present?" Akon asked, bewildered.

"Mister, are you ready to get a job or not? Don't waste my time." Olu drummed his fingers on the desk impatiently.

"E ma binu egbon. Please don't be angry. I just need one opportunity to prove myself. Please, give me a chance," Akon pleaded.

Olu sighed. "Listen, Mr Akete! This is not a dating agency where you must prove yourself in that fashion. This is a recruitment agency, and only the outstanding job seekers will get through the selection process."

Akon felt like crying. Another dead end and disappointing day. Olu noticed Akon's defeated countenance and sighed.

"Mr Akete, your accent is still solid, so you will come off as forceful and aggressive. Also, your personality may intimidate a recruiter. You need to polish yourself to suit the category of people recruiters are looking for."

"Please egbon, I need you to help me, sir. Just help me get an opportunity to be interviewed." Akon sat on the edge of his chair, nearly kneeling. He was sweating profusely even though the air conditioner was on.

Olu stood up and looked at his watch.

Akon stood up too, looking dejected. "Sir, I'm sure you passed through these stages when you first arrived in the UK. Please, help me," Akon pleaded.

"Have you ever worked in the sales department? If yes, include it in your CV. My friend, it's Friday, and I like to close early so I can enjoy the weekend," Olu looked at his watch again.

"I have worked in the sales department, sir. After my NYSC."

"Okay, let me be honest with you. Many Africans and Asians flock the UK on the Highly Skilled Migrant Programme, hoping they would be accepted as professionals and high-ranking bosses in their various areas of specialisation. But once they arrive in the UK, they find out they are competing with locals in lower-skilled jobs. Their hopes are dashed, and they end up settling for less. It is a shame." Olu shook his head.

Olu continued, leaning against his desk. "You were right; I have been through this stage before. I came in as a visitor eleven years ago. I applied to become a student and obtained a work permit. I had to work three different jobs to pay my bills. It was hard, but I struggled because I was determined to make it. I am currently doing a distant learning programme at the Open University.

"Listen, Akon, if you were in Nigeria, these qualifications and years of experience would get you a great job with a big pay without too much *gra*. From your CV, I can see that you had a great job in Nigeria. Why did you leave such a good, promising career in Nigeria to suffer here? If you really need my advice, then you should think about returning to Nigeria."

This was not what Akon wanted to hear from this man. He just needed help.

"You have lots of experience, but the UK is not child's play. It is better to return to Nigeria, so your life does not waste away. And I am not cursing you. It is too late for some Nigerians here. They cannot return home, neither can they make progress because the odds are against them at every turn. Aburo, staying here is not worth it," Olu said, placing his hand on Akon's shoulder.

"Thanks for the advice, Olu, but I have made up my mind to stay here and succeed," Akon cut in. If Olu was not going to help him, he could keep his advice. "I just need a stable job that can give me a good wage. That was what brought me to your office."

"In that case, it is up to you. I assume you are single and adventurous, right? You have no family that looks up to you?" Olu folded his hands against his chest.

"I am happily married sir, with a dutiful wife and a five-year-old son in Nigeria. I resigned my job, emptied my savings account, and sold lands to come to the UK. A lot is at stake here, and I simply cannot go back home. I need a job," Akon pleaded, nearly dropping to the ground.

Olu stared at him again with that piercing gaze, looking thoughtful.

"You know, you seem like a decent young man and, contrary to what you may think, I want to see you succeed. However, you need to understand the reality of this country. I want to see my fellow countrymen succeed, but most of them do not understand what they are getting when they come here. They come here mentally unprepared. All they can think about is: *first world country*, *greener pastures*, and things like that. Listen, you are not the first Nigerian to go through this. It is a difficult journey for everyone. Suppose you do not have anyone back in Nigeria to support you when you hit rock bottom over here, it will be even more challenging. Trust me, this is coming from someone who has seen it all," Olu said.

Akon sighed heavily and slumped into the chair.

"Anyway, I wish you the best. I must leave now; we have spent almost an hour talking." Olu patted his shoulder. "It is a few minutes past five. I'm going to an African restaurant in Peckham; you can come along if you wish." He grabbed his coat, and they both walked out of the door, which Olu locked with one of the keys in the bunch hanging by his waist.

When they arrived at the restaurant, Akon was taken aback by the number of Africans inside. Tuface's song, *African Queen,* was playing softly in the background. Olu was hailed here and there, and he stopped to greet several people. The restaurant seemed to be Olu's regular hangout. Olu was eager to introduce Akon to a few people.

Despite the earlier disappointment, Akon felt alive. He saw a familiar face, a man who used to be his colleague during his NYSC in Kogi State.

"Abu!" Akon exclaimed, moving closer.

"The GQ! The GQ!" Abu hailed back and hugged

him. The GQ was Akon's nickname because he was a stylish dresser.

Akon introduced Olu, and they chose the table next to Abu's. Abu was at the restaurant with a British woman, so he sought permission from her to chat at the next table. Abu joined their table and interrupted their conversation.

"So, where have you been, my friend?" Abu asked, leaning forward.

"In Nigeria, Lagos to be precise. I came into the UK four weeks ago, and I'm still trying to find my way around the system," Akon replied.

"We just met today," Olu chimed in, "and I've been trying to school him on how things work for Africans in the UK. Maybe you should share your experience with him so he can understand," Olu beckoned to Abu.

"See, GQ," Abu started, "it's not just about acquiring skills and starting from the bottom. No, my friend. It is more complex than that. This *Abrodi* can drag you in the mud; it will humble you. If you are not careful, you will find yourself in situations you never thought possible. You must work on the tone of your voice; otherwise, you come across as aggressive. Everything you do—the way you walk and speak—gives off a sign. Remember the saying, 'When you are in Rome, you do as the Romans do,'" Abu said with a smile.

"You've got to learn how to speak softly. Work on your gestures, and you will be alright. Also, it depends on the job and work environment. If you work in a predominantly white environment, your integration will happen faster, and this will help your career ambitions," Olu added.

Akon nodded and thanked them. They were all drinking Guinness Smooth beer. It was a Friday evening, and everyone was in a good mood, anticipating what the weekend would bring. Akon realised that these people had made their way up the ladder, and there was little or nothing they could do for him besides offer words of advice.

Abu stood up to leave, and exchanged numbers with Akon, informing Akon that his official name was Fred.

"Oh, why?" Akon asked, surprised.

Abu laughed. "I learnt the hard way that my Muslim name would get in the way of me securing a professional job. Once they see those kinds of names on a CV, it puts them off. I had to change my official name to Fred. My middle name is Alfred. I switched it with Abu and made it my first name. So, I am Alfred, Fred for short."

Akon leaned back and sighed. He wished he had known these things before coming to the UK.

"Don't look so downcast, my friend. Everything will

work out," Abu said as he stood up to leave. "Also, if you are bored and want to talk, just ring me." They shook hands, and he left their table to join his partner.

Bosa, another member of the Nigerian community, was listening to their conversation. "Sorry, I don't mean to be rude, but listen…" turning his face towards Akon and eager to talk. "You need to forget all the plans you made before you came here. It is good to have plans, but they are likely to fail if you are not ready to start all over again!"

Akon focused his attention on Bosa and listened intently. "If you have nothing to lose again while leaving Nigeria, you may think *'ah, what could possibly go wrong?'* he said in a mock voice. "Bros, you will cry, I swear, that nothing in Nigeria will look like gold dust when the reality of life bites you. At least, you had family and friends to turn to, didn't you?" he asked with a raised brow. "In this place, you are on your own because everyone has their own issues."

"It's not as bad as it seems bruv. It is all a bittersweet experience. You can't have it all," Bosa's partner, Ijay, chipped in. "The good thing about this country is that no matter what kind of job you end up doing, you would live and eat well. You would not have to pay school fees for children or pay for medical care, unlike where we all came from. Think about it…" Ijay continued. "If you are working, you can get a loan to buy a house or car and enjoy yourself. That is if you are modest," she ended with a smile on her face. "By the way, my name is 'Jay'," she said, extending her hand.

Akon shook Jay's hand and looked rather impressed. "You made my day sis. That is the positive energy I need. Thank you, ma'am."

"See you all later," Bosa said as he and his partner left the restaurant.

Victor identified Olu among the crowd and came to sit next to him at the table.

"More bottles of Guinness please!" Olu shouted from his table, his chunky gold chain dangling round his neck.

"Alowo ma j'aye..." Victor hailed as he started singing Ebenezer Obey's well-known song.

Olu cut in and sang along: "Eyin le mo." They clicked their glasses together.

"Victor, this is Akon, he is the newbie for London," Olu said, introducing the men to each other.

"Pleased to meet you," said Akon before extending his hands towards Victor.

"My piece of advice to you: if you are like many of us that have made promises to people back at home, better tell them 'ko le werk', it would never work," Victor said with a look of seriousness on his face. "The money you earned in Britain is for Iya Charlie o. If you keep working and sending money home, you will soon develop high blood pressure or a heart attack, and that is not a curse." Victor shook Akon's extended hand as he finished.

"Don't mind Victor, he is a comedian," Olu commented, making the three men to burst out laughing.

6

Akon straightened his tie as he stood at the entrance of the interview room. He blew out a nervous breath and hoped he would strike it lucky with this job. He had taken the advice of Olu and Abu on board and tried to work on himself for a whole week. He was physically and mentally exhausted and felt generally defeated.

He opened the door and entered. Two men were sitting behind a mahogany desk, perusing documents without acknowledging his presence. Akon cleared his throat, and one of them looked up. He had sandy brown hair and wore metal-framed glasses.

"Oh, are you the next person? Have a seat," the man said and nudged his partner. They leaned away from the table and stared at him, looking bored. Akon introduced himself and sat down. They took turns asking him some questions and when he was done, they asked him to wait outside for a while.

Although their faces were bland, Akon could bet they were impressed with his performance. He was glad he came prepared. He waited nervously, checking his wristwatch every five minutes. When he heard his name, he sprang up from his seat and entered the interview room. He sat down and looked at the two recruiters who were still talking to each other in low tones.

"Mr Akon, you passed the interview. You have been offered the position of a customer service advisor with two weeks of fully-paid training," the sandy-haired man beamed. Akon could not believe his ears. He realised they were waiting for his answer and quickly straightened up.

"Yes, yes. I accept," he said, standing up to shake their hands.

"Congratulations, Mr Akon," they said and gestured for him to sit back to discuss his salary and other things. After everything was covered, they congratulated him again and asked him to begin on Monday.

When Akon got home, he crumpled to the floor in relief, tears rolling down his cheeks. He was so happy. He had zeroed his mind, deciding that he would go back to Lagos in shame if this last interview did not work out. Now that he had found a job, he was determined to find his way up until he succeeded like Olu. For now, he was more than content with this job, earning £300 per week after tax deductions. He knew there was an unwritten rule about how junior employees interacted with managers and where to draw the line. He raced to the phone to call Lara and his son, adrenaline pumping.

*   *   *

Akon looked at his reflection in the mirror one more time before dashing out to catch a bus. He was excited to report for his new job. It did not matter that he would undergo two weeks of training as part of the induction programme. All he wanted was to start working as soon as possible. The job seemed promising too. He had imagined what it would be like to work as a customer service officer in the UK.

When he got to the place, he met some people who were also starting on the same day. It was not too long before he realised that the job was not the prestigious job he had envisaged.

Akon almost left when he discovered that his tasks entailed scanning products for customers, weighing and pricing vegetables.

"Is this not the same job people do for my mother in Nigeria? How can I do a job that is beneath me? I actually thought the customer service duty would involve sourcing for finances for staff, or insurance or any of these reputable offers," he said under his breath.

He felt a crushing weight on him. Back in Nigeria, he would never stoop to do this kind of job. However, he admitted the hard truth to himself. He needed a roof over his head.

After waiting for a while, the trainer, a lady whom Akon was sure could not be more than twenty-four years old, came in and started the training.

"Good morning, everyone,' she began. "My name is Shelly, and I will be your trainer. Today, as you all know, is the first day of your induction. I would advise you to pay attention to every one of our sessions as they will help you in the day-to-day activities. There are six to eight streams in the retail section, but for the purpose of this training, I would focus on two main roles—customer service representatives and shelving."

Akon and the other starters brought out writing materials to take notes. Shelly noted that delegates would be allocated to different streams at the end of the training. Akon observed that he and two other ladies appeared to be the oldest in the induction classes. He also noticed that the trainer used many post-it notes and flip charts during her sessions.

Shelly divided the inductees into groups to do some

work on cardboard. Akon kept mute as he noticed that those in his group were much younger; they enjoyed the activity and solved the puzzles where he struggled. *Mehn, this is not as easy as I thought.* Akon could not wait for the sessions to be over.

On the last day of the training, Akon felt relieved.

"This is the final induction day," Shelly told the new entrants. "I want you to complete the evaluation form. You don't have to write your name."

Akon awarded a score of three out of ten to the trainer. He also wrote *disappointing* in the comments section, but he dared not share his thoughts with any-body. At the end of the training, Akon was assigned to the shelving department. He preferred the customer service role to working in the basement of a shop. At least working face to face with the public would help him understand the system better.

Akon's job involved uploading items to the shop floor and moving them from the warehouse to the base-ment.

"Well," Akon sang to himself, "it is too late to quit."

7

Akon resumed on Monday and found himself in a department with six other recruits—four men and two women. They were all working under a supervisor called Marcus, a twenty-year-old man from Liverpool.

Akon soon learnt that Joro, one of the men working with him, was Kenyan. He was immediately interested in learning more about Joro. So, they met up for coffee during their break.

"Can you believe I was a financial consultant back in Nigeria? Now I am using my Masters' degree to do factory work; bottom-of-the-chain stuff," Akon said before sipping on his coffee.

"*Pole sana rafiki yangu.* I did not know I would end up here either. Everybody was excited when they waved me off at the airport." Joro was thirty-eight years old, three years older than Akon. He was tall and slim and had a little beard he never seemed to shave.

"What does that mean? You said something like sana yangu," Akon asked. The language had a melodious tilt, and he was curious to know what it meant.

Joro laughed. "That's Swahili for 'I'm so sorry, my friend.' Sometimes, I forget I'm no longer in Nairobi lecturing university students."

"What?" Akon gaped. "You used to be a lecturer in Kenya?"

Joro nodded. "I have a PhD in education. I was a lecturer at Nairobi University, but I quit when I found out that some lecturing jobs in the UK paid five times what I was paid back home. I never knew I would have to complete another degree in the UK before I could qualify to teach. Also, because I am not a British citizen, I would have to pay international student fees. I dropped the idea out of frustration. Nobody told me about the cost of living in the UK, and that jobs were not that easy to come by. There are thousands of people are seeking the same jobs."

"I thought it was easier for lecturers to move to the UK or any foreign country," Akon said.

"Lecturers encounter two significant challenges just like anyone else moving to the UK, USA or any other developed country. It is easier to move from one African country to another because we have much in common. But lecturers moving to the UK experience two main types of shock—educational and culture shock. Educational shock, in the sense that your work may be deemed to be of no marginal interest in the UK, even if it is recognised internationally, which can be discouraging. You may also find it challenging to get the support you need due to cultural differences. I am afraid that you cannot achieve much without the right support within the academic circles.

"The lifestyle, the people, everything is different from your home country. Now, imagine you finally get a job and students complain to the administration about your accent, or the students just do not like you for whatever reason! That is what many foreign lecturers go through."

Akon shook his head. "I had no idea your profession had problems with foreign culture."

"It cuts across all disciplines, especially if you do not have the UK experience, but once you learn the ropes, it becomes much easier... So where do you live? Have you found a place yet?" Joro asked.

"Not yet," Akon replied. "But I intend to find one as soon as possible. I am putting up with a friend, still sofa surfing. The sofa is tiring, I must add."

They both laughed.

"So, despite the trouble your lecturer friends who have found jobs here are experiencing, do you still want to be a lecturer?" Akon asked.

"I am part of the African brain drain," Joro frowned. "Some of us left Africa due to lack of opportunities, and we must make our new area work. It may take time, but it must work. It is a long, costly, and time-consuming journey. I was such a good lecturer, and my students loved my teaching style. It is challenging here in the UK. The educational system is different. Teaching or lecturing is different, you know. You have to spend hours talking to students who find your accent amusing. They also think that the way you speak may harm their grades. How demoralising that must be for a lecturer who loves the job with all his heart! By the time they realise there is a problem like that, it is too late to turn back. So, here I am, packing stuff in a warehouse. I have warned my wife, Amy, not to tell anyone what I do here. I left Kenya as a lecturer, and that's all anyone back home needs to know," Joro said.

Akon laughed. Finally, he had found somebody he could relate to. "That reminds me. I need to call my wife and tell her I have a new job," he said.

Akon knew he could not tell Lara about his job on the phone. Lara was a lawyer back in Nigeria, and if she heard about the kind of job he was doing, she would be alarmed.

Akon and Joro chatted some more and were laughing when Marcus, their supervisor, walked past.

"Some funny stuff, eh?" Marcus said as he approached them. He seemed to spend most of his time drinking tea, but he made occasional rounds. "If we can laugh and work at the same time, it would be ideal for the company, right, Joro? Con?"

"Yes, Marcus," they chorused and hurried back to their duty posts.

Still, Akon felt great to have somebody he could talk to. The other four men in the department were natives and could not understand Joro and Akon's experiences. The men were young, probably looking for work experience or extra cash for a holiday or so. For Akon and Joro, it was a make-it or break-it situation. They had no other option for now.

The next day was Friday, and Joro invited Akon to join him for a quick drink. They sat under a tarpaulin shade outside a bar called Tropical.

"I like the name. That is why I come here occasionally," Joro said.

"I think I might get to like the place too, although I don't drink much."

"Neither do I. Iko poa. That's sheng for it is cool."

"Sheng?" Akon frowned.

Joro smiled and said, "Sheng is a fusion of English and Swahili. It is common among Kenyans under fifty just as you have your pidgin. When you say *niko kwa airport nataka kufly*, it means 'I'm at the airport; I want to fly.'"

Akon laughed. "For every sheng phrase you teach me, I will teach you Nigerian pidgin English. One word or phrase a day."

Joro laughed. "We have a deal. I have a favourite drink here," Joro continued. "Tusker Cider. It has just 5% alcohol. It reminds me of home."

"I have never heard of it," Akon responded.

"That's alright, you can have one," Joro smiled. "Do you know why I haven't gone home for Christmas in the last two years I've been here? Expectations are so high, and I do not have the kind of money needed to meet those expectations. But once I learn the system and know how to save money and pile up a fortune, I'll be set. I am due for a promotion to supervisor in six months. Then I can save more and start a little project I have in mind that has nothing to do with lecturing. I could make fifteen thousand in a year with that project."

"And then, one day, you will board a flight to Nairobi. Once you get home, you will convert fifteen thousand pounds to your currency and seem like a rich guy," Akon said with a laugh.

Joro laughed too. "That would be over two million in the local currency," he said. "Not a bad start. And no one would know where I started unless they were close to me, and I wanted to motivate them."

Looking straight at Akon, Joro asked, "So, what's your story?"

Akon smiled fondly as he remembered his child-hood memories.

"My childhood was blissful, and life was perfect. My father was wealthy. He had a massive compound with three houses. My father's house was in the middle, and that was where I grew up. He had three wives; the second and third lived in separate houses with their children, while my mother and her children lived in the main house with my father. My father used to alternate between different houses. I think they had some kind of roaster." Akon laughed and took a sip of his drink before he continued.

"The second wife had two problematic sons, and for some strange reasons, my father spoilt them silly. The third wife had only one daughter before she left the house. While my mother and aunt were having a con-versation, I heard that my father was forced to marry her because he had had an affair with her. He had to bear the responsibility, which was the child. My father did not like her much, and he rarely visited her, which made her angry and sad. She fought the other wives over the title of who was the better wife from looks to cooking. We have an adage in Nigeria that says, 'The way to a man's heart is through his stomach.' And to be honest, my mother was a great cook. In fact, there were rumours that my mother may have given my father a love potion. She had six children—three boys and three girls. Two of the boys died from sickle cell anaemia, precisely one year after the other and soon enough, there were rumours that they were *abiku*."

"What is abiku?" Joro asked.

"Abiku, in Yorubaland, means a child predestined to die. The two boys died before I was born, so in reality, I am the third child. I never met them except through their photographs. The first child died at the age of three, and the second, born a year after, died at the age of two. In our culture, there are a lot of thoughts and beliefs about childbirth and destiny. So, when I was born, my parents took me to different places to make atonement to preserve my life."

Joro was enjoying Akon's story. He urged him to go on.

"They washed my head with some black soap for traditional rites that included bathing in the river as a child. I was told that my mother had to spend about seven nights in a great herbalist's house. I was given a mixture of herbs blessed by the priest. He invoked the god of Orunmila to cure the sickle cell anaemia that afflicted my older brothers. As I grew, my parents were overprotective of me. They spoilt me to the envy of my other female siblings. By the time I was ten years old, I did not have any sickle cell crisis aside from the occasional malaria or typhoid fever. However, I still have the sickle cell trait.

"Although the secondary school I attended was just a ten-minute drive or a twenty-minute walk from home, my father still ordered the driver to take me to and from school. The girls attended a different secondary school from mine. They complained that I was attending a private secondary school while they attended a state school. Even in primary school, I was not allowed to play with others without adult supervision. The headmistress was a family friend. Her name was Mrs Jayesimi; that woman was tough as nails mehn." Akon laughed fondly.

"My father had told her to keep an eye on me, and because I knew I was being watched, I was cautious. I missed out on some of the usual childhood fun, from climbing trees to picking up fruits, to playing with tyres and sticks. I remember when one of the trusted drivers was ill. I was fourteen, and my dad was sick also, so there was no way I could get to school. My mother gave me some coins and directed me to the garage where I would take the bus to school and back home. I had so much fun. After that, two of our maids misbehaved; I think they stole, so my mother sent them away. When they left, my sisters and I took over the domestic chores, but I was not the domesticated type. I always volunteered to go to the shop. One time, my mother sent me to a place called Oshodi, a famous market in Lagos State. They sent me to buy meat, vegetables, and all the ingredients to make traditional soup. I was surprised that I could navigate through the traffic by myself since I had never gone to the market alone with public transport. People were helpful at the time because I was decently dressed. When I finished from the market and saw that I had some change left, I stopped at the popular Mr Biggs for some doughnuts and meat pies. Of course, mobile phones did not exist in Nigeria at the time, so my mother couldn't call me or anything."

Joro adjusted his sitting position and sipped his drink.

"By the time I grew older, I started to learn life was not as easy as I had thought. Later, my father would complain that things were too expensive, and we are not to waste food, and all that. I was surprised. My father, who used to be a lavish spender, would think over a matter before committing money to it, especially with his wives. He did that because if he gave money to one to start a business and he did not give the other, all hell would break loose in that house. By the time I was in the university, I experienced strikes by students, lecturers; everyone was asking for a pay increase. Sometimes the students would protest over lack of light, water, and other things; the police would get mad and spray tear gas at them. Eventually, the school would close. I was active in student union politics. We would sing songs like this: 'Solidarity forever, solidarity forever, solidarity forever, we shall always fight for our rights.'" Akon stood up and sang out loud. Then he shook his head and became pensive.

"You know, in one of those riots, I lost a close friend of mine; he was shot by the mobile police. The mobile police force was an anti-riot police set up to counter civil disturbances, but they often killed innocent citizens. I think they still exist in Nigeria. During riots, you have to show you are on the side of the students or they may deflate your tyres, break the windows of your vehicle, or burn your car with you inside."

"Wow. So how do you show support?" Joro asked, looking puzzled.

"You show your support by putting tree branches on the windscreen of your car." Akon sighed, his eyes twinkling; his sadness gone.

"I remember those times with joy, but trust me, Nigeria has changed. The student union does not represent the students' voice anymore, and democracy has gone down the drain. It is now easier to bribe the students and silence them, so they do not fight for their rights. My father was a politician, and he would always say his mind. That behaviour used to get him in a lot of trouble, and it was not until he learnt to keep quiet that he was able to secure good contracts for his business. The system in Nigeria works like this; if you do not know the people in the corridor of power, anything you want to set up will fail. Corruption and insecurity are what brought Nigerians like me to the UK. It is a case of classism and a race to keep up with. Over there, foreigners are worshipped by locals."

"Literally?" Joro asked.

"I'll explain. For instance, if you visit a restaurant and a white man comes in to eat, the waiters would be all over him, while you are there, waiting for someone to attend to you. We love to protect foreigners but treat our own shabbily. When I was growing up, my father's wives would always fight. My dad had to settle quarrels, and this caused him to develop high blood pressure. Even though that was not what killed him, I made up my mind that I would be a one woman's man and I would never fuss over the sex of a child. My wife is still in Nigeria with my son, and I cannot wait to have them here. But right now, I've got to grind." He laughed as they ordered another round of pepperoni pizza.

Joro nodded. "The journey to success in my home country is not smooth. Tribalism is still a problem even though we look alike. You already know it will be hard, especially if you do not belong to the elitist group of the society, so you are prepared for it. But getting here with your hopes high and everyone's expectation raised, and then having to eat humble pie is something else. Yet it is the struggle, resilience, and immigrant faith that make your success remarkable, enjoyable, and inspiring."

"So, let's hear your story," Akon said as he sipped a glass of freshly made tropical juice.

8

"You know what? I have documented my story in a journal, which I am planning to publish in the future. My story is over 300,000 words. It'll be a widely read book." Joro said to Akon, caressing the journal with pride.

"It had taken me a lot of resources, and a long time to finish the journal, and I want to make it into every language possible. I want to sell more than a million copies. I documented various experiences, starting from 1996, including conversations with my wife before we got married. I have written the experience of other tourists and life generally in Nairobi." Joro said.

Joro explained that he wanted to use his story to narrate that classism exists in Kenya and that the issue is common in all African countries.

"I remember a vivid experience in my childhood," Joro said. "My father once injured his foot when we went to the farm, so we could not stay long at the farm. On our way back home, we stopped at my grand-father's house. He brought out some fruits but warned me not to swallow any seed, and I should throw it out. You dare not ask an elder why. You do as you are told in those days.

"When I was much older, I found out it was generally believed that if you swallow a seed, the fruit will grow in your stomach," Joro joked, and they both laughed, realising they once lived carefree.

Joro looked at his bottle of cider and shook his head with regret.

"I am not ungrateful even though life has often been unfair to me. The only thing that throws me off every time is knowing that my people back in Nairobi are oppressed. After I started working and stepped into the world of my dreams, everything got even more chal-lenging. I was happy; I was ready to work hard every day to get the experience and knowledge needed to become a great lecturer. It was hard at the beginning, but I did not complain. I had a dream, and I knew this dream would come true. However, every time I decid-ed to go out to my beloved Nairobi's streets, to be drawn into nostalgia, my heart would get heavy and sad. I always wondered if these people's dreams would ever come true, if these people would get what they deserved—appreciation, safety, and security.

"Here is one of those stories. It was just another simple day. I woke up feeling excited. I would work only up to noon that day, and I could either stay indoors and watch movies in the afternoon or drive around the parts of Nairobi I had not visited for many days. Hmmm. Of course, I chose to explore parts of Nairobi. If there was ever a city with a conflicting land-scape and a big divide between riches and poverty, this was it. But also, many African cities are like that. All along, while earning my Bachelor of Arts and Masters' degrees, I had known that I would be a lecturer in an institution of higher learning. At that time, I worked as a human resource officer because I had not secured a lecturing job yet despite my qualifications. My salary was not what I had imagined it should be, but at least, I had something to do. I started learning what responsi-bilities, hard work, and obligations mean.

"The strange thing about Nairobi was the division between the west and the east. The west was rich Nairobi; the east was middle-class and poor Nairobi. This divide started right inside the CBD, the Central Business District, which was in the middle of the city. Western CBD had beautiful skyscrapers and parks, including a National park with animals. The eastern side of CBD had industrial areas, more cluttered houses, and worse roads. But I liked the diversity—the CBD in the middle, the eastern lands, and west Nairobi. If you made enough money, you could move to the west side of Nairobi and get a four-bedroom house with your own lawn, garage, and gate, and you had better buy a western-class car or you would be frowned upon. And trust me, most of us, kids, dreamt of moving there one day. Our whole world was Nairobi. We had no idea that in other parts of the universe, people lived differently."

Joro smiled and continued, "You could be allowed to be rich in eastern Nairobi—moderately rich. You could rent a three-bedroom house and have your gate, car park, and a small walled compound, but there was a limit. They call it the lower, middle, and upper-middle class. But some upper-middle class were moving west to estates like Karen. They felt they were close enough to the rich. Some lower middle classes were in danger of relegating to poor estates like Kibera, where they might forfeit things like electricity.

"Once you parked the car and walked out, you assumed an attitude of suspicion. Suspicion was an unwritten rule in this city. Everyone was a suspect until proven innocent. There were only two criminals out of every thousand people, but you do not know who those two were, so you do not take chances.

"A pickpocket or a person going to do a regular job looked alike. Anyone could be a conman or a businessman. They were suspicious of you, too, no matter how well-dressed you were. You do not wave or smile at strangers. Friendships and acquaintances were restricted to the estate back home or the office. Not out in the streets.

"If you were poor, you have to live in individual estates built for the poor, where you could get a house for about £30. Your biggest worry was food for the day. The crime rate was high, and almost everybody did manual jobs. If you were in the lower middle class, you moved to a different estate. From there, you could catch the train quickly, and houses were better at about £50. If you joined the middle middle-class, it meant you had a better job. You could drive to town, and you could live in Donholm or a similar place. Most of your friends went to work, and you had grand plans. Unfortunately, you have no money to bring those plans to life. Most people in this social class had car loans to pay, and investment capital was one big worry. Nevertheless, they could afford to save and purchase a few luxuries."

Joro's voice cracked from time to time, as if he were about to cry. It was no secret that Nairobi's big flaw broke his heart.

"Then I left," Joro continued. "I left, searching for a brighter future, for something adventurous, fairer, and happier. I knew leaving my country was for good; I knew I deserved a better life, but..." Joro looked up at

Akon, and with his whole heart decided to explain, "Despite the bad side of Nairobi, I was in love with my hometown. I had a hard time leaving it because I wanted to see this place become one of my dreams when I was younger. I did not want to search for this life somewhere else. I love Nairobi, and I could never escape it. Nairobi is always in my heart, and I will always feel regret while thinking about these dark stories of Nairobi."

Akon tapped Joro's shoulder. "I understand. It is hard to leave something you love so much, knowing your home country is still dealing with unexplained tragedies and finding happiness elsewhere. But we should look out for ourselves. We should at least try to survive and not drown in these tragedies." Akon's words made Joro feel less guilty about leaving Nairobi behind.

"The hardest part was abandoning my students," Joro looked sad as he spoke. "These youngsters were thirsty for education. They know there are only two ways to having a life: being a bad person who robs and kills others, or becoming an educated person, equipped to chase your dreams. My students had chosen the latter. They wanted every single bit of knowledge I could share with them. They squeezed me out like a lemon, asking me questions, debating with me, sharing their stories, and demanding more information. Every lecture was productive.

"When I worked with new classes, the students all said they had heard about me and looked forward to working with me. I never thought I was the best lecturer, but these children felt a two-way wish. They wanted to study, and I responded by teaching them. That is when I heard that they learnt from my stories. They said I made learning easy. I always believed that a teacher has not taught, except the students had learnt," Joro's voice got deeper and dreamier, "Some of them even wept when I was leaving."

"Wow!" Akon exclaimed from astonishment. "This memoir of yours should win a Nobel Prize," he said with confidence.

* * *

Akon observed the street outside the bar. There was so much to see and experience in the city. The people, the way they talked, the way of life... everything seemed to move seamlessly. It felt like he was viewing life from the outside. He watched a woman in a short green dress walk past until she was out of sight. He checked his watch and looked outside again. He hissed. He took a gulp of his cider. From where he sat, he could monitor the door and a part of the street. He kept his eyes out.

Akon always found something to compare with being in Nigeria. And as he sat in Higgy's Bar, in the dim evening light, he imagined what he would be doing if he were in Nigeria. He closed his inner eyes and shook his head, forcing himself to shut out the thoughts. There was no need to live in the past like many immigrants. He is here now.

He checked his watch for the eighth time that evening and sighed. Moments later, someone walked in, but Akon was disappointed it was not his friend. He took another gulp and then, almost frustrated, he decided to finish it and order another.

"Ah! No one is chasing you o!" Joro said behind the raised glass. Akon dropped the glass, grinning. Joro shook his head and sat down. He stretched his hand over the table to Akon, and they shook and snapped fingers.

Akon's eyes widened as he wondered when Joro entered, but his friend was already thinking about other things.

"Want another?" Joro asked. "I have gist for you, bro!" He seemed excited. Akon accepted the offer for more cider. He watched Joro leave their booth and walk towards the bartender. Akon turned away from him and watched the street again. This time, his eyes caught a couple making out on the other side of the road. He smiled. He was used to it already. He wondered what Nigerians would say about that, but before the thoughts developed, he pushed them away. He watched them for a while until Joro snapped his fingers, which made Akon jump.

"Stop snooping," Joro said, smiling. He nodded at the refilled glass in front of Akon and sat down. He took a sip from his drink. Akon could not remember the name of the drink, but he recalled that it was a plant's name. It was Joro's best drink even though he had not been taking it for long. Joro took a sip and closed his eyes. He had told Akon about the drink before they dined out, and when he got it, he told Akon to taste the *magic* in a glass. Akon did not think there was anything special about the drink, but he told Joro it was the best thing he had ever tasted.

"What's the gist?" Akon asked.

Joro put a finger up, asking him to wait. He nodded at a girl on the other side of the bar. She was sitting with a couple of friends in a booth directly opposite them. Akon looked slowly and caught her looking. He turned to Joro and smiled shyly.

"I just walked in and noticed she's been looking this way. I don't think she is checking out the colour of my shirt," Joro said. Akon laughed and shook his head. Akon looked again, and this time, he saw her typing on her phone. He shook his head and chuckled.

"Tell me the gist," Akon asked again.

Joro sighed and shook his head. He took another sip of his drink, adjusted himself in his seat, and grinned.

"So..." he paused.

Akon waited for Joro to continue, but Joro was looking out. He had a frown on. He was about to tell Akon something when they heard an ambulance approaching. Akon looked out the window. He had noticed before that there were cars locked in place in the street.

"I think something happened out there," Joro said. His feigned English accent was back, and he was looking a bit worried. Akon stood up too. He was conflicted between sitting still and leaving the bar. He looked back at the girls. The girl on the phone and her friend had gone to check out what was happening. Another girl was still in the booth, straining to see through the glass wall. Akon looked at Joro and saw the same conflict on his friend's face. When he heard the sirens from police cars, Akon stood up, leaving his drink. He would put the money on the table, but Joro shook his head and gestured for them to go to the bartender. They paid and went towards the door. They did not speak. They did not need to.

Outside, they were greeted by a cool evening breeze. Sista Avenue had never been this busy in all the time Akon had been there—never this busy and full. Cars honked their horns and people came out of their vehicles to see what had happened. The ambulance was parked at the intersection, and there were policemen everywhere. Akon was worried. He knew what it meant for him to be in a place like that. He could not tell what had happened. Was it a theft gone wrong or worse? It could be a murder. He could see the back of the girl that had been staring at him. She was taller than he had thought. Her skin stood out from the near-black tee-shirt she had on. Joro touched Akon, and he jumped. They could hear police cars racing far down the street.

"Let's go," Joro said. Akon nodded and followed him. He knew how it would have been in Nigeria; there was no need to think about it. But here, in London, he either found out about things like this on the news or forgot about it. They walked quickly, making sure to stay away from anywhere they heard the sirens.

In the middle of the blaring sirens and police uniforms, a woman, about seventy, with a small frame, was pulled up onto a stretcher. She was saying a lot of thing at once and crying. She had a lot of blood on her legs, and as they put her in the ambulance, she called a name. A police officer picked her bag and gave it to one of the Emergency Medical Technicians (EMTs).

The ambulance left immediately, and the police officers stationed there to keep the public away from the woman joined in the pursuit. It was a hit and run, and a police officer had been there to see it. It happened so fast, almost as if the contact did not happen. One minute the woman was walking across the street, and the next, she was flying in the air. The police officer called it in immediately and ran to the woman. She was yelling and screaming. She could not move her legs, and it seemed her right wrist was broken.

"Christ!" the police officer had shouted. He screamed at a man standing on the other side to call for an ambulance, but the man looked just as confused as he was. The police officer cursed and stopped all vehicles coming towards where the woman was. He was about to call for an ambulance when he heard them coming.

He ran to the woman and knelt by her. She was crying now, pleading with him not to leave her. When the ambulance came, she held his hand in hers, squeezing it every time the pain got worse. Then the other police cars arrived, and the street that was welcoming the darkness of evening was thrown into a chaos of blue and red. The police officer checked and confirmed that the Vauxhall car was being chased. So far it had run two reds lights. He cursed again.

Who would do something like that? It seemed like the driver of the car was racing through the city. If they did not catch him soon, he would hurt another person. The policeman sighed. When he turned around, the ambulance was driving off in haste. He wondered if the woman would be alright. The other police cars were gone too, and he waited, listening to see if there was any way he could join the chase. He looked at where the woman had fallen. He could still hear her screaming and begging him not to leave her. He shook his head, looking away from the blood.

The radio crackled, and a woman's voice came on. The police officer waited, and when he heard how far the car had reached, he wondered if they were ever going to catch it. He still remembered the number, the car itself and how it had accelerated after hitting the woman. He imagined someone else being hit, and a shudder ran through him. He started his car and moved slowly. He felt sick.

The police officer sighed as he nosed into the next street. He heard the sirens and the radio calling for back up. They needed cars to stay at strategic places to cut the Vauxhall car off. He did not think; he stepped on the pedal and drove off in that direction.

9

If anyone had told me that life would become even more difficult now, I would have fought them tooth and nail. Akon thought about the difficulties he was experiencing even though he had come into the UK as a qualified professional. *What a life! It seems like I only moved from one trouble to another. Haven't I suffered enough?* The thought usually popped into his mind at the oddest of times. It was as if his mind was mocking him for the many wrong turns he had taken recently.

Akon no longer lived with Kay. He was practically homeless. He had saved enough money for a deposit of one month's rent, but that was just about what it could do. What next at the end of the month?

Penning down some notes in his diary, he wrote, "Akon wasn't supposed to suffer like this. But as you must have guessed, he put all his money into a bad deal, and it all went south." At times like these, he remembered his wife warning him not to gamble with all their savings. He did not even tell Lara that the money was for a business venture until it was too late. He lost £25,000.00 in a business he knew next to nothing about. He remembered how he excitedly, stubbornly, and doggedly convinced her that it was a no-fail deal. To this day, that heated argument rings in his head. He remembered as Lara waved her hands in disgust and exasperation. "I am your wife, for Christ's sake!" she had said. "Please listen to me, even if it's just this time." If only he had listened, maybe life would not have been so difficult for him.

Now, he was back to struggling, just like every other newcomer. What about the months he spent hustling, taking up multiple jobs, coming home tired and exhausted from work? What were the months for? As he struggled to answer these questions in his mind, he noticed tears spilling down his cheeks. His throat was blocked, and he just wanted to give in and cry like a baby. He wanted to cry to his heart's content. He wanted to cry till he felt as empty as his bank account. This was not his plan when he left Nigeria; he did not come to England to work like an elephant and live like an ant. His goal was not to struggle forever. But here he was, with less than a penny to his name and no place to call home.

Akon picked himself up. He needed to get a place to live first. He reminisced on how he had struggled to find a place in the past few weeks. This was primarily because he had only spent three months in the UK and could not get two references. Conversely, some landlords demanded six months' worth of payslips, which he did not have. Other estate agents wanted a guarantor. He could not provide one either.

And I thought Naija was hard; this country is on a level of its own! To ease the negativity and pressure, Akon decided to stay away from everyone who knew him or discouraged him. *Bad energy, stay far away.* He also wanted to prove everyone wrong; he wanted to prove that he could do it independently.

Just then, his phone rang. It was Uncle Bode, the one person he could always talk to. Not that he could not speak to his wife Lara, but he would rather not concern her with his current situation.

"Hello! Ekaaro, Sir," he greeted in his local dialect.

"How are you?" Uncle Bode responded likewise.

Akon took a few minutes to explain all that had happened in the last few weeks—how he had been sleeping in hostels at £5 per night with different kinds of people, how he did not like it, and how he had his things stolen a couple of times.

"Ha! This is serious. What do you want to do now?"

Uncle Bode questioned.

"I am still trying to secure a small place, a room or something. I have an appointment with another property agent this morning. I need a place to call home, but something I can afford," Akon replied. "Na who get money dey get choice. Soup wey sweet, na money kill am."

"It is well. Whichever way things turns out, just keep me posted. I have exhausted my call card. Odabo," Uncle Bode quickly said as the call dropped.

Not long after the phone call with his uncle, Akon boarded a taxi. It was a sunny day, and everything seemed right. The traffic was light; the driver was amiable and lively. If Akon believed in astrology, he would have said that all his stars were properly aligned today. He felt like something good would happen. He did not know what, but he just felt something great was about to happen. As he stepped into the agent's office, he heard a deep, enthralling male voice about thirty metres away. This caught his attention, and he looked up to identify the person with such a friendly voice.

He found a slim man of about forty years in a flowery yellow and orange shirt with long dreadlocks. He looked like a freedom fighter that had gained his freedom. He was in a bubbly, celebratory mode. Akon recognised his style and manner of talking as the Jamaican *patois*.

"Mi soon come, mi dear, mi need fi mek money ya so enuh. Tek it easy honey, yuh a gwan good out dehwidout mi. Big up yuhself," the man said, speaking into his mobile phone. "Wagwaan! Bless up! Bless up."

As the man ended the call, Akon and the housing agent stared at him, quite entertained by his lively demeanour.

Greg's voice brought Akon out of his reverie, "Bomboklaat! Seven hundred pounds for a one-bedroom flat? You must be kidding me!"

Greg turned to the agent and said, "C'mon man! It is too much, wagwaan! I came to the UK to survive and better my life, not spend all my life savings." Bemused, Akon could swear he heard the man say *kilode.*

While Akon was still amused by the gentleman, Greg turned to him and said, "Welcome mi fren. Wehyuh ah seh?"

Akon seemed confused. "What?" he replied?

"Wehyuh ah seh, mi fren. Wahgwaan. Small up yuhself an make room fi mi. Two black men ah help each odda."

Akon stilled. Confused, he tried to put Greg's words together. He then realised the man was offering to share the one-bedroom flat so they could split the rent.

"I think it's cool," he replied.

To date, he still does not understand how it

happened. Greg had such an infectious and cheerful personality. Within ten minutes, Akon and the Jamaican were riding inside a car with the agent to view the one-bedroom flat. It turned out to be bigger than he had imagined, and they decided they would partition it.

A day later, Akon and Greg moved in and settled down. Greg turned on his music from a small sound system he carried around. He engaged Akon in a conversation. "You will taste our cuisine, my friend. I'm a chef in disguise," Greg told him, unpacking some food-stuff from a bag.

"Oh, really?" Akon replied, even though it took him time to understand Greg when he spoke. He was beginning to enjoy his company, which made him think moving in together was not a bad idea.

"So, apart from being a good cook, what do you do?" Akon asked.

"Mi make good paintings, ma picture on ya wall," he replied.

"Photography?" Akon inquired.

"No, no mi man, mi don't do photograph. Greg is a fine artist." Greg showed Akon some of his recent works. He had arrived only a week earlier and was an outstanding artist. Akon could hardly believe he had drawn the paintings when he saw them. Greg said he had sold a picture for £300 the day before.

"British people appreciate art," he said. "Jamaicans buy a painting for £50. The British buy the same painting for £300, mi back foot!"

Akon felt that Greg would be an amusing companion, and he indeed was. Greg was about 58 years old. He was an artist and a musician, but he had come to the UK as an art exhibitor.

They soon settled in the one-bedroom flat. The living room was partitioned, so it became Greg's room. At the same time, he used the other part, the dining area, for his art exhibition. Greg asked if Akon would like to take the bedroom, and Akon agreed. He had to share the bathroom with Greg, which they both agreed was not a problem.

Akon came back home late from work most evenings, while Greg came home earlier. This was ideal for them as Greg had ample time to do the cooking, and he loved it. True to his word, Greg was a great cook. Sadly, it made Akon miss Lara and her sumptuous delicacies even more. On seeing another man do the cooking, Akon felt that he should try to help. So, Akon decided to wash the dishes after meals, clean the bathrooms and toilets and try his hand at easy meals. He was not confident enough to prepare main meals, so he shied away from them.

On the other hand, Greg was a complete bundle of entertainment. *This guy will make sense in Naija sha. Even with no light, he will still entertain everybody.* He was always like, "So, this happened to one of my friends some years ago." He always had a funny story for every situation. Greg never seemed to run out of tales and did not try to change his style or accent to fit in. He did not care who knew he was Jamaican. This helped him in his painting business.

Akon, on the other hand, could not stop thinking about Lara. "Lara would be very worried," he thought. He had been calling her three times a week, but now he was calling once a week. Between transport fares, utility bills, meals, and rent, he barely had any savings. He wondered how he would have survived if he rented the flat all by himself. Besides the rent, he needed to pay for council tax, water, light, and gas. The bills never stopped coming. He remembered the words of his cousin, Henry: "It is not easy to be a man." He decided to do another professional course in Accounting. He needed to be a qualified accountant despite his other papers. That meant more expenses. He had to deny himself, even if it meant calling Lara once a month. However, Akon promised himself to contact Lara via email once a week. Unfortunately, Lara was not regular with her emails.

*   *   *

Akon's heart raced as he stared at the man sitting across the desk from him. He was nervous, and his palms were sweaty. Harry Taylor, a well-known and successful accountant in the finance industry, was the head of finance in a huge company, and he was currently sizing Akon up. Harry was Lebanese, and his company was an international firm. He looked at Akon closely, picking up every detail about him, from the beads of sweat on his brow to the way he struggled to maintain eye contact. *Are all Africans untrustworthy? Is corruption flowing through their bloodstream? They seem to reek of it. The company needed a professional African to join their team, and Akon seemed good enough.*

"Ours is a fast-paced environment, and we need professionals who can work with limited supervision and show initiative. With your current qualifications, all you need is to do your ACCA professional exams." He held up a hand as Akon opened his mouth to speak. "Although you have passed your ICAN exams, I am afraid we cannot accept that here.

"So, Mr Akon, can you do this job? We are continually expanding our offices; therefore, be assured you will get a space, but you will need to devote time to prepare for the exams. I can see that all your experience was obtained from abroad. We have two offices here in London, one in Abu Dhabi, one in Cairo, and another in Canada, which is where our head office is located.

We have just opened our branch in South Africa, and we are working on expansion in Africa. So, we need somebody who understands the African market. How does that sound?" Harry asked.

"It sounds perfect, Mr Taylor. I am grateful for this opportunity. It's a rare one," Akon gushed.

"Good, I will have your name placed on our waiting list while you work to obtain the necessary professional qualifications. Once you register for the course, let me know. Who knows, we may be able to offer you a trainee or voluntary role. You could come in once or twice a week to learn about the company in preparation for your job. Do you think you'll be up to the task?"

Akon nearly collapsed with joy. "Yes, yes, I can, sir. That sounds perfect, sir."

"Now, I'll ask you one more time. Are you certain you are not going to disappoint me if I offer you this job? From what I can see, you are the right man for the job. That's why I picked you out of many other applicants." Harry looked at Akon with doubt in his eyes.

"I won't disappoint you, Mr Taylor," Akon assured him.

"Alright then. Get me two referees and proof of work permit. I will let you know the start date for the trainee role. Sounds good?" Harry asked.

Akon pumped Harry's hand in a handshake and left

the office. He was interested in the job position and knew it would be a long-term goal. He would need some money to buy textbooks, attend a few lectures, and sit exams. He decided he would call Lara and see how much she could raise.

If I can set my feet in this prestigious company within twelve to fifteen months, I would be unstoppable. Akon was so excited that he quoted Harry Taylor word for word as he spoke to Lara on the phone.

*   *   *

Akon watched as the old woman walking towards him gave him the side-eye and abruptly crossed to the other side of the street. She was not the first person to treat him that way, and he had a gut feeling she would not be the last. He walked into the corner shop, moving towards the shelves. He noticed one of the clerks following him around, glancing furtively at him.

"For God's sake, I'm not going to steal anything," he wanted to shout. Instead, he acted as though he had not noticed the clerk. Maybe because he was lost in thought, he did not see the man moving towards him until they bumped into each other.

"Oh, sorry! Sorry man!" the other man apologised. Akon noticed that the man was black, although his accent sounded American. Still, it was better than before when he was the only black person in the shop.

"No problem," Akon told the man, waving his hand.

He was about to move on when he noticed the other man staring at him in surprise. "You are new here, ain't ya?" Akon nodded, shooting the man a nervous smile. "Cool. I'm Zach," he announced, holding out his hand.

Akon shook it, relaxing at the man's friendliness. "Akon. Nice to meet you." Akon glanced at the clerk and realised the man was no longer looking at them with suspicion, eyes flicking back and forth between them as if one of them was going to pull out a gun.

"Right back at ya. So," Zach said, pulling some packets of pasta from the shelves. Akon turned his attention to the man. "How are you finding things?"

Normally, he would not share his feelings with a stranger. But his frustration had driven all reservations from his mind. "It has been difficult. Every bit of it— finding a job, getting a good house, even walking down the street. Everyone seems to have an attitude, and it's just because I am black. I am tired of it."

Zach let out an exuberant laugh that drew the attention and disapproval of other shoppers. He slapped Akon on the back and opened his mouth to speak, but the laughter started up again. He even doubled over with it. "Funniest thing I've heard all day, man."

Akon stiffened, wondering if Zach was making fun of him.

"What did you expect?" Zach asked, finally serious. "That they'd roll out the red carpet?"

Akon frowned. "No, but that doesn't mean people have to treat me like I have a disease or something." As if to emphasise what he was trying to say, the clerk suddenly approached them.

"Er... I'm sorry, but our customers are bothered by your presence in the store. Please, make your purchases quickly and leave."

I've had enough! Akon stormed out of the shop, without purchasing anything. He had walked for about a minute when someone touched his shoulder. He whirled around, ready to pour out his anger, before realising it was Zach.

Zach smiled. "I don't have the time right now, but maybe we could meet up later?" he asked, handing Akon a business card. They arranged for dinner before going their separate ways.

10

Zach and Akon sat in a restaurant and had been deep in conversation for hours. Zach speared a piece steak with his fork and placed it in his mouth. "I kinda get that you were angry and stuff when you left the other day. You gotta learn to hold your anger in. Don't let it push you into rash actions, you know," he said amid mouthfuls.

Akon sighed. "I know that, but it's not fair. One of my new neighbours complained to the building owner; he does not want to live beside me. Then there are the police officers stopping me, for being on the streets at 1.00 am. I had to show them my work ID, telling them I do night shifts. It is disgusting. Do you blame them? Some of our black people are into drugs, fraud, and these people believe every young black man is like that.

That is a wrong assumption. Why paint all black people with the same brush?"

"Look, bro, I know what you are talking about. It is the same in America. You got the whites hating on blacks and Hispanics and everyone who is not exactly like them. Not gonna say it is fair cause it ain't. But we just gotta live with it.

"You know," Zach continued as he sipped his wine, "Back home, before I came to the UK, I know someone who got killed by a police officer. Friend of a friend kinda thing. He did nothing. You know what I'm saying? It was some big party, full of these kids who had just finished high school. So, some people called the cops, and the kids heard the sirens and stuff, and they started bailing, you know. Got all of 'em running away, and that type o' place, the police don't bother to take anyone in because they'd be arresting everybody, yeah?"

Akon nodded, intrigued.

"You got the cops watching these white kids as they ran out and jumped fences and stuff, but then this guy followed some of his friends out the gate, running and laughing. Know what I'm saying? It was one of the girls who told us what went down. So, here's this kid, running and laughing, and the next thing, he's stumbling, and there is a splash of red everywhere."

Akon shuddered. He had heard this kind of story before, and it never got easier to bear. He waited as Zach wiped his eye before continuing. "They took the cop in, and he said he thought the boy was committing robbery, said the shooting was an accident." Zach laughed, but there was no joy in the sound. "You got kids running away from a party, and you say you thought it was a robbery. He got two years, if you can believe that. In some pansy prison."

"That's… That is horrible."

"Yeah, that's what I'm saying. You complain about how they stop you on the road or run when they see you, but it could be worse, yeah?"

Akon nodded as his throat choked. "Yeah, I know that."

"So, maybe life sucks, you know what I'm saying? Like, I'm always gonna be a minority as long as I wanna live in the US of A or in the UK. It ain't fair, but what are you gonna do? Just gotta keep on living, doing what you can, yeah?"

"Yeah," Akon echoed. He just had to keep doing what he could for himself and his family.

Zach nodded. It was then that he began to reveal to Akon the details of his life story. Zach had lived on his own since he was twenty-one, but he still felt the excitement of freedom as if it was his first-day independence.

Back in the US, Zach went through a lot under the Fosters. His parents died in a car crash when he was fifteen, and his father had believed that Mr Foster was the best friend and neighbour he could ever have. In his will, he left his son in the care of the loving Fosters in the unfortunate event of his death. K Marshall, the attorney, had handled it, not knowing that Zach was due for the worst six years of his life.

Zach Wilson was to inherit fifty-six thousand dollars with interest earned, but not before he turned twenty-one. In the meantime, he was to remain under his appointed guardians' care. According to the will in the event of his parents' death, Zach's guardians would receive a goodwill payment amounting to twenty thousand dollars.

When Zach's parents died, the wonderful neighbour, who had often visited his father and chatted with him over the fence, became his guardian. Though Zach knew that twenty thousand dollars had been paid to his guardian, he was not aware of the fifty-six thousand that had been transferred to a trust, which K Marshall decided would be his twenty-first birthday surprise.

The next six years were unbearable. Keith Foster, his father's *good* friend, turned out to be a monster with two oversized brats for sons. Mrs Foster died when Zach was seventeen. She was kind to Zach. Even though Keith was not nice to him and the sons, Sam and Shawn, bullied him, she always defended him and made him feel like he belonged.

When she died, Zach turned into a house-help who was always picked upon. He often prepared the meals, especially when Isabella, the maid, did not come. He received a little allowance, and if he got home late, he had to make his own meal or go to bed hungry. He would often stare across the house that used to be home, longing for those days of peace and happiness.

On one occasion, Shawn, who was three years older than Zach and a year older than Sam, sprayed pepper into Zach's eyes. The brothers laughed as he screamed, fell, and tried to find his way to the tap water. That was just one of the many times Zach experienced cruelty at the hands of his newfound *family*.

Zach had told K Marshall he wanted a new guardian, but Marshall had explained that he had to respect the will's conditions until he turned twenty-one. He also said there might be five thousand bucks somewhere when he turned twenty-one. Zach had not been impressed, but he had kept quiet, knowing that his parents had wanted the best for him and that the Fosters were fully to blame.

Zach had always wanted to sing so he joined two high school friends to form a band, but Keith Foster soon put an end to that.

It was a relief when he got a call from Marshall on his twenty-first birthday. Shawn sometimes dropped him at the L.A. School of Library and Information Science, where he took a course that had not been his choice, but Keith's. Shawn sometimes left him behind, and he had to take the bus.

Zach was about to head for home for another boring birthday celebration, one that he was not allowed to invite friends, when he got a call from K Marshall. The latter sounded happy and asked to see him. When he got to Marshall's office, he found him in a great mood. Zach would never forget that day in 2000.

"I have waited for years to get this off my chest, Zach," Marshall said.

"You are making me nervous, Mr Marshall," Zach said. "Do you know it's my birthday? I'm twenty-one today."

"I know that. Happy birthday, Zach," Marshall said. "You came to me when you were seventeen, and you were going through a hard time at the Fosters. You were always confused because it was your Dad's wish that, should anything happen to your parents, the Fosters would take care of you. I know it has not turned out to be the ideal home that your father wanted for you. I tried to encourage you, telling you that you were due for five thousand bucks when you turned twenty-one."

"Oh, man! I forgot all about it," Zach replied. "Twenty-one seemed like a century away back then."

Marshall nodded. "Well, besides the college fund that your Dad left behind."

"Wait a minute! Do you mean my parents paid for my college education and not the Fosters?"

"Yes. Your Dad had it all planned. Twenty thousand to your guardians. He took care of college for a course of your choice."

"You mean my dad gave me the freedom to choose? Sounds like my dad alright! Mr Foster forced me to take a different course! The only reason I did not run away from the Fosters was that I thought they were paying for my college education! You should have told me, Mr Marshall."

"Never mind that. Some experiences make a man of you."

"Not many men had to go through that," Zach argued.

"As I said, never mind that. The truth is, your dad did not leave you five thousand, but fifty-six thousand, deposited along with the will when you were only ten years old, which today, plus interest, is seventy-two thousand dollars. You are a man now and you no longer need a guardian. You can take control of your life. All legal fees and dues have already been settled.

This is your money, Zach, and I am proud to hand it over. Your dad would have been satisfied with my work."

Zach cried uncontrollably. When he gained control, he said, "I have no words, Mr Marshall. You have been extremely kind. My dad made many great choices in life, except the day he chose to drive behind a drunkard. He made a great choice in choosing his attorney or solicitor, should I call you that? I will pay you."

"You will do nothing of the sort, Zach. I am the happiest of happy men to have settled this matter with my long-gone client. Go and live a better life; you deserve it. Do you have a bank account?"

"I do."

Years later, when Zach was twenty-eight, he had moved to the UK. Maybe his lifelong desire to fit in would be fulfilled.

Akon waited until Zach finished narrating his story before asking: "Seems your story had a happy ending. So why did you leave?"

"Let me tell you something about being a mixed-race person. Because you are neither a straight African nor Caribbean or English, you always try to fit in. I thought this was just a US problem and that I might finally be able to fit in if I came here. Turns out it is a global problem. It is the same way you find yourself dealing with many problems as an outsider trying to fit in. I have been trying to fit in all my life."

* * *

Greg believed he had found the right job. Sam, the boss, seemed like a nice guy. Greg had a tinted-glass office that stood above a green warehouse. Here, trucks would arrive from Felixstowe, bringing freight containers packed with low-quality dried Robusta coffee beans. Once in the warehouse, the coffee would be processed and repackaged as Blue Mountain Jamaican coffee, one of the world's best brands. Greg hated when he had to talk to clients in his Jamaican accent. He did not like to lie, but he was helpless. People thought he was a manager, but Sam was paying him less than half of what he deserved. It was the price he had to pay for staying here without proper documentation.

Greg was also unhappy with other aspects of his new job. Mike, one of the warehouse supervisors, had told him they had a process of making the coffee taste like the real deal, and it involved some mixtures that Greg was afraid might be harmful. Even though Mike insisted they were all-natural, it did not ease Greg's worries. He wished he could explain the situation to his mother back home so he could take this weight off his shoulders, but he was afraid of discussing his illegal status on the phone. *You never know who would be listening.* And he had no intention of letting his London friends, including Akon, know. He felt they might view him differently.

Sam had informed Greg there was a meeting on Friday at 10.00 a.m.

"This is important," he said. "We are introducing a new angle to this business."

"Let us do legal business, man. Mi nuh wa fi guh a jail, man."

"What does that mean?" Sam asked impatiently.

"I don't want no brush with de law, man. I don't want to go to jail."

"Don't worry. My plan is failproof. No jail."

Sam knew a lot was riding on in this meeting. He had cast the bait, but he needed to make it stick. He had to sell the idea. He had managed to turn low-quality coffee into high-quality coffee. Now, he was ready to take things a notch higher. His friends would be at this meeting. They probably doubted he was street-savvy enough to come up with an idea that involved deceiving the customs department. Perhaps they did not believe he had the guts for it. Being successful in business was one thing; but getting away with criminal activity was a different ballgame.

Greg was concerned as Sam explained his plan to the other men. It sounded like a smuggling scheme.

Which was more dangerous? Being an illegal resident or part of a smuggling ring?

"Mi wi hide. No criminal things for me. Mi wi hide."

So, when Akon arrived home, he found a note in place of Greg.

"Sorry, my friend, I left. I'll pay you a visit one day."

Akon frowned. What was going on? One day, Greg was there, laughing with him as they made dinner. The next day, he was gone along with most of his things.

Greg left Akon's place because Sam knew where he lived, and he had no intention of working with Sam again. Also, Sam might make good on his threat to report Greg to the authorities.

Greg was worried about something else. He knew Sam was going into smuggling, and Sam might try to silence him. The best idea was to stay away.

* * *

Zach brushed his way into the Royal Parcel office. Glancing around to ensure that Danny Mitchell, the director, was nowhere in sight, he bowed mockingly and grinned at his colleagues in the open office.

"How are you doing, everyone?" he greeted. Zach liked to joke around. His colleagues called him Zach, and the name had stuck. "Guess who had an awesome weekend?" He pointed at his head. "This guy! London is cooler than I thought. When I was in Los Angeles, I always said, 'Those UK peeps, they don't know a thing!'"

He had met a girl over the weekend at a dinner he had been invited to. She seemed nice, and their lively discussion and the fact that they had exchanged numbers had dramatically improved his mood.

"The only radiant thing on your face is sweat, Zach," Claire, the secretary, said with a roll of her blue eyes.

The others laughed. There was Andrew, who was Zach's boss, and Pete. Four people were enough to run the Royal Parcel office, the administrative branch of the parcel company Zach now worked for. Most of the other staff members were at the warehouse below.

"Please do some work," Andrew said, his eyes glued to his computer. "You waste at least three hours every day on silly jokes."

"I think Zach's funny," Pete protested.

"Funny!" Andrew snapped, shooting Pete an angry glance. "I should take you to see a real comedian later this week so you can stop laughing at primary school jokes."

"Oh, you mean grade school," Zach said. "You are trippin, bro."

"It's not called grade school. This is the UK, not the US," Andrew said. "It's one thing to take a man from America. It's quite another to take America out of a man."

Claire laughed. Zach snorted and moved to his desk.

"Many people struggle to secure jobs in London because of unappreciated talents. You cannot see new talent coming up and kick it to the curb," Zach said.

"I'll kick you to the curb if you don't forward yesterday's report by midday," Andrew replied.

Claire's laughter was interrupted by Zach's phone ringing in his pocket. He frowned at it before answering. "Hello?" a gruff voice said. "Hi, Zach. Are you proud of what you did?"

Zach frowned. "What? Is that you, Abe?" Abe was the internal auditor whom they referred to as the *spy*. Zach had begun to suspect that Abe hated him. He felt it had something to do with his skin colour. *I thought this racist bullshit was only American. A brother is blacked in LA and blacked here too? Damn!*

"Never mind who I am. Are you proud of what you did?"

Zach was getting impatient. This guy was just being a nuisance. "I will hang up on you in six seconds unless you begin to make sense," he said into the phone.

"A week ago, five hundred pounds that were being refunded to the company expenses account, which you oversaw, went straight into your pocket. I have the records, Zach. You used it for your own purposes and did not issue a receipt for the cash. You banked it in your account and sent an email to your friend Elvis telling him how lucky you were. I'm looking at the message on my screen right now."

Zach gulped. He was speechless. He got up and walked into the corridor. "You are looking at the email I sent from my phone?" Zach paused for a minute, his stomach flashing with sudden fear. "Hey, I'm talking to Abe, right? Are you an internal auditor or a spy?"

Zach recalled the money. He had transferred it to his account to qualify for some bank vetting by a certain lender because his friend, Jeremiah, who was supposed to lend him business capital, had not deposited the money. It would probably take more than forty-eight hours.

"I'm cleaning up the company, Zach. You are not in some Inglewood gang. This is London, and a crime is a crime."

"I have never been in a gang. Not every black person in America is in a gang," Zach said, clenching his fists. Yet he did not want to lose his job. "To be honest, I only borrowed the funds and intended to refund it within forty-eight hours."

"That is fraud. Oh, embezzlement is a casual thing where you grew up, is it? And how do you intend to return it? Got some money coming your way?"

Zach breathed heavily. "Believe me within forty-eight hours, the money will be in the account."

Half an hour later, Zach's phone rang. It was Jeremiah. "Just deposited the £500 into your account, bro."

"Thank you. Can you believe I am still black across the Atlantic? One of my bosses thinks I'm a former Inglewood gang member."

His friend chuckled.

"It's not funny," Zach continued. "One of the main reasons I came to the UK was so I could be treated like me. Not as Zach the black. I had a racist employer in LA." He sighed into the phone before saying, "Thanks for sending it. They had already found out that I used their money to settle this issue. I'll just replace it."

"There you go. You are acting like the gangster you do not want to be. You shouldn't have used the company's money. If your employer has that kind of attitude, everything you do will be interpreted through that prism. Take care, bro."

Zach logged into his account and transferred the funds to the company's account.

"Zach, did you deposit five hundred pounds into your account instead of the company's account?"

Avoiding the actual question, Zach said with a deadpan expression, "The money is in the company's account, sir. I am sorry about that. I was desperate to make the right impression to a potential investor. I knew my friend was sending replacement funds in hours. My account had to appear to have the money in it. I had borrowed it as I waited for my friend to send me the funds."

"Don't pull a trick like that again."

11

Akon stared at the 2007 calendar on the wall. Life had been humbling in the three years since he moved to the UK. Akon had experienced things he never thought he would experience in his life.

The son of Otunba Akanni Akete, brought up on the lap of luxury and comfort, could only afford to eat chicken once a week. He even struggled to buy groceries! He had to travel by bus or train. He now cherished the little things he once took for granted when he was growing up. He had never gone to bed hungry back home. He now knew what it meant to worry about long and arduous nights because often he had to sleep on an empty stomach.

What would his friends in Lagos say if they get to know about his situation? They knew he was comfortable in Lagos, and they believed he must be doing much better now.

Akon had managed to keep away from people who could spread rumours about his condition, at least until he could confidently say that he had "made it." He had promised Lara that he would visit every six months, but this had not been possible. He was only able to speak to Jabez through Skype, and the little champ always asked the question: "Dad, when are you coming back?"

Akon consoled himself that whatever needed to be done must be done well. He needed to settle down in the UK so his family could join him later. He had told Lara not to tell anyone about his situation. Bad news spread quickly in Lagos.

Akon sighed when he thought about the assets he had sold. The sacrifices seemed necessary today for future stability. The lack of security back home was one of the reasons he wanted to move his family to London. He had his own brush with *area boys* and crime when he was a teenager growing up under his father's roof. Being the chief's son, he had been shielded from crime most of the time, yet he had not managed to escape it totally.

He recalled an experience he had while growing up. It was still vivid in his mind. It was a time when he was close to his two sisters, before they realised their father loved him more than any other child, and jealousy and animosity had driven a wedge between them. He could not remember the last time he had spoken to either Folu Dunni or Ibukun. Bose was the youngest sister and was kept out of the sibling rivalries. Akon remembered his friend Tayo, who was his best friend when they were younger, but they had since lost touch.

They had lived in an affluent neighbourhood in Ikoyi. They resided in a beautiful mansion, and his father had owned a lovely silver Benz.

Akon's mind focused sharply on a memory from when he was fourteen years old.

"Akon, please drop this briefcase at Uncle Diran's place on your way back from school," his mother had called to him one Tuesday morning, just before Akon left for school. It was a sealed A5 khaki envelope. Sometimes, Akon rode his bike to Uncle Diran's place, which was only about a kilometre away from his home.

"What's in it?" Akon inquired.

"I have no idea," his mother replied. "And I don't think they wanted anyone to know or they would not have sealed it, don't you think?"

"Who brought it here?"

"Your usual curiosity is in top gear today, I see," his mother sighed. "It arrived yesterday along with a parcel your Dad sent. You know he's away at some conference this week."

"Did you open the parcel?"

"Are you a detective now?" His mother pushed Akon towards the door. "Your father called me and said he is in Abuja. He forgot to deliver it before he left. You and your sisters were at school. Sorry, I forgot to tell you last night."

Akon and Folu did not go to the same school. Sometimes she left earlier or later than Akon. The driver drove her and Ibukun to school most of the time, while Akon's father drove him to school. This was one of those small things that would later cause a rift among the siblings.

Folu and Ibukun had begun to wonder why Akon attended a better school, one that was closer to the house? Why didn't father bother to drive them to school as he did Akon? But when they were younger, these things did not seem to bother them.

So, after school, Akon took his bike and rode off. He loved his bike. Uncle Diran lived alone in an apartment along Gbagada Road. He was no family man, and his best moments were spent inside a van he drove around town when he was hired to deliver merchandise. Akon found his way to the stairs that would take him to the fourth floor of the apartment. If Uncle Diran were not in, his wife would be, or Isiatu, the house help who often looked after eight-year-old Teju.

Akon rang the bell. After a minute, a man he had never seen before opened the door. Two things seemed strange. Why didn't they switch on the light as they opened the door? Who was this man, opening the door to Uncle Diran's house?

"Yes?" the man rasped in a voice that told Akon he was not welcome.

"I'm here to see my uncle," Akon said. "Who are you? What are you doing in his house?"

"This is my house." The man suddenly grabbed Akon by the collar. He pulled him close, and Akon could smell stale garlic, cigarettes, and beer on his breath. It was enough to make him feel faint. "If you want me to be your uncle, just ask nicely instead of forcing things, okay?"

His words would have been funny to Akon, but the last thing he felt like doing was laughing under the circumstances. He realised he should have called his uncle's home before visiting. The "garlic man" pushed Akon roughly, releasing the boy from his grip, making Akon stagger backwards.

"That's a terrible way of welcoming people," Akon retorted. "My uncle lives here. Or has he moved?"

A hand grabbed Akon by the collar, lifted him off his feet, and hurled him into the dark passage that led to the living room. A foot kicked the door shut.

"Who sent you here, kid? The police?"

"No! My uncle used to live here. Maybe he switched houses, but he used to live here!" Akon's voice was trembling. The air reeked of a nauseating smoke he was not familiar with, which he thought might be weed. A friend at school had introduced him to it, but he decided he did not like it after taking a few puffs.

The man seemed to pause and consider the situation. Perhaps he did not want Akon to make a scene or call anyone.

"Wahidi! Close that door!" a voice snarled from inside the dark house. "Are you crazy?"

"Don't talk to me like that!" Wahidi snarled back. Footsteps approached them and a man, so big he made Akon catch his breath, appeared. He grabbed Akon's captor, just the way the drunkard had held Akon by the collar. He shook him and banged his head against the wall. The man yelled in pain.

The giant glared at Akon. "What do you want, kid?"

Before Akon could answer, the giant kicked the man into the dark living room, and Akon heard him stagger and fall.

"My uncle lived here, sir," Akon said, flinching away from those big hands. He did not want to mess with the new arrival. The dark living room intrigued him though.

"We moved in here three weeks ago. Why didn't this uncle of yours tell you he had moved? Not a very communicative uncle, is he?" the hefty man said to Akon with a sneer. He must have been over six feet tall.

Just then, somebody switched on the living room light behind the huge man. Akon gaped as he saw lots of Thousand Naira notes spread all over the seats, carpet, and tables.

"Who did that? Which idiot switched on the light?" the giant bawled. The light went off.

Akon knew he may have seen too much. As the big man turned towards the living room, Akon sprang to the door, ran down the corridor towards the stairs, and fled. He nearly knocked down an elderly lady coming up the stairs, who began to scream. Akon sprinted to the floor and burst outside. He slowed down once he realised no one was following him. Maybe the men had nothing to hide despite all the money.

The moment Akon got home, he told his mother and sisters about it all. "Trust you to turn a normal visit to an uncle into a sinister adventure," Bose shook her head in wonder. "Do you find trouble, or does trouble find you? I thought you knew uncle Diran moved. He is only a few blocks away in the orange house. So careless that we do not have the new number, and no one seems to pick up the old one."

"So, do I call the police?" Akon wondered.

"I would advise you to call as an anonymous caller from a booth," his mother said. "If you identify yourself, you may spend your future in courtrooms and police stations answering endless questions and identifying people. I don't want you to be directly involved."

Akon's father was respected in the neighbourhood. The police would probably not trouble Chief Akete's son. They were one of the most affluent families in the area and had a big yard around their house, surrounded by a wall. Yet Akon's mother was worried that if he witnessed a crime, the criminals might decide to take revenge.

This experience had stuck with Akon ever since. No matter how protected you were, if your neighbourhood were unsafe, you could get into trouble at any time. Safety at home does not mean safety on the streets. And if there was trouble outside those walls, who knew when it would jump over the wall? Perhaps the problem was not just the neighbourhood but the entire city. Maybe gates and walls were not enough so long as you were a resident of the town.

*   *   *

Lara stared at the TV, but her mind was far away. Maria, the house girl, had taken Jabez to bed and since retired too. The only other person in the compound was Adebiyi, who had his own quarters behind the large house.

Akon had called her earlier in the day. Admittedly, life had been tough for him, but now the future seemed bright. He had been promised a job as the coordinator for a multinational company trying to tap into the African market. A Regional Finance Controller sounded great. But first, he needed to obtain professional credentials in accounting. The CEO would wait while Akon took the course, which, due to the exemptions he would be granted for impressive qualifications, would take a year. The salary was great - five times his Lagos salary. But in the meantime, how would he survive for a year in the UK? How would he pay for the course? Education in the UK was more expensive than it was in Nigeria. So, he had called Lara to try and arrange his finances.

"You mean the reason you called is not that you miss me so much, but because you want us to arrange for some money to be sent over?" she asked, without sounding angry.

"You know I miss you," Akon replied. "I miss you every day. But I have not been able to afford calling you that often. We could not speak on the phone for months, and when we did, I could not stay on for long? I was worried. Suppose I called and you said you were married to somebody else?"

"Your faith in me seems to be little," Lara said. "Were you so broke that you couldn't even call?"

Akon laughed. "You have no idea how hard things can get around here. A phone card is £5, and that could sort meals for two or three days. After I was laid off from that packaging job because I could not keep up with the pace, I spent five months without a job. Then my housemate, Greg, disappeared mysteriously and left no forwarding address. I have no idea why. He was a great person."

"Maybe he got tired of you," she joked. Akon laughed.

"Your sense of humour always lightens my dark spirit," he said. "I wish I could just hold you."

"In a little while," Lara hoped.

12

Lara tried to listen to the song, but she was feeling a little faint. She told the driver to turn the volume down. She closed her eyes and tried to stay calm. The day had been like a wrecking ball, and she had been the wall. She was exhausted. She wanted to get home; she wanted the warmth of her bed sheets. She could already picture herself getting in the shower and slipping under the covers.

"Adebiyi, can you turn it off, please?" Lara said. The driver turned the stereo off. She sighed. The silence was better.

They were almost home. She thought about her husband who was struggling to settle in London, but that only reminded her she would later walk into a lonely house. Lara sighed again. Akon had been gone for long, and she was beginning to feel like he was gone forever. She pushed the thoughts away and tried to focus on seeing her son.

Lara turned on her phone and was about to call Maria when the car hit a bump and then another. It suddenly spiralled out of control. The phone flew from her hands, and Lara was flung against the front seat, her face hitting it so hard that her head exploded with pain. She wanted to scream but could not. The car swayed, and Adebiyi tried to regain control. Finally, the car screeched to a halt out of the road.

"Are you alright, ma?" the driver asked. Lara shook her head. She could feel pain all over, and blood was dripping from her nose.

"What happened?" she asked; her voice higher than she wanted it to be. Adebiyi had been driving her husband before they got married. He was a fantastic driver, which was why Akon had told him to stay and drive her around the city. She knew Adebiyi was careful, and this had been a mistake, but she was angry regardless.

"What happened, ehn?" Lara asked again. "What's going on? Are you drunk or something?" She could hear the man apologising, but she did not care. The day was already a difficult one. She tried to get out of the car, desperately needing some air. She needed to raise her head, or there would be blood all over her shirt. She was about to do so when she heard a knock on the window. Someone pointed a torch straight at her, and the blinding light blocked her from seeing whoever it was. She heard Adebiyi swear in Yoruba, "This is trouble."

Another man knocked on the window behind her, and Lara jumped. Her heart was racing. She turned to Adebiyi. The driver stared ahead, and when Lara looked up, she saw why. A man was standing in front of the car, pointing a gun at them. He gestured for them to come out. Adebiyi did not move; he could not move. But when he finally did, he opened the door and tried to step out, but the man pushed him back.

"Where you think say you dey go?" the man asked. Adebiyi shook his head. He turned to Lara, but she was too scared to look at him or even think. There was only one thing running through her mind: "not again!"

The man in the driver's seat unlocked the doors. He turned to Lara and grinned. The other two entered the car. All three were dressed in black, wielding guns. For the fifth time in Lara's life, she stared at what could be the end of her life.

"What do you want? I—" she began, but one of them hit her with the butt of his gun and everything faded. She could hear someone screaming, but it felt like it was happening far away. It was as if she could hear hundreds of bells going off at the same time before she passed out.

When Lara finally woke up, her head was pounding violently. She opened her eyes and then closed them immediately. The low light directly in front of her felt like it would pierce her brain. Lara blinked, pushing back a bit. She tried to move, but that only sent a shooting pain up her wrist and ankles. She looked down and saw the ropes, tied tight around her ankles.

"Madam?"

She moved her head to the left. She could recognise that voice anywhere. The rest of the room was pitch black. It seemed as if there was no one there. She tried to stare into the darkness, figure out if she knew where she was, but she couldn't. The light in front of her was just low enough to light up her feet, and the second pair next to them.

"Madam, are you alright?" Adebiyi asked, his Ondo accent making it seem like he was singing. She heard him try to move, struggling against the ropes. He groaned impatiently, moving against his confines again and again until he eventually stopped and settled down.

"Madam, I didn't… I no see… I no see them," Adebiyi began to cry. Lara sighed. Her head ached badly. She wondered what they had done to him. She had never imagined he would be the crying type. But she was scared too.

"Where are we?" Lara asked.

Adebiyi tried pulling against the ropes again. Every time he did, Lara cringed; she pictured the ropes digging into him, eating at his skin. He would start bleeding soon if he did not stop.

"Ah, you are awake," someone said. A door to their right opened slightly. A glimmer of light seemed to move up slowly until the individual was standing above them. The light grew brighter until Lara could finally see Adebiyi. At the sight of him, she flinched. His face was bloody. They had beaten him like he was a rogue beast they were trying to put under control. His mouth was bleeding. The light was not bright enough to see the rest of him, but she could only imagine how awful he must look.

"What do you want?" she asked, not looking away from her driver. The man walked closer, his footsteps making harsh sounds on the cement floor. He crouched beside Lara and pulled her face gently towards him. He was grinning when she finally looked at him. He had an exaggerated beard and thick eyebrows which concealed his face.

"You know what we want, Lara. I think you knew the moment you saw us," the man said. Lara shook her head. She did not know. Next to her, Adebiyi groaned. The man turned to look at the driver and shook his head.

"You give us what we want, and you can save him," he said, still holding Lara's face. She nodded.

"Good," the man said and pushed her face back. He chuckled, his voice a bit rough. He cleared his throat and stood up. "No games, we know all about you and your husband. We know that your husband is in the UK. We know you guys just sold your cars. Now, I no just dey tell you story because I be storyteller. I am telling you, so you know I did not pick you at random." Lara nodded.

"If you get us five million naira, you can kiss that sweet baby boy of yours tonight," the man continued. Lara froze. He looked at the man, but she could not see him properly with the hair on his face. The man grinned and turned to Adebiyi, pointing the gun at him.

"I don't need to beat him up; I can call my boys to go over there and play with your kid," he said. He was looking at Lara, but Lara was not looking back. She was thinking about Jabez being threatened with a gun. She imagined her son lying dead in his room just because someone thought she had five million naira. She could imagine Akon breaking down. She could hear herself going wild with grief and despair.

"Stop wasting my fucking time!"

"I don't… I don't have five million naira," she said. Her face was wet with sweat and tears. Her body shook uncontrollably. She was not scared for herself anymore, or even Adebiyi. She was thinking about her son. What was he doing now? What was Maria doing?

"Please, we don't have that money. I cannot get five million, sir. You can kill me. Kill me, but leave my son alone," she pleaded.

"You want your son to die because of five million naira?" the man asked. "You want Jabez to die because you want to keep your money?" The mention of her son's name pushed Lara to the edge. She started struggling against the ropes. She screamed as the ropes tore into her skin, but she did not care. She had to save her sweet boy. She wondered what he was wearing. Was he waiting up for her to come and tuck him in bed? She kept struggling and screaming, and the man watched her until her movements slowed and finally stopped.

"Please, I am telling you the truth. We do not have that kind of money. But I can get you something instead." She was talking fast. She coughed and then continued. "I can get about three hundred thousand naira. I can get that for you immediately. Please, don't touch my boy."

"All dis wicked people wey get money! Dem too dey pretend! You tink say I no know about the land wey you sell for seven million naira? You tink say I no know how much you take sell all the cars? If I confirm say na lie you dey lie, I go go your house, beat your house girl, and on top am, I go allow my men make dem do anytin dey like with her. I go even join your son too, before dem go kill two of dem. Den I go kon come back put bullet for all of una head. You get wetin I dey tok?"

"Abeg," Adebiyi begged, "no kill my madam son. Take anytin wey you like, no kill us o."

"What?" Lara asked. She was shocked that he knew, but she was more worried about her son. How was she ever going to live if they killed her son? How was she going to tell Akon their son had been murdered? What about his family? They would never forgive her. These thoughts were spinning around her head like a buzzing bee.

"I don't—" Lara sniffed and cleared her throat. She was tired. She tried to look at Adebiyi, but the man waved the gun at her, and she turned to face him immediately. "I don't know who told you about all that, but I sent the money to my husband. He needed the money for school. You think I have that amount with me? Take my phone and check my account. You will see what I have."

The man cursed and turned away from her. Lara took the opportunity to look at Adebiyi. The light was not bright enough for her to see him properly.

"Hey, she said she sent the money to her husband. You think say na lie? She said we can check her account." The man was speaking on the phone. He paused and nodded. "Okay," he said and ended the call. He stared at Lara for a while, gently walked up to her, and smacked her with the back of his hand. Lara screamed. The man slapped her again, but not as hard as the first time.

"If we check and it turns out you are lying, I will go to your house, beat your housemaid, and let my men do what they want with her before they kill them both. Then I will come back and put a bullet in your heads, understand?" Lara nodded. She just wanted to get home. She wanted to hold her boy; she wanted this night to end. She did not want to die. She kept saying it in her head, praying it. She let the words roll in her mind that she almost blurted them out.

The man left the room, and when he came back, three other men were with him. One had a mask on, and the other two wore subtle disguises. Lara watched the three men remove Adebiyi from the room, leaving her with the man she had been talking to previously. He sat on the chair her driver had been tied to and turned to look at her. She could see his face a little better from here.

"I know you have eight hundred thousand naira," the man said. "I know you have it at home. I know you do not want one of my friends to follow you home and kill everyone before taking the money. So, we will do something else. You will tell your maid where to get the money, and she will bring it to us. Either that or I blow your head off right now." He spoke these words calmly as if he were discussing where to take her on a date. Lara was not concerned that he seemed to know a lot about the money. She did not care anymore. She nodded her head vigorously in agreement.

When Maria later delivered the money, Lara told her to bring to her captors, the men decided to let them go. The man who was sent to the ATM to confirm that Lara's account had no money had come back with confirmation that the account indeed had no funds. Of course, Lara could not say she had given them the details of an empty account.

Lara had driven the car home because Adebiyi's left hand was bleeding. Lara suggested they stop at the hospital, but Adebiyi refused. "I will use engine oil and bandage," he had replied.

Adebiyi stood in the corner of Lara's elegantly built home. Lara had an eye for luxury. She was perched on a Chestermoon sofa in her living room, her eyes fixed on the floor with a vacant stare.

Adebiyi wanted to pat her back with his only arm or offer her any form of consolation, but it was not in his place to do so. He was just a driver. His eyes darted from her face when he saw a teardrop fall from his Madam's eye. He looked towards the noise coming from the kitchen. Whoever was behind the door wanted to make a dramatic entrance. Maria, the house-maid, emerged from the kitchen. Her face showed signs of concern, but her words were laced with detest.

"Madam, welcome," she said. Her eyes met Adebiyi's, and he was sure her countenance screamed satisfaction rather than worry.

Lara finally spoke. "Where is Jabez?"

"He is asleep, ma." Maria inched closer to Adebiyi. "Wetin happen? Na accident?" Adebiyi gave her a frown. "Madam, na robbers?" Maria continued.

Lara tucked her kaftan between her legs. "Maria, I need you to tell me the truth. How did the robbers get that information? This had to be an inside job. I'm sure those robbers were amateur because they were asking direct questions."

Maria shook her head. "I don't know, Madam. I don't know ooo. Maybe Adebiyi told them."

"Don't lie!" Lara snapped. "Adebiyi would never do a thing like that."

Maria feigned ignorance.

Lara continued to stare at the carpet as Maria began to defend herself. "No be me o; you can check my load. It's not fair, Madam. Maybe it is Adebiyi."

Adebiyi suddenly snapped. "I go kill somebody o even with my one arm," he shouted. He snatched

Maria's phone from her hand, and she struggled to get it back.

"Leave me alone!" Maria tried to squeeze Adebiyi's neck, but it was too late. He had thrown the phone to Lara, who got to her feet and scrolled through the messages frantically.

Maria crossed her hands on her chest defensively.

"Here it is!" Lara cried, "You sent a message telling one of those crooks what we have in the house!" Lara scrolled through the messages.

Maria: *"Madam go pick up two million naira from Stanbic Bank tomorrow."*

Received message: *"So wetin you wan make we do, kill am?"*

Maria: *"No kill am o. Just threaten them until they reveal where the money dey."*

Received message: *"So, how much is my cut for all this? You no say we go be four to share the money with you."*

Maria: *"Just give me my own share—one million naira. You go share the rest."*

"Ha, Maria!" Lara waved the phone at her maid. "Despite all the things I have done for you and your family, is this how you repay me? I am in trouble! So, it is the enemy within that opened the door for the enemy without. I am in trouble! By the time I finish with you and your family, you will all be locked up."

Maria became defiant. "Abeg which kind yeye police you wan call? The one we don settle? You should be happy that neither you nor your son was killed. You are chopping life, and you think I should not chop, you wicked human being."

Adebiyi, even with the cast on his arm, was able to overpower Maria and hold her down until the police arrived.

Two fierce-looking policemen marched into the house. They had been told by the Commissioner to take care of the case and inspect the crime scene. They were also told to guard the property till further instructions.

Lara tried to explain what had happened. "I wish you had come earlier," she told them.

The officers did not look concerned. "We will interview you so we can find out more about these thieves. We can round them up, Madam, but it is going to cost you," said one officer.

"I no suppose dey duty for this time; my wife dey labour right now. Na because our oga send us; that is why we came here," the other officer added. "I should not be on duty, but I need money to pay the hospital bills; if not, there would be trouble."

Lara gaped at him. *How is any of that my business?* "What is that supposed to mean?" she asked.

"Well, you could have come to the station yourself.

The police have a lot of work to do."

Lara apologised; she knew defiance would only worsen her problems. *Oh, I miss my husband, I cannot take it anymore.* These men were typical Nigerian policemen and would not do anything if she did not play by their rules. She reached into her bag and gave them an envelope containing about N15,000.

One of the policemen looked at the envelope. "Madam, please top am small for your boys," he said. "They never pay our salary for two months, Madam."

Lara knew this was a ploy to extort her, but she also knew she had no choice. Exasperated, she added another N5,000. One of them collected the cash, beaming with smiles. "Consider the work done!"

"Sorry about all of this, Madam. Most of these house helps are informants for robbers," the other officer said, glaring at Maria. "Young lady, you will follow us to the station for interrogation."

"No be me o; na the devil work. Please, I no won go prison o."

It was no use. The policemen seized her. Before they left, the officers assured Lara one of the policemen would return to keep an eye on the premises for the next few days. Lara thanked them. "Please, if you decide to release her, I don't want her to return here. I will take her property to her mother's house."

Maria screamed as the police hauled her out of the house into their van. As soon as they left, Lara called Akon. She was sobbing as she held the phone to her ear. "I just thank God that I had sent the money to you as soon as I received it. If it had been in the car when they came, the robbers would have taken it. To think that Maria could do this to us. I guess good people are hard to come by these days."

Akon fought back tears as he tried to console his wife. "Honey, please calm down. I am sorry I wasn't there to protect you and Jabez." He did not want to imagine the horror his wife must have been through that night. *Lara is strong; such an event would have broken other women.*

After the call ended, Akon sat in the living room and gazed into thin air. The TV was on, showing one of his favourite programmes. However, nothing seemed to interest him tonight. His mind was too preoccupied. This night's experience made him regret leaving his wife and son in Nigeria.

He was battling self-condemnation and guilt as he reflected on his wife's encounter. *What if the armed robbers had killed Lara? Of what use would this work be? I wish I could get Lara and Jabez here even if we must live on toast and baked beans.* Yet, he knew things were not as simple as that.

13

Akon leaned on the kitchen counter, sipping on a glass of water after a long day at work. He thought about a family friend, Aderonke, the wife of his close friend, from secondary school. He remembered when she narrated her ordeal from living in the UK as a single mother.

Aderonke's husband, Dele, refused to relocate to London with his wife, but his wife did not want to live in Nigeria. Despite much persuasion, Dele had adamantly held on to his business in Nigeria.

"I am too old to make changes, and I cannot allow one little girl or boy to be my manager. You know the Bible says, 'If your left-hand causes you to sin, cut it off.'"

Aderonke tried to get him to stay in the UK with her, but Dele refused to change his mind. He gave her the option of either returning to Nigeria or sending their son to him. Aderonke did neither. She stayed in the UK and worked as a midwife to support herself and her two children.

As a result, Dele and Aderonke lived apart for about seven years. Dele committed to visiting every Christmas, but for the last two years, he had not visited.

"You had better return to your husband. Is it not better to have your home than a job?" Aderonke's mum had advised her.

That was two years ago, but those words had stayed with Aderonke ever since. She had lived each day, wondering if she had made a huge mistake. Dele was born in the UK but grew up in Nigeria. He had every opportunity to return to the UK but insisted he could not leave his motherland to waste his life in a foreign man's land.

It was during this time that Aderonke met up with Akon.

"I know you are close friends with my husband. Please, can you persuade him to relocate to London?" she begged. "My son is growing up without his father, and this is impacting on his attitude." Aderonke was distressed by the situation.

Akon had been sympathetic. "Why don't you consider sending him home?"

"It is too late; social services are already involved. At this point, if I attempt to take Dami to Nigeria, I might get into trouble. Worse still, Dami may even resist."

"Really? That is unfortunate.

"Dele is angry with me. He blames my stubbornness for everything. Uncle Akon, Dele has threatened to divorce me if I do not return the children," she sobbed.

"It is okay, Madam."

Aderonke's two children were taken away by social services under an allegation of child neglect.

"They just don't understand our culture. What they call abuse means discipline to us. It does not kill. If it does, I would be dead by now. Abi, Uncle Akon, did you die?" she asked.

"What happened exactly?" Akon asked.

"Dami, my ten-year-old, went to school, and his teacher noticed some marks on his body. She questioned him, and he said I hit him with a wooden spoon. But that is not what happened. Even though I took the wooden spoon, I did not hit him. He tried to run away, but he stumbled on a metal chair in the kitchen. That was how he got the marks on his body. When I saw he was injured, I dropped the spoon and treated the bruise with antiseptic. His teacher, Ms Gregson, took him to the pastoral care unit in the school building. His sister, Nike, was also taken there where she was questioned by the Head Teacher and other staff."

"This is serious," Akon said.

"That's not all o. The police and children's services were informed. Nike told them I do not beat her, but I beat Dami because he is naughty. When the social worker learnt that Dami had been flogged, she wanted an investigation into his family circumstances. This was about One in the afternoon. The school would not take chances after interviewing the children, so they hurriedly took them along with them, telling them they would be going home. That afternoon, I heard a knock on my door and opened. I was shocked to see my children, the police, and the social worker at my doorstep." Aderonke's eyes blurred with tears as she remembered when her world fell apart.

The officers had identified themselves and asked to be invited in with the children. Aderonke asked them if there was a problem. The social worker informed her she had been invited to assess the family situation as there were concerns about her children's wellbeing.

"What concerns? I work double shifts to look after these children. There is nothing they want that I will not give them. Dami has a mobile phone. I buy him trainers from JD sports. I just bought Nike a Nintendo."

"We are not disputing that, madam," said the social worker, "but you have been whipping your child, and the law does not allow that the kind of discipline."

To make matters worse, they learnt Aderonke worked night shifts, which meant she sometimes left her ten-year-old son and eight-year-old daughter alone at home. They accused her of neglect and decided to take her children away from her. She was ordered to undertake a parenting course which she did willingly, hoping she may get her children back.

Akon shook his head. "I have to warn my wife so that we won't end up in a similar situation," he said.

"Uncle Akon," Aderonke continued, "maybe it is a blessing in disguise that your family is not here. I must work to put a roof over our heads. Business is not too good for my husband so he can only contribute a little. I refuse to depend on benefits. I work hard, Mr Akon. I work really hard."

Akon took a deep breath and tried to comfort her. Aderonke wiped her eyes and continued. "Their father blames me because he had instructed me to send Dami back to Nigeria. The boy is troublesome at school; he gets detention every month. The system is different. How can you train children without beating them occasionally? Is that not the language that children understand? Even the Bible says foolishness is bound in the heart of a child, but definitely not in London."

Aderonke's story made Akon think about his family. Should he have stayed in Nigeria and sent Lara and his son to London? Akon became afraid of how life would be when they were together in the UK. Would the British system disrupt his family life? In the UK, children belong to the government. How would he cope should things go wrong? *Well, I would just tell Lara not to beat Jabez. I do not believe in hitting a child anyway. My father beat the life out of me when I was growing up, and I have vowed never to beat my children.*

He remembered when he first visited the UK four years ago. He had attended a barbecue party hosted by his Old Boys Association.

"Forget about your children; they belong to the government. Children become your masters. They have rights and can threaten you," Mr Idowu had said.

"You cannot discipline your children the way you want. Yet, if they get into trouble, the parents get the blame. Their Head Teachers would not let you rest. How frustrating!" said Agnes Ibidele.

Her husband, Segun, nodded in agreement. "But we have to be balanced," he said. "Some parents beat their children out of frustration. They return home after work and shout on their spouses and children. I bet the system is trying to encourage African parents to be balanced."

"I am not married, and I don't have children, but I agree with Mr. Segun," added Gbuyi.

"Darling, how many times did we change Sam's primary school?" Agnes asked her husband.

"Twice," Segun answered. "They said he was violent and too lousy. They also said he always disturbed the class just because he defends himself against bullies."

"Dear," Richard said to his wife, Bisi. "What did we do with Dipo?"

"We sent him to school in Nigeria when he was thirteen and only brought him back to do his A levels. The boy is now sober and well-mannered."

Richard nodded and continued. "When Dipo turned thirteen, he began hanging out with bad boys and was always coming home late. I told him we were going to Nigeria on holiday. He had not been to Nigeria before and was concerned. 'Dad,' he told me, 'my teachers said Nigeria is full of poor children and that we should donate some money to charity so they can have water to drink.'"

"I told him that was not true and showed him photographs of Lekki and all the exotic places, including houses with swimming pools. My wife was cooperative; she made him watch Nigerian movies too, which made him excited and expectant."

"I made arrangement for Dipo to move in with my

elder sister. One day, while we were in Nigeria, his mother took him shopping and bought everything you could think of. We left him with my sister and took his passport with us. It was not easy, and I thank my late sister and her husband for their help. Dipo did not talk to us for a year because he thought we were cruel. Later, he understood we just wanted to save his future."

"That's very good of you," Philomena commented, Taofik's wife and co-host of the barbecue party. "My sister had two of her children taken away a couple of years ago. She had travelled to London and left the sixteen-year-old with his sisters, who were eleven and nine years old. My sister warned Chris not to leave the children alone, but he left them one Saturday morning and went for football lessons. By the time he came back, an ambulance and a police car were waiting outside. The little one had cut her hand with a knife, and the eleven-year-old had called 999."

"If anyone can send their children back home to school in Africa, it would help," Pelumi added. "At least, children will experience both cultures. Here, you train children one way, and the school is raising them another way!"

Akon had listened quietly to the conversations.

As he recalled these events and wondered whether it was best to leave Jabez with his mother until he was sixteen, his phone rang. It was Lara.

"Your old friend, Akin, has been offering to visit so we don't get lonely in your absence," she told him. She sounded amused.

"That crafty fox!" Akon snapped. "I hope you did not allow him. I do not trust him. He is loose with women."

"Don't make a mountain out of a molehill," Lara said. "I told him Jabez and I were okay. What would people say? Akon is in London, and his best friend keeps visiting his wife? I don't want such rumours to spread like a bushfire around the city."

"Listen, I got this new job. You will be able to join me soon," Akon said.

"I miss you so much. I cannot wait for us to be together again. It is just a matter of time, darling. I hope those 'British' girls are not eye*ing* you sha," Lara teased.

"Come on, Lara. You know you are the only one for me. Do not worry; we will soon be together again. I love you."

With that, Akon hung up. He sighed heavily because he knew he was lying. He recently stopped being celibate. He remembered Ela, a thirty-one-year-old Polish student he had met three months ago at the council library. She was studying part-time and working as an admin assistant in the office. Ela was pretty and friendly.

She and Akon had gotten along quite well. He was studying for his upcoming professional exams, and she was preparing for her exams too. Studying for weeks at the library together, a bond began to form between them. He always removed his wedding ring whenever they were going to meet. She had no idea he was married, and he intended to keep it that way.

She had invited him over to watch a film one evening. Akon knew Ela was attracted to him. He did not tell her about his intentions, but he liked her too. If he dated an African woman, the news might find its way to his wife in Nigeria, which would be a problem for him.

Akon had dressed up and headed over to Ela's one-room apartment. He walked up to the door and knocked. She opened the door and smiled at him. He leaned in and hugged her, breathing in her floral scent. "It's good to see you, Akon," she said in her exotic accent. She stepped back to let him into the room.

"I got these for you. I hope you like them," Akon said, handing her a box of chocolates.

"Oh absolutely! I love them. Thank you so much!" she said excitedly and leaned to kiss him lightly on the lips. That was the first time they had shared a kiss, and she was a little embarrassed. "I'm sorry, I was so happy, I just…" she stammered.

Akon kissed her just as lightly and looked into her eyes. "It's okay. Now we are even, right?"

She nodded and smiled, then took his hand and led him to the couch so they could start the movie.

Throughout the evening, they kept sharing shy glances, touching each other tentatively. However, nothing happened beyond the earlier kiss. It was evident that Ela wanted something more, but Akon was hesitant. He still felt guilty about the kiss. The movie ended late, and with as much restraint as he could muster, Akon refused to spend the night.

The following week, they did not see much of each other because their exams had commenced and there was no time to hang out. However, on the Saturday of that week, after their exams had ended, they went to see a movie. After that, they went to a pub to celebrate the end of the stressful exams. After a few glasses of wine, things got a bit intense. Ela pulled Akon down for a deep kiss, which he reciprocated with equal passion. They eventually made their way to Ela's apartment. As soon as they were inside her house, Akon realised what he was about to do, and Ela noticed his hesitation.

"Hey, what's wrong?" she asked him while planting kisses along his jaw line and neck.

"Don't you think we are going too fast?" he asked

her, feeling helpless to her charms. Lara's face flashed across his mind, and he was overwhelmed with guilt.

Ela laughed. "I should be the one saying that, silly. Unless you do not care about me?" she asked, looking up at him curiously.

"Of course, I care about you. I just thought…"

She silenced him with a kiss. "Don't think. Just go with the flow."

A few minutes later, they were in her bed. Ela's head was resting on his chest as he played with her hair.

"You are such a wonderful man, Akon. I think I might be falling in love with you."

"You are an amazing woman as well." His marriage hung over him like a cloud, and he hoped he would be able to keep it away from Ela. He had the opportunity to be close to a woman after four years, and he really liked her.

One afternoon, three months later, while they were having lunch at a restaurant, Ela brought up the matter Akon had been dreading.

"Sweetheart, Easter Sunday is in two weeks. I would like us to visit my family," she said, holding his hands.

"Hey babe, don't you think it's a bit too soon?" he said, avoiding her eyes.

"We've been dating for three months now. I think it would be a step in the right direction," she said.

"I know, but these things should not be rushed into, you know?" he said evasively.

"Oh," Ela said sadly. She pulled away from him.

Akon sighed and reached for her hands. "Babe, I'm sorry. I will visit your parents, I promise. I just need more time."

"Alright, I understand." She smiled at him.

They finished their meal and left the restaurant.

14

"I'm sorry, dear. It's not as if I did not want to call you. I have been busy with work and a lot of things," Akon said to Lara on the phone.

"This is what you've been saying for months. Akon, is there something I should know about?"

"I've told you. I have been spending a lot of time working overtime to raise money for your trip in two months. There are a lot of things I need to set up so you can enjoy your stay."

"Okay o. I just wanted to be sure nothing else is involved. Aunty sends her greetings too. She said you have forgotten about her. You don't call her anymore."

"Ah, no o. I did not forget her. Mama is also upset. She is getting old, and she wants to see me before she dies. Please help me explain to everyone that I have just been swamped. I will make it up to them."

"Alright darling, I love you. I can't wait to see you in two months," Lara said.

"Me too, my dear. I miss you. Alright, I will call you later. Bye."

He wondered how he was going to handle Ela's issue when his wife comes to the UK. He decided to break the news of his marriage to Ela.

Later in the day, Akon and Ela were having dinner at their favourite restaurant.

"Darling, I have been thinking. Why don't we go on a holiday this summer? Poland is lovely in summer. I'm sure you'd love it," Ela gushed.

"Hmmm, that's nice," Akon replied without enthusiasm.

"What is wrong, dear? If you do not want to go to Poland, we can choose somewhere else."

"Ela, I have something to tell you."

Ela looked alarmed. Akon hardly called her by her name. This did not look good. What could make him look so grave? "What is it, darling?" she said, taking his hand in hers and caressing it.

"I am so sorry, Ela. It wasn't my intention to hurt you."

"Hurt me? What are you talking about?"

"I... I have a... My wife is coming to the UK in the next two months."

Ela recoiled, a look of horror and betrayal on her face. "What?" she gasped, withdrawing her hands.

"I'm sorry, babe. I didn't mean for things to turn out this way," Akon said. He had come to care about her over the past few months.

"I can't believe this," she said, tears running down her cheeks. She stood abruptly and left. Akon held his head in his hands. He did not want to lose Ela, but he could not jeopardise his marriage. He stood from the table and left the restaurant.

* * *

Akon walked towards his front door, but his mind was far away as he thought about Ela and the news he just received from his wife regarding the approval of the dependent relative visa.

He was still contemplating what he needed to prepare for his wife and son's arrival, including getting a car on hire purchase, when his phone rang. It was Kay, his long-time friend. Akon answered the call with mixed feelings.

Kay wanted to see him urgently, and Akon gave him his address. About half an hour later, the doorbell rang.

Akon glanced at his watch. It was almost half-past eight in the evening. When he went to get the door, it was Kay. Akon hugged his old friend and invited him in. They had not met face to face for three months.

"How you dey, my brother? You must be doing well," Kay observed.

"I dey o, my brother. I am just trying; that's all. This city can toughen you or break you. I am determined more than ever to succeed," Akon replied. He could see that Kay looked unkempt. He wondered what could have made the ever-fresh Kay look this way.

"I have my own problems sef," Kay said. "I'm now homeless."

"What? What happened?" Akon asked.

"She called the police on me, and I was ordered out of the house," Kay explained.

"Who? Why?" Akon asked.

"My partner, you know her, Monica. She is not Nigerian, and her culture is different. She believes she must have a say in everything, and whatever she says must happen. She is from Trinidad, and I have learnt the hard way that you do not slap a *Dogla* woman."

Akon looked shocked. "You slapped her? What happened?" he asked.

"It's a serious matter. Monica is obsessed with travelling and getaways, and I told her it was affecting our finances. I work part-time due to my health condition, and she knows it. She is also addicted to cigarettes, and I warned her about this, but she would not listen. Monica goes on weekend getaways whether I approve or not, and that drives me mad. She told me she was not a *'yes sir'* Nigerian woman who will accept any-thing. So, on a particular Sunday evening, she arrived home from her weekend getaway and walked into the house. I was so furious that I did not respond when she greeted me. She just walked into the kitchen, opened the fridge, ate some leftover pizza, and went to the living room.

"I did not like the tension in the house. So, after two hours, I went to her. She ignored me and kept watching the television. I snatched the remote control from her to get her attention. At this, she yelled, 'What the hell do you think you are doing? Give me the remote control now!' But I held on to it. Then she grabbed my shirt's collar and gnashed her teeth at me. I thought she was going to bite me. I was so enraged that I slapped her. She screamed, and the next thing I knew, the police were at the door. I was charged with domestic violence. The good thing is Monica did not want to press charges so I would not have a criminal record, which is helpful. I was given a restraining order and sent out of my own house! It is illegal for me to be in my own home! Can you believe that? I mean, it is not my house in that sense. It's Monica's mortgage and in her name, but I have been paying for the house, so all my money has gone down the drain."

Akon opened his mouth in shock. "This is pathetic. You should have just left her alone." He felt sorry for Kay.

"Man, I was under pressure. This lady has taken me for granted for too long. How long was I supposed to endure it? I am struggling, and no one is hearing me out. The relationship is all about what she wants to do, not what is best for us. The issue is, I am in debt, and I am not creditworthy anymore. Hence, I hate to watch the way I spend. It is difficult to compromise when both parties are not thinking the same. Even though I was born here in London, you know I grew up in Nigeria."

Kay was five years old when his parents relocated to Nigeria. He was the firstborn and he had three younger sisters. His father had wanted another male, but after the third daughter was born, the medical team said his mother could not have more children. So, his father married another wife. Kay's father was Igbo, and the new wife was Yoruba.

Kay's father built a chalet for his second wife and built a life with her. The first child they had together was a male. The second and third were male too. His dad then focused more on his new wife and the home became a tug of war. Kay's mother struggled to feed her children with her teaching job because his father had stopped sending money for their upkeep. His parents fought regularly. His father even used a cane on his mother because both his wives fought.

"I was sent to a boarding school when I was eight, and my father did not visit me, not even once. My mum visited me once every three months. I spent my holidays with nasty cousins who treated me like a liability. I was tossed to and fro amid all the fights and sibling rivalry. I struggled with my school grades. My dad was not bothered, and my mother never showed she cared.

"When I had an opportunity to relocate to the UK through a late friend, I took it. I changed my name and adopted a new identity. I moved with diverse ethnic groups, and saw myself as a British man, not an Igbo man from Nigeria. Sadly, I cannot hide my identity in relationships. If you remember while we were in school, my name was Chukwurah Nduka Okwu. In Nigeria, they called me Chuks, but when I came to the UK, I changed my name to Kay Okwu. I make many sacrifices for people, but when it's my turn, they do not want to do the same!"

"That is terrible. No wonder you haven't kept in touch with your family in Nigeria," Akon said as he poured two glasses of wine.

Kay rubbed a hand over his face. "I wanted to start a new life and put the past behind me. Deep inside, I do not trust anyone. I have been used and duped financially by men and women, so what do you expect? I was once married to a Scottish lady called Isla, but it only lasted for three years. Both of us were in love, but her relatives did not accept me no matter how hard we tried. I observed this during Christmas and visits. Her relatives believed I was not good enough for her, that I would be violent towards her. I did all the shopping, laundry, and spent all I had to ensure she had a beautiful life. Oh boy, from ice skating to mountain climbing and other exotic holidays. I spent money on Isla. One day, she told me her heart was no longer in the marriage, and she wanted us to settle this amicably. She said she had also been seeing someone else for the past six months. She felt sorry we had to go our separate ways, claiming that we were no longer compatible. That broke me. I was devastated. I vowed to never marry again. The good thing was we had no children. If we did, it would have been difficult to put the past between us."

"Here you go," Akon said, handing Kay one glass of wine.

"Thanks, man," Kay said and took a sip. He sighed and continued.

"I was bitter. I guess I have been looking for love in the wrong places, and I never healed. When I met Monica, I thought this was it. She appeared mature and knew what she wanted, but little did I know she would boss me around. I really loved Monica. Even though I proposed to her, she did not want us to formalise the relationship. So, I played along. Now because of her, I am homeless and stranded."

"Wow! Life has really hit you hard. Where do you intend to stay for now?" Akon asked.

Kay stared at him uncomfortably. He seemed embarrassed and looked like he was struggling to say something. Then he said quietly, "My brother, I know I was not accommodating when you returned to London. I am so sorry. I understand this does not justify how badly I treated you. At the time, I had just lost my job, and I was in debt. I was confused; it sucked the life out of me. I did not want anyone around me, but because I had given you my word, I allowed you in. You can see that I moved to a smaller place. You were a bit complicated, and you thought I did not want you to succeed, so I thought it would be better to allow you to be. I wanted you to survive on your own as I did. Nevertheless, I am sorry, my friend. Can you find a place in your heart to forgive me?" There were tears in his eyes, and he looked genuinely sorry for all he had done.

Akon was quiet for a moment as he considered Kay's apology.

Kay's problems did not justify his cruelty towards him, but he was only human. "I forgive you," Akon finally said. "There is no point holding on to the past. What you did was not right, but I would also be wrong to hold it against you. After all, you allowed me to stay with you in the first place. So, I forgive you, my friend."

"Thank you. You are indeed a good man."

Both men embraced each other as they put the past behind them.

"I'm happy for you o! See how well you are doing. Your house is tastefully furnished," Kay said as he looked around in awe.

"It is rented accommodation, and it came furnished. I got it through another connection. I do not have my indefinite leave to remain yet, so I cannot buy a house yet. I am just managing this place," Akon said.

"Congrats, mate!" Kay said. "Akon, just as you needed my help, I need yours now. I have been sleeping in my car for the past three days, and you know how dangerous that could be. Please, can I spend a few nights at yours while I plan where next to stay? I'll be okay sleeping on the couch if you let me."

"Of course," Akon replied. "One good turn deserves another. There is enough space; and you don't need to sleep on the sofa."

"Thank you so much. My experience has humbled me, but your kindness humbles me the more. You are a friend indeed," Kay said with tears in his eyes.

"It is nothing, my friend. You are welcome to sleep here until you are ready. I think you should see a counsellor because what you have gone through from childhood could affect you psychologically. I will also advise you not to start a relationship for now."

"You are right. As soon as I get back on my feet, I'll see a counsellor."

"Oh, and something else," Akon said. "My wife and son will be joining me in two months. Hopefully, you would have sorted yourself before then."

"Of course," Kay replied.

15

During the night, Akon thought about what Kay had said. Was he trying to get sympathy from him? Akon stared at Lara's picture on his bedside table. He missed her so much. She was his safe place and would cover up for him no matter how much distress it caused her. She was dutiful and did not make unnecessary demands on him.

He smiled as his mind flashed back to when he started to court Lara. There had been another lady he was involved with before they met. Her name was Precious, and their parents had introduced them during his father's political dinner party. Precious was engaged in hotel and café franchises. She had won the heart of Akon's sisters because she always gave them huge discounts whenever they bought meat pies and drinks from her continental café. She was from a wealthy background; her father was a business mogul based in New York. She had also graduated from the University of California with honours.

Precious was beautiful and smart, but she was not Akon's type of woman. She had extreme feminist views and was annoyingly bossy. She once told him that any woman who allowed a man to control her was weak and not a *true* woman. She always wanted everything to go her way, from the restaurants they visited to the clothes he wore. Precious monitored his movements and was jealous of him. She even stopped him several times from hanging out with his old school mates. It got so bad that Akon's friends called him a *woman wrapper*. Dating her was stifling, to say the least. They always argued. The only reason they stayed together was to please their parents. Moreover, Akon had always wanted to travel out of the country and getting married to Precious would give him the green card.

On the contrary, Lara was a breath of fresh air. He had fallen hard for Lara the first day he saw her in a court session he attended. His friend's sister, Moyeni, was Lara's client, and he had gone to court to support his friend. Moyeni had been sued for embezzlement by the company she worked for. Akon had fallen in love with Lara's confidence, her solid stance, and the way she spoke. She won the case that day, and his respect for her grew. He searched for her on Facebook and sent her a friend request. She accepted it, but she did not reply to his messages. He made another move and got her number from Moyeni. He called her and fell in love with her voice too.

"Hi. Um, this is Akon, Moyeni Coker's family friend."

"Oh. Alright."

"So, I was in court the day you won the case against Moyeni's company. You were brilliant, and you deserved that win," he gushed.

"Thank you."

He had expected a little enthusiasm from her. "Would you like to go out for dinner? Tomorrow night? I would like to pick your brain."

"I appreciate it, but I can't. I have prior engagements. I must go now; thanks for calling. Do take care," Lara said before hanging up.

Akon felt disappointed. *She seems like the type that plays hard to get.* But there was something about her that drew him like metal to a magnet, and he kept calling her until she warmed up to him and accepted to go out with him on a dinner date.

On their first date, he could not stop staring at her. She did not dress up glamorously even though she knew they were going to one of the most expensive restaurants in Lagos. Still, there was beauty in her simplicity. She wore stone-washed ripped jeans, a red t-shirt, flat sandals, and carried a simple red and blue bag. She looked exquisite in the candlelight, like cake waiting to be eaten. "So, tell me about yourself," he had asked her.

"I was raised by my grandmother in Ilora, here in Nigeria. My grandmother was enterprising; she sold charcoal, salt, soft drinks, and water. From the time I was eight, I learnt the art of selling. I did this after school. I went to a government school and was the best in my class. I passed the common entrance exam and had double promotion. By the time I was fifteen, I had done my WAEC and passed. I sat for JAMB examination, and my results were one of the highest. It sounds like bragging, but that is the truth. However, I did not go straight to university; my aunt said I was too young. So, I stayed at home, helping my grandmother.

"Three years later, I gained admission to study Law at the University of Lagos. In the first year, I stayed with my mum's younger sister and her family in Yaba. In the second year, I moved to the hostel. While there, I joined the Student's Christian Union and was much involved with evangelism. I graduated with a first-class LLB," Lara finished with a smile.

She did not disclose her entire story to Akon, why it took three years to gain admission to the university.

When Akon asked, Lara explained that she had taken a gap year before she eventually studied law.

Akon nodded and said, "A story with a sad beginning and a happy ending." He took her hand across the table and rubbed it comfortingly.

Falling for Lara had been effortless because she was different from Precious. Lara was kind and brilliant in every aspect. She was an outstanding lawyer and the personal assistant to a top manager in an oil company. She had graduated top of her class with first-class honours.

Unfortunately, Akon's mother preferred Precious to Lara and had urged him to marry her. Akon was against the idea. In addition to all her other undesirable qualities, Precious was not a good cook. She was always ordering food from her hotel chain. She believed there was no reason for her to cook if she employed cooks who could do a better job than her. Even when Akon urged her to learn, she waved him away and told him it was too late. But Lara was a fantastic cook; she made delicious food, just the way he liked it. She could even bake bread, biscuits, and mouth-watering pastries in her spare time.

When Akon introduced Lara to his parents, his mum sneered. She said Lara did not belong to the elite class and had never heard of her father's name among her class of friends. Akon tried to explain that Lara was an orphan raised by her late grandmother, but his mother would have none of it. Akon's mother believed Lara was a gold-digger who pretended to love her son. She even said to Lara's face that Akon already had someone to marry.

Lara had won the heart of Akon's father with a delicious meal of pounded yam and *efo riro,* garnished with goat meat and peppered snails. Even his mum had cleaned her plate, noting how good the food was. Yet, his mother preferred Precious because Lara was from an average working-class family. Lara had decided to step back because she did not want Akon to have problems with his mum.

Akon continued dating Precious but realised he could not do it anymore. Precious was a difficult person, and Lara had become his best friend. He broke up with Precious with an apology and explanation. She did not accept his explanation at first, threatening to destroy his relationship with Lara.

"You will not enjoy that relationship, Akon. You're dumping me for that low-class thing!"

"Try to understand me, P. It is not just about Lara. In fact, it is not about her at all. You and I cannot work in the long run. This ship will sink eventually."

"I do not care! It's either me or no one else, Akon. Get that into your head," she had said before storming out of the restaurant.

She started to show up whenever he had a date with Lara. After a while, she conceded and wished him the best of luck, telling him she hoped they would still be friends. Akon's mother had been disappointed, telling him to get back with Precious or she would disown him. After several threats, she finally accepted Lara, because her views about Lara put a strain on her relationship with Akon.

Twelve months later, Akon and Lara got married. Their wedding was a nice one, and even Precious attended with her fiancé. Chief Akete had presented a car to Lara and Akon as their wedding gift and one of his houses in Anthony village, which came with a swimming pool.

Akon grinned. He had never regretted his decision because Lara made him happy ever since. He could not wait to see her. He was looking forward to when she would join him in the United Kingdom.

*   *   *

Lara sighed softly as Adebiyi drove her home from work. She missed her husband so much. She had to deal with the security man, the driver, and mechanics all by herself. The mechanics could make ridiculous demands just for repairing little things. She was tired of handling these technical issues.

Besides being her husband, Akon was like the brother she never had, always quick to defend and protect her. Her life had taken a downhill spiral since he left, and she was all alone, having to jostle different activities while working with the little money at her disposal. Calling the UK from Nigeria was expensive, and Akon did not call as often as she wished. Lara tried her best not to doubt her husband, but she knew how charismatic he was and how women could easily fall for him. Sometimes, she questioned whether he was being truthful when he claimed to be busy or if his heart was with another woman. Living alone as a woman in Nigeria was tough.

Lara sighed again. She was facing a huge problem and had decided against telling Akon. She was thinking of resigning from her job and did not want to trouble Akon with the issue.

Lara's boss, the general manager, had been making advances at her since he learnt Akon had travelled to the UK. There was little she could do except avoid and refuse him repeatedly. She did not have any other job opening, so she could not just leave her good-paying job. She knew she would have to think fast. She was getting choked up in that office. When she got home, she brightened up at the sight of Jabez on the Persian rug, doing his homework. He was her only consolation amidst the stormy terrain.

Whenever she considered how vulnerable she had become because of her husband's absence, she often felt sick to her stomach. Akon had been away for nearly three years now, and things had been hard for her. Nowadays, no matter how tired she was, she would find time to tell Jabez folk stories and help him with his homework. She used to organise play dates at the amusement park between Jabez and Koko's children, Nife and Jaiye, who were their family friends. However, since the Koko family had moved to South Africa, she hardly took him to the exotic parks.

Furthermore, Akon had used up their savings. So, Lara focused on keeping Jabez in his British private school until they could join Akon abroad. Her entire salary went towards Jabez's school fees, the household staff salaries, and buying groceries. There was hardly enough to go around. Akon, who was still trying to make ends meet, could rarely send money home.

In raising their son, Lara wanted to balance the Yoruba tradition with English culture, even though her husband preferred the latter. She believed a person's culture was a person's roots, and any other culture is secondary. Lara took pride in the fact that her aunt and grandmother spent time telling her stories when she was younger.

"Mummy, I miss my dad," Jabez said to Lara one evening after dinner. "It has been long. I miss everything we used to do back then. Going to the stadium, looking at animals, and watching Daddy play *ayo* with his friends over a keg of palm wine. I want to see him now."

"It has not been that long, my boy." Lara patted his cheek. "He'll be back before you know it." Lara knew that Jabez was saying the truth. Akon's "six months" had gradually become three years.

"That is what you always say, mummy. When exactly is he coming back?"

"Do you know there were about eleven children in the same house with my grandmother?" Lara said, deliberately changing the subject. "I never knew my parents, so my aunt took care of me. During the long holidays, I would go to my grandma's house where there were eleven other children."

"Must have been fun." Jabez's eyes grew wide as saucers. He had forgotten about his dad for that moment.

"Well, it was a lot of fun, but there were a lot of fights too. Children are born selfish, you know. My late grandmother, popularly known as Mama Oyo, always had a story and lesson for every situation. If a child woke up late, she would have a story on laziness. She had a story for stubbornness, fights, and lots more. One day, one of the children who lived with her, Idowu, urinated on the sleeping mat, but instead of drying it out in the sun, he kept it there. The room was stinking. Mama Oyo called all the children, and they all denied knowing anything about it. Idowu did not know Mama could identify the mat because she knitted the mats herself. She asked Idowu to confess, but he did not. She brought out a small mortar and pestle and pounded red pepper, threatening to pour it in Idowu's eyes. Idowu was five years old at the time, and he started crying because of the pepper. He eventually confessed."

"Was she really going to use the pepper on him?" Jabez asked.

"No, it was just to scare him. Mama Oyo was strict, but not wicked. Idowu had to miss his dinner that night."

"It's not good to lie, Mum," Jabez said thoughtfully.

"No, it is not." Lara patted his head.

16

"Mum," Jabez looked puzzled. "Why are the stories always about animals like leopards, lions, monkeys, ants, and Mr Tortoise? Animals don't talk in real life, but they do in cartoons because they are animated."

"You are smart, Jabez. It is because the animals are innocent, and they cannot defend themselves. The aim of these stories is to teach moral values to children and stop them from being naughty and disrespectful to elders. Children will also learn to tell the truth always."

"But adults tell lies too, Mummy." Jabez looked suddenly sad. "Daddy said he was coming in six months, and it's been three years. Daddy lied to me."

Lara took a deep breath. "He did not lie to you. Your dad would never lie to you. Adults usually have good reasons for not keeping promises, but they do not lie."

"But mum, the other day you told the security man that if anybody asks for you, he should tell them you were not home. You lied, mum," Jabez accused.

Lara felt like shutting him up. "You are too smart for your age. Yes, I could not see anybody, and I was not lying because there was a good reason. Young man, it is 9.00 pm, and it is bedtime!"

"But tomorrow is Saturday, mum! I don't have school."

"It doesn't matter, darling. Bedtime is bedtime," she said firmly. They prayed before she took him upstairs to his room.

Lara stretched out on her bed but could not sleep. She kept tossing and turning. She was troubled by her boss' sexual advances and how he made her life miserable. He made her dread going to work. She could not tell Akon because his calls were few and far between. She could not call him either because of the cost. She also had to deal with her dishonest servants, especially Maria before she was dismissed. She did not have the energy or time to look for replacements, so she managed them like that. It had become rampant—missing pieces of meat, missing naira notes, and even Jabez's snacks. She had questioned them so many times, but they always maintained their innocence.

Lara felt bad she did not have enough time for Jabez.

As she lay on the bed, she remembered the last story she told him three weeks ago called *Olurombi*.

"Jabez, today we are going to learn why you should always keep your promises and not let people down," she said to Jabez as she tucked him into the bed.

"Today's story is about a woman called Olurombi," she said as Jabez looked at her in anticipation.

Drumming passionately, Lara began to sing the song, thereby heightening Jabez's interest. She was a master storyteller and knew exactly what to do to make the most boring stories exciting.

"Once upon a time," Lara voiced immediately she ended the song.

"Time, time," Jabez whispered.

"In a certain village in Yoruba land called Ajangbe, the villagers looked up to the tree for their needs. The name of the tree was Iroko Olu Were. The Iroko tree would grant all the wishes of the villagers. It would also give children to women who wanted them." Lara took a dramatic pause.

"One day, a woman named Olurombi, who was also desperate to have a child, joined other women, and traders to ask Iroko for a child. All the other women promised out of their wares but Olurombi promised to give a big goat," Lara said, using her hands to describe the size of the goat.

"So, what happened?" Jabez asked excitedly.

"Iroko was very happy with Olurombi because of the gifts she brought, and vowed that she would get a child," Lara answered.

"Mum don't tell me Iroko did not keep his promise," Jabez asked with a raised brow.

"Of course, he did. The Iroko gave her a baby girl," she said, causing Jabez to smile.

"But you know what's sad? Olurombi did not keep her promise after she got the child. She forgot the promise to give Iroko a goat," Lara said as Jabez's smile turned into a frown.

"Iroko was annoyed so he visited the house and took Olurombi's daughter away."

"What happened next?" Jabez asked, desperately wanting to know the rest of the story.

"We would continue with the story next weekend. It is time for us to go to bed," she said as she planted a kiss on his forehead.

*   *   *

Lara had been preoccupied with work all week and forgot about her promise to finish the story of Olurombi. She thought about it now with a heavy heart. It seemed everything was going wrong at once. She closed her eyes and prayed that her family would be together again. She was still praying when she drifted off.

The next day at work, she avoided Architect Fayati as best as she could. She sent her secretary to his office with all the files she needed him to sign only for the personal assistant, Miss Iyabo, to come back with a message that the boss asked for her. She groaned inwardly, her heart thumping hard. She wished she could disappear. She straightened her skirt and went to his office. She knocked twice before opening the door. He swivelled around in his chair to face her, his elbows in the armrests.

"You sent for me, sir?"

"Yes, my dear. Please, sit." Mr Fayati gestured to the chair in front of him.

"How is your husband? And your son?" He smiled at her, revealing his yellow teeth. Lara felt repulsed.

"They are fine, sir," she replied, her hands in her lap.

"Without further ado, I want to know your answer to my request. What have you decided, my dear?"

"I cannot remember what we talked about, sir." Lara played dumb.

His mouth tightened into a thin line. "Don't pretend with me, Lara." He stood, leaned on the table, and tucked a strand of hair behind her ear. Lara flinched.

"Be my mistress. I know your financial state; I can help you. There is no guarantee that Akon is going to come back for you. I will treat you like a queen, much better than your husband ever has," he said, trailing his finger down her neck.

She gulped and slapped his hand, bristling with anger. "Don't you ever put your hands on me! I have told you no over and over. Even if Akon never comes back, I still will not date you! And that is not going to change, sir," she snapped.

"Then get prepared because I will make your life miserable in this office!" he shouted, wagging a finger at her.

"Do whatever you want. I do not care anymore. The worst you can do is sack me. I am not going to sacrifice my integrity!" She excused herself and walked out of the office. She locked the door when she entered her lavishly furnished office, collapsed on the small sofa, and cried her eyes out. She did not need a genie to tell her she was in trouble. She will have to look for another job quickly. She reached for her mobile phone to call her friend, Bunmi.

*   *   *

The following weekend, Lara was at home playing a game of charades with Jabez. She had turned in her resignation after Fayati embarrassed her during a conference with another company. Her friend, Bunmi, had helped her to secure a secretarial job. The pay was not as good as her former job, but at least she had peace of mind. Suddenly, the doorbell sounded and Maria hurried to open the door. She ushered in Akon's close friend and former business partner, Alade.

"Iyawo wa!" he called out gleefully. "J, how are you?"

"Very well, thank you, sir," Jabez replied politely.

"That's good. That British school is doing you well," Alade said grinning.

"What would you like to drink, sir?" Lara asked.

"Anything is fine." She stood up and gestured for Maria to follow her.

In ten minutes, Lara microwaved a plate of coconut rice garnished with liver and turkey, which they had cooked that morning. She set the food on the dining table and invited Alade to dine.

"Iyawo wa! It is for this reason I liked you from the very beginning when Akon married you. You are a gem ojare!"

Lara smiled politely and curtsied. Alade finished eating and picked his teeth with a toothpick.

"Jabez, go and have your afternoon snack in the kitchen with Maria," Lara instructed.

"Okay, mum. Can I have the chocolate chip cookies?"

"Anything you want, sweetie." Lara patted his cheek. Jabez left hurriedly.

"So, Uncle Alade, we weren't expecting you, but thank God there was some food at home," Lara stated.

"Yes, my dear. I was in the neighbourhood and decided to check in on my friend's family. You know there's no man with you now, so someone has to be checking in on you."

"Thank you, sir. We are doing fine."

"No need to be so formal, Lara. I've always had a fondness for you," Alade said, fumbling in his pocket for a handkerchief as he had begun to sweat.

"Thank you, sir," Lara replied primly.

"Lara, you should understand what I mean now. You are not a baby anymore," he said and reached for her hand. She withdrew her hands immediately.

"Lara, what is even wrong with you? Let us have some fun while your husband is away. I know Akon very well. We have been friends for a long time. He is cheating on you too. Let us have fun with each other. No one will know about it," Alade continued, mopping his brow with the hanky.

"Get out of my house while you can, Alade. You are a shameless man. You have a beautiful wife and daughter at home, and you are here telling me this nonsense. Please, get out!"

Alade stood up and leered at her, grabbing her wrist, and pulling her to him. "Come on. What is in your body that you are proud of? Shior!" Alade kissed his teeth.

Lara yanked her hand away and slapped him. "Get out of here now! Shameless old fool."

Alade looked at her and made to grab her, but she moved away.

"Beautiful Lara, bye for now. But I'll be back." Alade moved towards the door, rubbing his burning cheek.

Lara ran upstairs and collapsed on her bed, sobbing uncontrollably. "What kind of life is this? I am not a *runs girl.* Even if Akon chooses to go with another woman, I will count my losses and raise my son myself." She stood up, feeling determined.

Lara thought about her secret life. Ranti. No one knew about Ranti except her aunt and uncle. She tried to console herself that if her marriage ended, she still had Ranti and Jabez. What was the joy in a marriage without children anyway? Lara had never been out of Ranti's life and had been responsible for Ranti's feeding and school fees. Akon knew she sent money regularly to her aunt, but Lara had told him it was appreciation for how they helped her when she was young.

Akon had met Ranti twice, and that was when he and Lara had visited to inform her uncle and aunt about their relationship. *How would Akon react if he heard about my secret from a third party?*

Lara became energised and said out loud to herself, "It doesn't matter. I'm going to make the most out of my present."

*   *   *

Lara held Jabez's hand as they left the embassy after a three-hour wait. She did not mind the wait; in fact, she was overjoyed. Their visa had been approved, and they were set to join Akon in the United Kingdom. Akon had sent the paperwork two weeks ago, and she had been scheduled for an interview today. Initially, there had been a long queue at the embassy, but when it got to their turn, the interview went smoothly. They were granted the visa almost immediately. She saw people wail in anguish as their application for visas got rejected. She was glad theirs had been approved. Lara and Jabez got to the car park, entered the car, and Lara drove home.

"Can I have some ice cream, mum? It's been a while," Jabez asked, looking up from his gaming tablet.

"Sure, sweetie," Lara replied, smiling at him. The drop in her income, selling of their lands, and emptying of their savings, had meant they had not had any luxuries for a long time. Even the simplest things like ice cream or eating out had been cut off.

"Thanks, mum. I want the mint chocolate chip. So, we are going to meet dad soon?" Jabez spoke up again.

"Yes, honey. Isn't that wonderful?"

"Ripper!"

Lara laughed and leaned over to kiss his cheek.

"Come on, mum. I'm not a baby anymore."

"Hey, if you complain, no ice cream for you," Lara said. Jabez promptly shut up and focused on his game.

Lara smiled. She had decided she would keep the great news all to herself. *Besides,* she thought *there isn't anyone to tell. I don't have many close friends.* She was not even going to tell Akon's family. His sisters had not been nice to her. Her mind flashed back to the time Akon's sister, Bose, who was studying at the University of Lagos, stayed in their house for a while. Bose was ill-mannered and unruly towards her and the house rules. Eventually, Lara had asked her to leave. Akon's family were not happy about it, and the rift between them further widened. Lara sighed.

Lara pulled up in front of Cold Stone Creamery at the Ikeja city mall. Jabez jumped out and raced inside. She unbuckled her seat belt and took her purse before getting out of the car. She went in and saw Jabez already ordering his ice cream.

"I want French vanilla with dark chocolate pepper-mint and a banana mixed in. And oh, with waffles please," he said to the guy at the counter whose name tag read Ola. "Mum, can I have a cupcake? Please?"

"Sure honey," Lara said, holding back a laugh. His childlike enthusiasm was endearing.

"Thanks, mum! And one chocolate cupcake." He finished his order. "What will you have, mum?"

"Just a cupcake, thanks," she told Ola.

"To take away?" he asked, grinning at Jabez, who nodded, his head bobbing up and down in excitement.

Lara paid for their purchases before leading Jabez out. When they got home, Lara called Akon to tell him the good news. He was elated and told her he was almost done preparing for their arrival. Lara almost cried in relief. She could not wait to be with her husband. She would start afresh in London. She was also happy that she had started a distant-learning law course to work in the UK. She had resigned from her job to dedicate the remaining days to prepare for the journey. There were many last-minute details to take care of.

Jabez and Christiana, the maid, helped her with most of the packing. As Jabez was in 7th grade, he had already taken his final exams and was free to stay home. She had warned him not to tell any friend or classmate about the move. So, he only told his classmates he would visit his dad soon but did not include further details. Lara was still wary of armed robbers in Lagos.

On the day they were set to leave, Lara packed a suitcase full of Nigerian food, such as Indomie noodles, dried ponmo, dried fish, dried locust beans, and portions of garri and yam flour. She packed some Nollywood movies and all their framed pictures and photo albums into another bag. The largest suitcase was full of clothes.

As they piled everything into the car, Lara looked back at the house where she had so many good memories, and she shed some tears. She braced herself and got into the car where Jabez was waiting soberly. She did not tell Adebiyi she would not return. She only told him that she was going there for a visit.

Meanwhile, she had persuaded one of her friends to employ Adebiyi as a driver. She felt it was the least she could do for him. As for her new maid, Christiana, she also found a good place for her employment.

When they got to the airport, Adebiyi helped them with their suitcases. He then waved goodbye and drove off. Lara and Jabez got through the check-in point with no issues. The customs officers even joked about her suitcase that was full of Nigerian food. She was glad she did not have to bribe her way through. She was so happy they were finally joining Akon.

Lara dozed off during the flight and woke up as they were about to land in France. Jabez was still in the same position, playing with his gaming tablet. After they disembarked the plane, they were supposed to board the KLM to Gatwick Airport. They walked briskly to the immigration desk to stamp their passports, but encountered some problems.

The immigration officer said something in French, pointed at the picture on the passport, and then to Lara, shaking his head. Lara was confused.

"Pour qui me prenez-vou," the dark-haired immigration officer said.

"Sorry," Lara shook her head politely. "I don't speak French."

The officer beckoned to another officer for assistance.

"Where are you going?" the new officer asked.

"To join my husband in London."

"You do not look like the person in that passport photograph," the officer said stonily.

Lara had anticipated something like this happening, which was why she had meticulously compiled all her documents and receipts. She brought them out and showed the officer one by one as evidence. After a lengthy perusal of the documents, the officers let her board the next flight.

17

The KLM flight touched down at Gatwick Airport at exactly 6.50 am, but it took about two hours before Lara and Jabez got to the arrivals gate due to a luggage issue. Akon had been at the airport since 6.30 am. He had parked in the car park and paid for a long stay. He was waiting for them with a cardboard sign that read "Mummy and Prince."

Jabez screamed as he spotted his dad and ran to meet him. Akon was exhilarated. He grabbed Jabez and squeezed him before turning to Lara, who was crying. He hugged her and wiped her tears with his thumbs.

"You're okay now, baby. You're with me now," he said and hugged her again.

He turned to Jabez and hugged him again. "You are

so tall now, champ. Just like Dad. I hope you have been good to mummy."

Jabez laughed. "I was good, dad. Trust me."

After piling their suitcases into the car, Akon drove off.

"Why don't you have a driver? We had one in Nigeria," Jabez asked his father.

"Well, we don't need drivers in London. The roads are good, and cars are easy to drive. Also, you do not need a car everyday like we needed one in Nigeria."

"Dad, did you get my PlayStation 3? Mum said it's less expensive here."

"Yes, I did son. We will set it up once we finish unpacking."

"Yes!" Jabez pumped his fist into the air.

Lara chimed in. "Actually, you can only play when I give you permission. Okay?"

Jabez groaned. "Mummmm…" he drawled.

"Babe, you still have your headmistress behaviour," Akon laughed.

"Yes o!" Lara answered.

Akon laughed and turned to his wife. "How was your flight?"

"It was fine but tiring. Jabez had fun though." That was the incentive Jabez needed to cut in, telling his father about the teenager who somehow sneaked some cockroaches and spiders into the plane. One of the air hostesses who saw them fainted and another ran into the bathroom and refused to come out.

Akon was laughing uncontrollably by the time Jabez had finished his comic narration. Even Lara, who saw how it happened, laughed till tears ran down her face. Seeing his chance, Jabez asked, "Daddy, is there food in your house?"

"Don't mind him," Lara said before Akon could answer. "He ate a big plate of fried rice and chicken just before the flight, and an air hostess even gave him an extra pack of snacks. I don't know if there is a well in his stomach."

"My teacher said growing children eat a lot," Jabez replied petulantly.

"Because he is not the one feeding you, right?" Lara asked with a snort.

Akon interrupted them. "Don't worry, when we are closer to the house, I will order pizza for you, okay?" He exchanged glances with his wife, and they both smiled when Jabez let out a loud whoop.

They drove for a while longer before Akon took a final turn and entered a street marked "White Road." They drove until they got to a compound and Akon parked in the driveway. Lara sighed in relief as Akon parked adjacent Piers Close.

Akon had not realised how much he missed his family until they were there with him. Just as Akon started to show them around their new home, the doorbell rang. "That should be the pizza delivery man," he said. He turned to Lara. "You can look around while I get it." Jabez followed his father though, leaving Lara alone to take in the decor.

The house looked a bit disorganised, but it was clean. The decor was plain; she would have to work on that. She glanced into the rooms. Her husband slept in the master bedroom, and she smiled when she saw framed pictures of Jabez and herself hanging on the walls. There was another bedroom that looked lived-in, and she assumed that was where Kay, her husband's friend, slept. Akon told her a while ago that the man had some accommodation issues.

Lara walked back out into the hall and moved to where Jabez and Akon were talking in the kitchen. Akon put three slices of pizza with most of the chicken nuggets he ordered on a plate for Jabez, along with a bottle of Pepsi. "Do you want ketchup?" he asked.

"No, Daddy, thank you," Jabez replied, and he dashed out of the room.

Lara was surprised until she heard the TV come on and she laughed. "Jabez and cartoons!"

She opened the fridge and just stared at it in shock.

"Why is the fridge empty? Don't tell me you've been eating pizza all this while."

"Is pizza not food?" Akon asked, taking a slice from the box. "Come and eat."

"Pizza is not food. It is just bread with spices. I am talking about food like proper Nigerian food. You know I'm not a fan of junk food."

"Sorry," Akon muttered. "Maybe I should have ordered something from a Nigerian restaurant."

Seeing the frown on her husband's face, Lara realised she was acting rather ungrateful. She moved to peck him on the cheek and said, "Don't worry, I'm here now. You'd better get used to eating Nigerian food again, or you will starve." They laughed, and Lara took a piece of garlic bread because she was starving.

The next few days were like a whirlwind. Akon had taken three days off from work. He took his family on a London tour, showing Jabez the famous places he had read about when his mother told him they were moving to England.

They went everywhere—the London Eye, London Bridge, Oxford Street, Hyde Park, museums, and galleries. Jabez's favourite place was the London Eye; he enjoyed the view from the top of the ride. He cajoled Akon into buying souvenirs from each place they visited and decorated his room with them when they got home. Akon laughed when Lara told him her new life goal was visiting all the shops on Oxford Street at least once.

About four weeks after they arrived, Akon decided Jabez was settled enough to start school. He took them to the school he had registered him in. "I want him to be safe and close to the house. The school is a ten-minute walk from the house. This way, either of us can walk him to school in the morning. And in the afternoon, you can pick him up, or I can when you start working."

Lara nodded. "Yes, it is safer that way." Then she voiced something that had been troubling her. "Do you think I can get a good job here? I'm afraid no one will hire me because I am a foreigner."

"Don't worry, dear. I am also a foreigner, and we are not the first immigrants. Others have come before us, and others will come after us. They succeeded, and we shall too. You just have to get used to the system, and I am sure you will find a great job."

"I hope so," she replied.

Meanwhile, Jabez was outside on the street, attempting to make friends. "Hey, hello!" he called out to a boy across the street. The boy looked at him, looked away, and went into his house.

The same thing had happened with a few other kids. Soon enough, Jabez realised people kept to themselves in the UK. Many neighbours seldom accommodate those who seemed different from them. Back in Nigeria, he could go to neighbouring compounds and play with the kids, but it was different here. The kids already had their friends, and because Jabez was different, they did not welcome him in their circle.

Jabez was nervous and excited to start school. He hoped it would be easier to make friends in school than it was at home. Maybe he would see other boys who were from Africa too. His parents had bought his school uniform and all the things he needed to start.

"How do you feel about starting school today?" Lara asked Jabez as he dressed up.

"I'm happy. At least, I will get a chance to see other boys my age and make some friends," Jabez said.

"I'm sure you will, darling. You are a smart boy, and I know you will fit in well," Lara said with a smile.

Lara and Akon believed Jabez would not have any issues adjusting to his new school since he had attended a British school in Lagos. They did not think they needed to prepare their son for the challenges he may face in school. They thought that Jabez's brilliance would outshine any prejudice that his teachers and other pupils might have.

On his first day, Akon and Lara took Jabez to school and dropped him off at the school reception with one of the school administrators. His parents supported him as much as possible while trying to figure things out for themselves. The only thing that seemed to embarrass Jabez was the confusing city transport.

The administrator put a call through. In a few minutes, a lady appeared at the school reception.

"Hello. My name is Ms Whitestone. How are you?" she asked Jabez, smiling.

"I am fine, thank you, ma," Jabez replied, feeling nervous.

"Just call me Ms Whitestone next time," the lady said as she led Jabez to his class. "What is your name?"

"My name is Jabez."

"Nice to meet you, Jabez. We'll be going to the assembly in ten minutes." She showed him where he could put his rucksack and asked if he brought lunch or was entitled to free school meals.

Jabez looked blankly at her. It was hard to keep up with her accent. Later, when he was narrating his first day experience at school to his parents, he told them Ms Whitestone was just churning out words like a robot, not considering the environment may be strange to him.

Ms Whitestone ushered him to join the other children at the assembly. Left on his own, Jabez looked around, not knowing what to do next. The other students gathered and chatted in groups. Not belonging to any of the cliques, Jabez felt a bit intimidated. He stood on his own and was thinking of how he would strike a conversation with someone.

Some minutes later, a brown-haired Caucasian boy approached and greeted him. "Hello, you alright?" The boy was about his height but a bit slimmer.

"Hi, how are you?" Jabez asked shyly. He was glad someone was talking to him.

The boy frowned as if something did not sound right. He adjusted his uniform, maintaining eye contact with Jabez. "My name is Josh. I guess you are new here," the boy said.

"My name is Jabez. Yes, I am new here. Today's my first day." He had to listen carefully to make out the boy's words, but he realised the more he talked with him, the easier it became to communicate. Hopefully, in a few weeks, he would have conversations with anyone without sounding strange and looking confused.

"My family recently moved here," Jabez continued.

"No way! Wait. Say that again?" Josh asked.

"Say what? Sorry?"

"Anything, just keep talking!"

"What do you want me to say? What's going on?"

"Tom! Michael! Come over here for a second, you guys need to see this!"

Jabez felt his cheeks burning as his anxiety built up. This was not going to end well. He took a step back, but two boys joined Josh and cornered him.

"Listen to this guy talk," Josh said to his friends. "It's the funniest thing you'll ever hear!"

"Just leave me alone!" Jabez cried. The boys laughed out loud, calling him names as he walked away. At that moment, a teacher interrupted them, and announced where each class should head. The boys kept quiet, giggling between their teeth while staring at him from afar. Throughout the day, Jabez avoided talking to anyone, particularly the boys who picked on him. They were a year older, so he did not bump into them too often. But that was just the start of his purgatory.

Lara was furious when Jabez narrated his experience. Was it a mistake coming to London? Was it going to be too much for her son? Why aren't the teachers prepared for these situations? After all, Jabez would not have been the first kid to move in from another country. Akon rubbed her shoulders, trying to comfort her. In exchange, she looked back at him with tears in her eyes.

"What are we supposed to do now?" Lara asked.

"Support him the best we can," Akon replied in a soft tone. Lara could not believe this.

In the following week, Jabez was the main protagonist in three fights, according to the head teacher's claims. Akon received a phone call at work, asking both parents to come over for a serious discussion. Akon took time off work and managed to get there in time. Lara was already waiting for him. When they entered the head teacher's office, they were asked to take a seat.

"Thank you for coming here so quickly," Mr Rose, the head teacher, began. "I appreciate the effort. The reason behind this is we needed to ask you a couple of questions about your son." Jabez was also in the meeting, sitting on a chair.

"Sure, please go on," Akon encouraged the head teacher as he was getting impatient.

"We have had some complaints about your son's behaviour. Are you aware of the fact that Jabez was in detention three times this week?"

"Three times? For what?"

"The history teacher saw him pushing another boy. On another instance, he got into a fight with two classmates. These were the first two detentions. A third fight occurred during a lesson!"

"This must be a mistake. Our son would not do anything like this. He has always been such a lovely kid!" Akon insisted.

"I understand your frustration. But we have many witnesses."

"Jabez? Is this true?" his mother asked, full of pain and embarrassment. Jabez stared at his feet. He wanted to hide from this terrible moment. Things were not that simple. While it was confirmed that he pushed the boys and wanted to beat George, this was not in vain. They had pushed his last nerve until he had broken down. There was no other way for him to cope; he had to fight back. Akon gently shook his arm, demanding an answer.

"C'mon, son. Come clean. Tell your mother what happened."

"It's not fair. The kids at school always laugh at me or act so mean. I pushed Adam because he was making fun of my accent. I asked him to stop, but he did not. He kept imitating me and calling me names. All his friends were pushing me, and I wanted to get away. That's why I pushed him!"

"What happened next?" the Head Teacher asked.

"George took my backpack. I looked everywhere for it. I was almost late for class when I saw him taunting me. I asked him to give me my backpack because I knew he took it. He headed to class without telling me. I later found it in the bathroom hidden away in the toilet stalls. When I finally got it, he was still laughing at me."

"Is that why you wanted to slap him?"

"Yes, Mr Rose. The kids hate me! I don't like it here!"

"Wait. So, these kids are bullying you and you are the one in detention? What else happened? How come we didn't know about this?" Akon was angry.

Lara tried her best to keep calm as Akon's voice echoed through the room. Mr. Rose could not leave things like that, so he reminded them about the school's policy.

"We do not encourage aggressive behaviour under any circumstances!" he insisted.

"What about racism? Do you encourage that?" Akon demanded.

"No, Mr 'Con. We will discuss with the other children's parents and take appropriate measures if needed," Mr Rose replied.

"The teacher didn't say anything when they laughed at me in class, Dad. I was assigned to read a paragraph out of a book. They all mocked me. The teacher was right there but he did not stop them!" Jabez said, tears in his eyes.

"This is my fault," Lara intervened. "He told me he had no friends here and that his classmates were mean. I told him to ignore them. I had no idea how severe the situation was."

"Don't blame yourself, honey" Akon said. He turned back to face the Head Teacher. "Mr Rose? How is this possible? You have other kids besides my son that study here. They are not all native English speakers. Why don't you do more for them? It's a big change to come to a new school, and these kids need help."

"I understand your point of view and will take it into account," Mr Rose replied. "Before that, is everything going well at home? Are there any problems?"

"No. I can assure you nothing bad is happening at home. Why do you even ask?"

"Jabez is an excellent student. His only problem is aggressive behaviour."

"It is stress," Akon noted. "The other kids are making him feel like a fool. Surely, this would take a toll on him. I am sorry if he has been fighting, but I brought him up to defend himself."

"I understand," Mr Rose said. "I will suggest that your son engages with the Pastoral Care department at the school. I can arrange so they can offer Jabez the support he needs during this period of settlement. I understand your son may be finding it difficult to settle into a new class, especially when he is new to the school and has no friends. On the other hand, you can seek alternative counselling for your son to help him temper his emotions instead of encouraging him to practise violence. It might prevent this from happening again, and it's in your best interest."

"That sounded like an ultimatum," Akon replied coldly.

"Please, understand that this is necessary. If your son does not behave and we receive one more report, we are obligated to expel him."

Lara and Akon were terrified. They could not believe this was happening to them. The Head Teacher walked them out of the meeting without further explanations. With so many things going on, the parents needed to take a moment to breathe. Jabez was waiting for someone from Pastoral Care to arrive while his parents took a seat in the car.

"Talk to me," Akon asked Lara. "Do you have a better idea?"

"No, not for now. Did you see Jabez's face? He was shaken. Maybe we should start looking for a new school," Lara said, with tears in her eyes. Akon's eyes were red too. Both parents were visibly shaken.

18

The Pastoral Care department was a new world waiting to be unveiled. Jabez looked around the room and noticed that students were learning in pairs, tutoring each other. Some larger groups were gardening outside, while a handful of students were having tea at a table. After everything that had happened, Jabez could only think of how he had disappointed his parents and how this whole episode would affect his future education.

Absorbed in thought, Jabez rubbed his palms against his eyes, trying not to cry. All he wanted was to attend a good school, make friends, explore the city, and have fun! The feeling of being an outcast was killing him. There was nothing more in this world that he wanted other than to be a part of this country. He loved the tall, gothic buildings, variety of foods and the London atmosphere, especially the language, the way it rolled off the tongue with an ease he was incapable of. For a moment, he loathed Nigerian culture and wanted to embrace the British. Otherwise, how could he be part of this environment?

"Hello? Have you been waiting for long?" the Pastoral Care attendant, Mr Brighton, asked him. His voice sounded harmonic, full of kindness and typical English politeness. Jabez wanted to say something, but words would not leave his mouth. Knowing he would be expelled if he did not adhere to the rules scared him. He was also embarrassed by the way he spoke.

"Come on, don't be shy. I'll show you around."

Mr. Brighton had already been briefed as to why Jabez was there. He had a lot of experience with troubled kids and believed goodwill would always find its way into broken hearts. That is why he created an extracurricular group in which students were encouraged to make friends and work together. A psychologist helped him plan the activities so that the children could connect with others and regain trust. This was a non-judgmental place where children were encouraged to be themselves and respect other members of the group.

The programme's first step was to assign a community buddy that would have weekly meetings with the student. The activities were not always school-related.

The two buddies could go to the movies together, jog or share lunches. The children were also encouraged to visit the place whenever they felt like it. Mr Brighton told Jabez all of this and asked what he would like to learn from his potential new friend.

"I want to talk like you! My type of English doesn't sound right, does it?" Jabez said.

"Alright. Well, I think your English is not that bad, Jabez. But if that is what you want, I know a literature student that might be able to help."

Although Jabez knew his problem was not English, the British knew better than to challenge this. Jabez was introduced to Jonathan, a tall, ginger-haired boy with big blue eyes. It was the friendliest face he had seen since he moved here. They started talking, and Jonathan tried to find out what he liked so they would have something to talk about. Slowly, Jabez warmed to him. It was hard to trust someone after everything he had been through. But Jonathan was not there to laugh at him. He wanted to support him, be his friend, and learn more about his passions. He explained he was also a troubled kid who had come here to get better. Someone finally understood Jabez's misery and treated him with dignity and care.

A new routine was put into place. Jonathan would meet Jabez three times a week for English lessons.

Every other weekend, they would go out together to learn about English culture.

They shared burgers, sausages, and chips, and laughed at how different things were voiced in their upbringings. Jabez realised he did not have to give up his roots; he just had to embrace his new lifestyle and incorporate it into his everyday activities.

Because of his new friend, the bullying diminished day by day. At first, Jonathan would intervene each time Jabez was in trouble. The bullies tried to attack him in many ways, but Jabez refused to meet their violence with violence. Jonathan encouraged him to keep calm and tried to keep an eye on him. Then, he introduced him to other members of the group who invited him to sit at their table at lunch or during breaks. Now that he was always surrounded by people, the bullies lost the courage to provoke Jabez.

However, Jabez still felt uneasy when he was alone. He would jump at the slightest touch and would run away from any confrontation. It took him a few months before he was able to walk alone during breaks. His friends, however, were there to support him.

Three months into Jonathan's lessons, Jabez's language skills had improved significantly. He was another person. Confidence and practice made him sound almost like a native speaker. He was grateful to Jonathan, and they continued to be friends. He even made a couple of new friends independently. Things were stabilising.

Lara could not believe how much her son had adapted to his new culture. She was glad that she trusted her instincts and judgment.

Jabez's Nigerian accent would be almost gone within a year. He was an excellent student, tutoring many pupils at the pastoral care centre. A new school year was about to begin when he saw another Nigerian boy trying to talk to his new classmates. They were laughing at him. Jabez saw himself in that boy's shoes and could not tolerate it. All he ever wanted back then was someone to stand up for him. This new boy could certainly become his friend.

*   *   *

Soon after her move to London, Akon invited Lara to his office. She had been in London for almost a month now, and it was time that she found out where he worked. It was nearly 6.00 pm, and most of the staff had left. While they sat in the office, the phone rang.

Akon grabbed it, said "Hello" and frowned. "What did I tell you? I am married! Don't be a doubting Thomas. In fact, you can speak to my wife right now."

He handed the phone to Lara.

Lara spoke. "Hello."

"Who are you? I want to speak to Akon!"

"I am his wife."

"Keep dreaming. Akon isn't married."

"Did he tell you that?"

"Stay away from Akon!" the woman at the other end of the line snapped.

Lara hung up and turned to Akon.

"What is going on?" she asked. "Who is this woman? How come she does not know you are married?"

"She is a nuisance," Akon said with a shrug. "She does not believe I am married. Her question has always been, 'Why don't you live with your wife?'"

"She sounds determined," Lara said.

Akon smiled. "I knew her in Lagos. Then we met in London."

"And then?"

"I told her I was happily married, but she never believed me."

"Then you should introduce me to her, face to face."

"And start a fight? No way."

"Fight? Why should we fight? Tell her I am your wife, and that would be it. Hasn't she seen your wedding ring?"

"You know I sometimes take it off even at home. The

first time we met, I did not have it on. Now she says I only put one on to discourage her."

"She is shameless," Lara said scornfully.

She had never caught Akon cheating on her. But he had always been insecure about her, perhaps because she was a beautiful woman. He had always thought she might go out with one of her male friends.

"You have changed, Akon," Lara continued. "London has changed you. How would I know if it has not changed your taste in women as well? Maybe you want to replace me with whoever that is."

"That is nonsense!" Akon cried, becoming annoyed. "How has London changed me? I am still Akon, the son of Akete, and I am still your husband. Who planted ideas into your head while you were in Nigeria?"

Akon had been uneasy about leaving his wife in another continent while he was in the UK. He also noticed that Jabez was closer to Lara than him. He knew that would happen because he had been away for so long. It was going to take a while before Jabez got used to him again. That did not stop Akon from feeling a bit isolated and neglected.

Well, that is a price I had to pay for relocating to London. Akon had bigger things to worry about now—the challenges at work and Lara's suspicion that he was a serial cheat. Lara had seen Ela's text, the Polish lady he broke up with shortly before she arrived in the UK. Since that incident, Lara could not trust anything he said. He tried several times to convince her that she was the only woman in his life, but she could not believe him. These days, there was tension in the house, which was affecting their marriage.

The other night, Akon had left his laptop open on the dining table, and Lara had seen a Skype message from a lady who asked when the "next meeting" was going to be. This was two months after she had arrived in London. Since then, she had become even more distant and cold.

"I no longer feel secure in this marriage, Akon. You keep giving me reasons to doubt your commitment to me," Lara had said, looking furious.

"Please, my darling, don't let us ruin our love having come this far. How many marriages would have lasted this long? Do you not know that 40% of long-distance relationships break up and we are lucky to still have ours? I bet you don't know how much I worked, sixty hours a week for five years, so we can both be comfortable, and to think that all I get is an accusation of infidelity," Akon said. His eyes were red with anger because Lara did not seem to believe him.

"I have no reason to believe a word that comes out of your mouth. You cheated once. Why should I believe you won't cheat again?" Lara retorted.

"Okay, you swear on your father's grave that you too did not cheat on me.

Lara sighed heavily. "I did not, even when I had opportunities to."

"Babe, please listen to me, okay? Sandra is a gym instructor. I met her through Kay, and she was trying to help me cut down on my belly fat through aerobic exercises. Tell you what? I will invite Sandra to come over next weekend if she is free so we can put a stop to these accusations!" Akon was tired of trying to prove that he was not unfaithful. Maybe it was time to show her some evidence.

"Oh, that is not necessary," Lara said, her face lighting up.

Nevertheless, Akon called Sandra to come over for dinner on Saturday night. Sandra arrived with her partner, whom she introduced as Jeffrey. She presented a bouquet of flowers to Lara. She also came with two packets of scones and strawberry jam. Lara was surprised to see how friendly Sandra was.

Lara drew her into the kitchen while the men talked in the garden. Sandra was chatty and interesting. She told Lara about two of her lovely cats, Bin and Kit. She had owned another cat, Pinto, but she had died.

"Oh, I'm sorry about that," Lara said.

"It's fine. It happened a long time ago. What is that

orange stuff you've got in the dish?" Sandra asked, pointing at one of the bowls on the kitchen counter.

"Oh, that is jollof rice. Would you like to have some?"

"That would be nice, thank you. So, how do you pronounce your name?"

"That's easy. It is La-ra."

"Laura," Sandra said. "Did I get it right?"

Lara pronounced it again, but Sandra kept pronouncing it as Laura. They both laughed about it.

"I am sure I'll get the hang of it soon," Sandra said.

"Sure," Lara said.

"I am glad you made it to London, you know. Akon was eager to have you here. He talks of nothing except his wife and son, and he really wanted to stay in shape for you, Lara. You have got a nice guy there. You are lucky," Sandra said.

"Thank you," Lara said. "So, where are you from?"

"I am from Ireland. My dad is Irish, but my mum is from East Sussex. I was born in England, not Ireland. I have only been there two times in my life."

Lara smiled. She was glad to know Sandra was not dating her husband.

* * *

It was already late in the night, but Akon knew Lara had a habit of waiting for him to arrive. She sat in an armchair, reading a book. But Akon knew every minute of lateness meant a little nervousness in Lara's heart.

"Hi, honey," Akon said and kissed Lara.

"Hi," Lara smiled at him, "How was your day?"

"It was alright, but I am exhausted. I'll just go to bed."

Your dinner is on the table, won't you eat?"

"Thanks, dear. I am too tired." Akon said, walking towards the kitchen for some hot water. "I would have some chocolate drink." Lara joined Akon in the kitchen as she packed the dinner and placed it in the fridge.

Before lying down, Akon had a habit of checking his emails one last time. He opened the website on his phone, and to his surprise, there was one new email for him. It was from corporate. Nobody sends work emails at night.

Akon opened the email with shaky fingers and started reading. "We regret to inform you that your post has been dissolved. Please, show up at work on Monday." It was no longer viable to keep Akon's role, but the company would find something for him to collect his salary until a new position is found for him.

Akon froze. He could not believe he had just lost his post through a short email. Akon checked the email once more, thinking there was further explanation for this decision. Nobody tried to convince Akon that this was the right decision. It was as if corporate did not care about what he thought.

Akon did not discuss the email with Lara. Neither did he allow it to disrupt his plans for the weekend.

On Monday, Akon walked to his new ugly-looking desk. The new requirements floated in his head: "Do not talk about structural changes," the paper said. Everybody had been warned against discussing the changes among colleagues. So, they were all in hushed tones.

Akon took a seat. He did not even greet his new colleagues. The pain of losing the job had turned into anger for unfair treatment.

As the days went by, Akon still did not talk to his new colleagues. He would sit at his desk and do those boring accounting tasks, which only triggered his anger the more. New office rules also meant Akon's days were even more stressful.

19

"This is chaos!" the area manager stamped her palm on the desk, papers flying into the air.

"It is Jake's fault. He spent money on unprofitable company expansions," someone mumbled.

"Well, Jake's era is over. Now I decide where the funds go. And my first task is to close all the international offices in three months. From now on, we will be working only on domestic offices. Whenever we have the chance, we will re-open those international ones," the manager stood up and straightened her skirt.

"But, Mrs Murphy, hundreds of people are employed in those offices!" the workers started complaining.

"If you don't do what I say, all of you will be left

without jobs!" Mrs Ciara Murphy looked around angrily, "Do you understand?"

Everybody nodded their heads.

"We need to focus on this management change, and the restructuring of roles and posts is part of the process. I will evaluate each of our employees and review their roles." Without waiting for a response, she left the room.

Everyone knew significant changes were about to happen. But Akon never thought this company would fire someone as hard-working and dedicated as he was. However, walking into the office became hard for him because he always felt nervous. He did not know how long he had left in the job. And the last thing he wanted was to disappoint his family, especially his loving wife.

Akon was staring at the blank screen of his work computer, lost in thought. He did not realise his colleagues were staring at him sympathetically. Akon was close to tears. *What did I do wrong? Why are things going south for me?* He was still lost in thought when one of his colleagues walked up to his work desk.

"Hey, man. Would you like a cup of coffee? It is lunchtime," Habib Mohammed asked.

"Sure," Akon said reluctantly and turned off his computer. They took the elevator and walked to the nearest coffee shop. Habib ordered two cups of Espresso.

"Listen, man. I did not want to talk about this in front of others. I see your pain, and I know how you feel right now. But you must be strong. You have become bigger than this company, and I think you should chase up other opportunities. Everyone knows you were immersed in the company. You worked during lunch. We saw you take work home to make sure you met deadlines. You were a good manager. No one knows why your post was dissolved, but you need to chase your dreams somewhere else. This place has nothing to offer you anymore."

"Thanks, Habib."

I just need to be strong, Akon said to himself, managing a smile.

*   *   *

The new area manager banned music during office hours and reduced lunchtime from one hour to thirty minutes. He mandated staff to take five-minute breaks every two hours, so they do not strain their eyes on the computer.

It was now payday after a torturous month in his new job. Akon smiled in anticipation as he opened the envelope that contained his wage cheque. Akon's smile turned sour as he saw the amount he was paid.

"What?" Akon whispered after realising his salary

had been reduced. He had lost about thirty percent of his previous salary and was short by almost £450. "That's it!" he said loudly and jumped from his chair. No one looked at Akon because they were all in the same boat.

After three cancellations of a meeting with the new Area Manager, Akon decided to knock on her door. "Come in!" the woman said.

"I am sorry to bother you," Akon was shivering, "I wanted to draw your attention to my grade." Akon placed his paycheque on the woman's table. "You told me it would not affect my wages, but upon receiving the payslip, I was paid thirty percent less than my usual pay."

Mrs Kistrel looked at the paycheque, then at Akon, who was standing in front of her with arms crossed. She breathed in deeply and responded, "I am sorry your wages were downgraded. I bet you may want to take it up with the human resources department. But remember, in the new policy, salaries are performance related. So, if you did not get your exact wages, it might have to do with your ability to do your job."

Thousands of thoughts ran through Akon's mind. But the only phrase he could mumble was, "But I am a great worker."

Mrs Kistrel looked at him with a cold facial

expression. She sighed once more. "Mr Akete, can you please take your grievances to the human resources department? I am running late for a board meeting," the woman said and pointed at the door.

"Mrs Kistrel, I beg your pardon," Akon tried to talk as loudly as possible because his voice almost disappeared from nervousness.

"Can you please learn to say my name properly?"

"I am sorry, ma'am. I just wanted to find out what areas you want me to improve on so I can address this and earn back my grades and salary in the future."

"As I said in the last team meeting, everyone would receive an email advising them on their position in the company," the manager talked while typing something on her computer. She did not even look at Akon who stood in front of her like a schoolchild. Akon's patience was wearing out. He knew the time had come for him to look for another job.

*   *   *

Akon had started applying for other roles. At the same time, it had been two months since Lara arrived in the UK. In the last four weeks, she had tried, to no avail, to secure a job. She was sitting on the sofa, checking the job advert section in the newspaper when the phone rang. She picked up on the third ring.

"Hello." A female voice with a British accent was speaking. "Am I on to O'Laura Holuu Kete?"

"Sorry, you've got the wrong number." Lara responded politely and hung up the phone.

Akon was working on his laptop, listening attentively to Lara's phone conversation. "Are you sure you are not the one the lady was asking for? Let us wait for a while, she might just call back. And when she does, do not hang up. Okay?"

"I don't think it was for me, honey. She asked for Laura. Besides, it might be one of these cold callers again. Just last week, somebody called and said that he has been informed that I was involved in a road accident and have broken my limbs. I dropped the phone and rejected their curses. That is why I hung up on this lady. It's too early in the morning to receive curses."

"It's okay, darling," Akon assured her, chuckling. "People market their products all the time, and if you aren't interested, you can just decline politely."

Five minutes later, the phone rang again. Lara rolled her eyes heavenward and gestured for Akon to pick the call. Akon stepped forward and put the cordless Panasonic phone on loudspeaker before picking up.

"Can I speak to O'Laura Holuu Kate?" The female voice said again. Akon knew that the call was for Lara.

He cleared his throat and feigned a female voice.

"Yes, Laura speaking."

"Alright. We received your application to work in our law firm, and we would like to invite you for an interview next Friday. Is that convenient for you, ma'am?" The lady on the phone asked.

"Yes, it is. Would you please send me the details?" Akon answered.

"Of course. We will put it in the post to you first class, and you will receive it tomorrow," the lady said and hung up.

"Omolara Oluferanmi Akete," Akon said in a sharp tone. "I had a feeling the caller was asking for you. That was a job opportunity you almost missed after months of looking for a job. You better learn to listen well and stop playing dumb."

Lara rolled her eyes again. "I'm not dumb. How am I supposed to know it's for me when the caller asked for Laura Kate?"

"Sweetheart, we are in this race together. I get called *Con*, but it does not matter if my salary is getting paid. Who cares what I am called?"

"I am not Laura though. I am Lara. They call me Laura at work, and it's annoying." She was referring to where she worked as a waitress. "I have corrected them severally, but they just don't listen."

Akon grinned and shook his head. His dear wife did

not know what was up. "I am leaving. I have an interview this morning," he said, carrying a bag that contained his PC.

"An interview? What happened to your job?" Lara asked alarmed.

"I'm just pushing my luck. I am not getting along with my manager. She finds fault in everything I do and is never happy with my work. She is always snapping at me. Funny thing is, she is just twenty-nine years old. I'm paying homage and trying to please someone who is almost twenty years my junior." Akon lamented some more before saying, "I'm off."

"Bye," Lara said and stood up to clear the table.

* * *

The following week, Lara met up with one of her friends, Aina, at a restaurant. As they ate and chatted, Lara kept scratching at the persistent itch in her hair until Aina noticed. "What is wrong with your hair, Lara?" She asked, giving her a quizzical look.

"Oh, I have been carrying this weave for two months, and my entire head has started to itch like crazy. I had to buy a cream to relieve it a bit."

"Loosen it and make another one," Aina replied. "Once you wash it, the itching would go away."

"That's the problem. Where will I make it? You

know this is not Nigeria. I don't want someone to do nonsense with my hair."

"No way! This is not like the eighties when I first came here. Then, you would have to go to Peckham or invite the stylist to your house. These days, many places cater to African Americans and blacks from other countries."

"Wow! I came at the right time then."

"Yes, you did." They both laughed as they finished their meal. "If you want," Aina continued, "I can make an appointment for you at a salon in Woolwich that I use. When would you like to go?"

"Saturday would be okay. I want to have ample time to loosen and wash the hair."

Aina nodded, and they made some small talk before leaving.

*   *   *

The following Saturday, Lara gasped in awe as she stared at the building. *This place is just like Lasgidi!* As she approached, she stared in amazement at the people who looked and sounded just like her. Some of them were even conversing in Yoruba and pidgin—two languages she understood. She wanted to talk with them, but her innate wariness around strangers would not let her.

As she stepped closer to the building, she saw the signboard bearing the name, *4inOne Unisex Salon*. Curious about the strange name, she stepped in. The place was well organised with two floors divided into clear sections. She saw the barber shop, hair styling sections, and nail fixing points.

Some men and women were sitting on waiting chairs at the reception hall. She moved over to the receptionist who greeted her with a large smile. "Hello. What service are you here for?" she asked.

"I want to braid my hair."

"Okay. Do you have a reservation?"

"A friend made a reservation for me." She told the receptionist her and Aina's name, and the receptionist checked through her computer. She beckoned one of the girls to come over.

"Dana, this is a *special* customer. Please, take her to Madam's station." She looked at Lara and said, "Please, you might have to wait for a while. The stylist you were booked for is still working on another customer, but she should be done within a few minutes. Dana will take you to a comfortable waiting room."

Some of the customers who had been waiting before Lara came were angry. Lara overheard the receptionist telling them that those with reservations have precedence over walk-ins.

Dana took Lara upstairs to one of the few sections demarcated from the rest of the room by a wall. Lara sat and took out her earpiece. She recalled a conversation she had with some of her old school mates. One of them mentioned how, in a bus, one would see an average British passenger with a paperback novel or Kindle in their hand. On the other hand, blacks were often seen with earphones.

Someone else had replied that blacks did read, but Africans preferred to get information from friends and relatives rather than books because they consider experience far better than book knowledge. Lara laughed as she recalled the humorous conversation.

Suddenly, there was a swarm of salesmen and women, holding out different items ranging from fancy jewellery to food items, shouting prices to the salon's customers. Lara was shocked when she saw a woman, who looked to be Chinese, obnoxiously holding out pirated blockbuster disks in the faces of customers. Most of them refused, of course. Another Asian was advertising jewellery and perfumes, claiming he bought them from Dubai.

Lara was surprised. She had not realised there were things like this in London too. She did not buy any of the items and she was amused at how customers haggled over prices just like they would in any other Nigerian market.

"Ma'am," the girl called Dana called her attention. "I am sorry about the delay. Please, be patient. It will soon be your turn. You can go out to buy snacks if you want."

Lara smiled and waved at the girl. At first, she was surprised she was being asked to leave the salon to buy snacks when there were food vendors right there. Then she understood they would not want any liabilities if there were unsafe elements in the food. *How sad.*

After about an hour of waiting, she was taken in to see the stylist. "Hi," the smiling black lady said as Lara stepped in. "I am Evelyn, the owner of this humble establishment. How are you?"

"I am very well, and you?" Lara said, surprised that her stylist was the owner. Maybe that was why she was called a special customer. The woman's accent was also surprising. Most Nigerians still had their accents imprinted even as they spoke English, but Evelyn's accent was flawless.

"Very well. I am sorry for the long wait. I hope you are not offended."

"Not at all," Lara replied in her easy-going manner. Soon, she was settled, and Evelyn began to make her hair. Somehow, they got talking, and she was able to find out a lot about the stylist, including the fact that she was not a mere stylist. She was a professional beautician and fashionista with a degree in hair, makeup, and fashion. She also had various fashion houses and salons in the UK as well as Nigeria and Ghana. When she mentioned the name of her beauty shop in Lagos, Lara realised she knew the place. Evelyn even had British stylists and employees from other countries working under her. It was astounding how much the woman had accomplished. Lara was impressed.

They were in the middle of their conversation when a woman ran past the building screaming. At once, people started fleeing the building like passengers deserting a sinking ship.

Lara became panicked, wondering what was going on. The stylist managed to calm her down. "Except you do not have your papers, there is no need to worry. It's the immigration officers that come around occasionally to do spot checks."

"Oh! You mean these people running out don't have complete papers?"

"Yes. Either that or their papers have expired. It is sad, but many people are desperate. They come here under any pretext so they can find work. But if they are caught, they would be detained and deported."

Just as the woman finished speaking, a man ran in, breathing heavily with sweat pouring down his face. "Awon ile nla ti block gbogbo street o," he said in

Yoruba. "If you know anybody planning to come to Woolwich today, tell them it is not safe; immigration officers are everywhere," he added before running out.

Lara shook her head sadly.

20

Lara sighed as she glanced at the clock for the ump-teenth time that night. It was almost 10.30 pm, and Akon had not returned from work. Lately, he had been coming home late, and Lara did not like it one bit. She tried to talk about it several times, but he claimed he needed to put in extra time at work to support the family. She had gotten tired of explaining to Jabez why his father was not always home to say goodnight.

After about half an hour, Lara heard Akon's car pulling into the driveway, and she let out a sigh of relief. When he came inside, she heard him switching off the lights and checking the electricity metres. That had become his habit too. He always said things were expensive in the UK and they could not afford to be wasteful.

There was a clear difference between the Akon she married and the Akon she now knew. UK seemed to have turned him into someone else, to the point that Lara could not help but feel like she was losing the man she loved. Lara sat up as he came into the bedroom.

"Welcome home, babe," she said.

"Thanks." He barely looked at her. He entered the bathroom and had his bath. Lara went to heat up his food, which had grown cold after being laid out for so long. She had prepared his favourite—pounded yam and egusi soup.

Akon came out of the bathroom, wiping a face towel across his face.

"Babe, your food is ready," Lara said to him.

"What did you make?" Akon asked.

"Your favourite—pounded yam and egusi soup," Lara said with a smile.

"I don't think I have the appetite for anything tonight. I'll just have a smoothie," Akon said with an irritated look as he walked into the kitchen.

Lara's face fell as she sighed in disappointment. This was getting too much for her. Lately, he had refused to eat their native dishes that he used to enjoy. Now, he preferred to eat out or eat something different from what he used to eat. It was as if he was distancing himself from the person he used to be.

The next day, a Sunday, Akon dropped Lara and Jabez at church and drove back home. Lara was troubled by his behaviour. She could not concentrate on any of the church's activities. Her family seemed to be falling apart. Her husband no longer cared about her and their son. He did not spend time with them anymore. He had set ridiculous boundaries between them, claiming he needed his privacy.

When she got home from church, Akon was sipping a glass of wine and watching TV. Later that evening, they sat in the garden together. The garden had a nice green lawn and a green hedge. Akon found it refreshing. It was better than their old Lagos neighbourhood where he always heard hooting cars.

"Babe, we need to talk," Lara said.

"About what?" Akon asked, not paying attention.

"About everything. About our family. About how you have changed. You are no longer the man I used to know."

"How do you mean?" Akon asked defensively. He was attentive now.

"A lot has been going on, but I need to ask you something first. Do you really want me in the UK? There is a strange tension here that I cannot place my finger on. You are not excited to talk anymore, and you have become very formal with me. What's going on?"

"I don't understand what you are getting at," Akon said. He was becoming uncomfortable.

"For example, when I talk to you in Yoruba, you reply in English. As a matter of fact, you do not even use endearing words for me anymore. Darling, do you realise that such behaviour can build walls between us? I even brought all our *Naija comedy night of a thousand laughs*, but I cannot remember you sitting to watch them with me. What is going on, my dear? I thought you wanted me with you in London."

Now Akon laughed. "Maybe you have forgotten how I used to be."

Lara snorted. "Nawa ooo. Forgotten how you used to be? I remember everything. When my husband changes, I can spot the difference a mile away. You are easily influenced by the things around you. If you moved to Brazil today, you would end up absorbing a bit of their culture."

"Are you saying that I don't have a mind of my own, woman?" Akon said, feeling irritated.

"Of course not! I just want to be carried along with any changes you are making. After all, you were living here long before I came, but you should not forget where you came from," she challenged. "You should not discard your old culture to embrace a new one."

"I did not discard my culture! Just because I have not

spoken Yoruba doesn't mean I have thrown away my culture," Akon snapped. "What else has changed? It seems you have made up your mind to profile me today."

"You said each of us should have individual phones and we shouldn't bother to pick up or check each other's phones. The same rule applies to letters that are not addressed to me. I thought we were one regardless of location. I am confused Akon."

"How is respecting each other's privacy a big deal? Why are you blowing things out of proportion?" Akon asked.

"We need to talk about this, Akon."

"What is there to talk about, Lara? You are just being paranoid," Akon retorted.

"I am not being paranoid, Akon! I have every reason to be suspicious. You are no longer the man I married! You have changed into a different person. I don't even know you anymore."

"Changed, you say? Change is constant, Lara. There is nothing wrong with change." He was going to say more, but Lara cut him short.

"Only if the change is in the right direction! I never had a problem with you visiting the gym and adopting exercise routines. That is a good kind of change. But any change that would make you reject my food and not have time for your family and even the Church is not good change! As a matter of fact, you pay more attention to the aquarium than your own son. What do you expect me to make of that, Akon? Even your diet has changed. I was excited to make your favourite pounded yam and egusi only for you to tell me that the locust beans I used in preparing the soup is making the whole house smell and that it would be a nuisance to our neighbours. You did not care about that before now, Akon. This side of you is strange."

"Lara, please try to understand. This is Britain. You give to Caesar what belongs to Caesar. When you find yourself in a new environment, it is only wise to assimilate their culture and code of conduct. Know and accept how things work or you will be left behind in the scheme of things. Most of our Nigerian meals like pounded yam, eba, rice, plantain and even the oil you use to make soup are unhealthy accumulations of carbs and fat that our bodies can do without! We should stay away from them or eat them on special occasions.

"My dear," Akon continued, "do you know why Africa is still the way it is today? Two things, Lara—religion and tradition. That is why I am trying to move away from these factors to embrace a life of challenges and endless possibilities. I know what I am doing; just trust me on this. In time, you will see that I do everything in your interest and for my son," Akon said, half convincing his wife.

"Are you sure that's all this is about, Akon? You are sure there's nothing else to this?"

"I promise, Lara. That is all there is. Believe me. Embrace these little changes so we can move forward as a couple. You are my wife, Lara. I need your support now more than ever."

*   *   *

Things seemed to be going well until one night when Lara brought up a topic they had avoided since she arrived in London.

"You know, there is immense pressure for us to have another child, Akon."

"Yes, but I am not a magician," Akon replied. "We should prioritise how you would get a job so you can contribute to the bills. Do you know how much child-care costs? Jabez has only one year to go until he starts secondary school; but then, we cannot leave him alone. We will have another child but let us settle things financially first. Did you get Jabez by magic?"

"I know we have tried, but I think it is time you visited a Urologist about this. I'll go with you," Lara said, refusing to give up.

"What? Who said I'm the problem?" Akon asked.

"While in Lagos, I was cleared by a doctor before we had Jabez and again, before I joined you in the UK. I have the medical reports. I should have no problem conceiving."

"Are you trying to say it's my fault?"

"How many times did I plead with you to get a test? You refused and told me you were okay. Akon, please be reasonable. I am forty-one years old for crying out loud. The older I get, the more difficult it becomes."

"So, what do you want me to do?" Akon asked.

"The doctor said you should have a sperm count check," Lara replied.

"I'll think about it." Akon paused before suddenly asking, "Wait a minute, Lara. If I cannot impregnate you, where did Jabez come from?"

"What are you implying?" Lara retorted. "The doctor said you can still father a child if you have a low sperm count, but it may take many tries."

"I see," Akon said.

Akon was worried that the two specialist Doctors he and Lara had seen had come up with the same conclusion. They had both said that he had a low sperm count, and he just could not bring himself to accept it.

Akon loved Jabez dearly, but that did not stop him from wanting more children. He had daydreamed of playing with his children, a boy, and a girl, but now the dream was threatened, and he could not help but wonder what could have gone wrong.

His mind began to wander. In the first year at university, he had a throbbing pain in his stomach and could not take in any food without throwing up. The university had been on a strike because of non-payment of lecturer's salaries and he was at home when the pain began. His mother had rushed him to the hospital with the help of neighbours, as dad was not at home.

Akon's mother could not hold back the tears as she watched her only son groan in pain. "This is my only surviving son, I hope nothing befalls him," she had said under her breath, holding back tears.

"This must be the work of my enemies who are jealous of my son's success. May God punish all my enemies!" Akon's mother prayed. She hit the taxi driver's seat and urged him to drive faster.

"Where are we going ma?" the driver asked politely.

"We are going to the party ni, are you crazy? Can't you see my son is in pain?" Mama Akete lashed out at the driver. "We are going straight to the City hospital, his Auntie's hospital," she said as she refocused on her son. The driver apologised and tried to go a little faster.

As soon as they arrived at the hospital, Mama Akete ordered the driver to stop in front of the gate as she hurriedly jumped out of the car.

Akon was so weak he could not walk by himself. He had to be held by his mum and the taxi driver, who had been moved by compassion by the current situation. As soon as they entered the hospital, one of the nurses recognised Mama Akete immediately and ran towards her to assist her with the sick boy.

"Stretcher!" the nurse screamed as she got closer to her. Within seconds, Akon was laid on a stretcher and wheeled away, with a consultant walking behind in hurried steps.

After a few minutes of the consultant examining him, he diagnosed that Akon had a hernia and needed to undergo surgery immediately. Mama Ekete broke down in tears. "My enemies have gotten me!" she wailed loudly. The nurse quickly ran to her to calm her down.

Within 30 minutes, Akon was moved to an en-suite ward and placed on drips. "He's already dehydrated," the doctor said. "We would need to conduct some blood tests too."

"That's fine, as long as you are sure my boy would be okay," mama Akete said in ragged breaths.

"We will carry out the surgery in two days, but we need to stabilise him first. His blood pressure is high," the doctor said calmly. At this point, Mama Akete could no longer hold herself.

"Mo gbe o! Mo daran! Jesu! I am in trouble! Please save my only son!" she continued to cry out.

Again, one of the nurses tried to console her. "Mama Akete, your son will be alright. He is in good hands. This is about 6 pm. Why don't you go home and rest?" she asked.

"Rest ke?" Mama Akete gave the nurse a puzzled look. She was determined to stay next to her son, who was drifting in and out of consciousness.

By the next day, Akon felt a bit better. The pain-killers seemed to have worked.

"Can I go home now? I feel better," Akon asked the nurse, his mother looking at her with expectation.

"No way," the nurse said. "You will be here for a couple of days because we need to conduct a series of tests on you," the nurse said as she turned to leave.

Akon was about to raise further objections before his mother interjected. "My son, please listen to the nurse," she said with a sad look in her eyes.

"But Mummy, I am hungry," Akon said, hoping he could persuade her.

"You cannot eat yet," Mama Akete said, "not before the operation."

"But why? Oh no! I don't want one," he tried to argue.

After debating for a while, Akon finally fell asleep. Mama Akete decided to quickly use the opportunity to get some fresh supplies from the house. She took a quick glance at him as she walked out of the room, wiping tears from her eyes.

When Akon woke up a few hours later, he was shocked to see daddy, Otunba Akete, and his second wife by his bedside. He looked around the room in search of his mother.

"I have just spoken to the consultant and they said they would be performing the surgery tomorrow." His father's voiced boomed around the room. "Take heart, my son." His father continued. "Ko si ewu. No fear at all," he tapped on Akon's legs before taking his leave.

The operation went ahead as scheduled and was a success. Mama Akete could not hide her joy as she kept thanking the doctors and nurses. Five days later, Akon was discharged from the hospital.

However, after only a few days of being back home, he noticed his testicles were swollen and hurting, and his mom decided it was best to go back to the hospital.

On getting there, the doctor prescribed some antibiotics and after a few days, Akon was back to normal and he quickly forgot about the whole episode.

Looking back now, Akon wondered if that ordeal had caused the issue of his low sperm count. He wished he could investigate his medical records, but in a country where records are not kept, that would prove impossible. "What can I do?" Akon asked out loud.

Meanwhile, Lara, who had been crying her eyes out in a corner, looked at Akon with disbelief. "You knew you had this problem and went ahead to marry me without discussing this first. And you ignored your family's attitude over our childlessness, forgetting it takes two to tango!" Lara tried to steady her voice.

"I didn't know, babe," Akon said as he tried to defend himself.

"Even then," Lara protested.

"Okay, how did Jabez come? Common babe, be reasonable!" Akon was now starting to get upset. "Are you saying I am impotent or what?" He questioned. "Well, maybe Jabez is not my son. Because if he is, what's the fuss?" Akon threw both arms in the air.

"Okay," Akon continued, "let us do a DNA. I double dare you if you doubt where I conceived that boy. He is my carbon copy with my birthmarks. Let us do a DNA, then we would know who is telling the truth." Akon screamed as he continued to pace around.

"Did I put any pressure on you? I am the man here, the head of the family. If I am not making a fuss, why should we care about what any other person thinks?" Akon lowered his voice a bit and looked straight at Lara. "You think I do not know what I am doing when I said we should leave Nigeria? We are here to build our lives and not carry along cultures that would put us under pressure. An average British person lives simply with their pets, no qualms. Do you not just love the simplicity of their culture? I love the culture mehn," Akon shouted.

"So, what are you saying?" Lara retorted. "Should we give up looking for children and substitute all the animals in the safari for kids?" Lara screamed back at him and stormed out of the room before Akon could give a reply, tears streaming down her cheeks.

21

Akon searched online for a private clinic and booked an appointment with a consultant urologist that week. When he and Lara visited the urologist, it was confirmed that Akon indeed was the problem. They asked the doctor if he would ever be able to father another child.

"It is possible," the doctor said, "but it may be arduous work, and you will need to be patient. It may take a year, two years or even three."

Akon said they should visit another urologist who had more positive reviews, and Lara agreed. Akon booked an appointment. They were to do some tests before the meeting.

Akon held Lara's hand as they stood in the reception,

waiting for their turn to see the consultant. It was a busy day at the clinic as the doctors ran back and forth. There was tension in the reception; couples were waiting for their results. Seeing people comforting or congratulating each other made Lara even more nervous.

"I don't want us to be like those couples who came out of the doctor's office with hopeless faces and teary eyes," Lara whispered to her husband.

"We won't," Akon said. He smiled at his wife and placed his hand on Lara's palm.

The warmth of her husband's hand reduced Lara's stress. She sighed and decided not to over think.

"Mr & Mrs Akete!" a nurse called, stepping out of the doctor's office.

"Finally!" Lara tightened her fingers around Akon's hand as her heart began to beat faster.

They walked to the doctor's office and peered through the door.

"Please, come in," the doctor said. He smiled at them and searched for something in a bundle of papers on his desk.

Akon stepped inside the room before Lara. He wanted to know the results before his wife because he knew Lara would feel miserable if it was terrible news. He knew she needed emotional support. However, it was impossible to read any answers in the doctor's calm and welcoming eyes. As soon as they sat in front of the doctor's desk, Lara said nervously, "Doctor Sai, please tell us that everything is okay."

Dr Sai smiled again, but this time, Akon noticed his expression was a pity smile. He looked down, not wanting his wife to see the nervousness. Lara did not let go of Akon's hand.

"Firstly, you should be grateful that you have a healthy twelve-year-old son," Dr Sai began. "People who have been trying to conceive for twenty years come here."

Akon was breathing heavily as he knew where the conversation was heading.

"Moreover, you spent five years moving back and forth between Nigeria and the UK. You were apart for a long time, and immigration issues can be extremely stressful. This might be another reason you did not become pregnant again," Dr Sai continued, looking straight into Lara's eyes.

Lara's heart pounded so forcefully that she thought it would burst. The doctor's eyes were full of kindness and support.

"But we have found a concrete reason for why you are not conceiving," Dr Sai said as he slid some documents towards the couple.

Akon took the papers and read the results of the various tests they had taken.

"I am sorry, Mr Akete. Our tests revealed you have a low sperm count, which makes your chances of conceiving slim."

Akon froze. All these years, Akon had thought Lara was the one who could not get pregnant. This was unexpected. Akon's family had always talked about how Lara was unable to conceive, so this idea had consumed Akon's mind as well. Finding out that he was the one with the problem was shocking. Akon slowly turned his head to look at Lara. She was still with her head hanging down.

"I am sorry, but if you want to have another child, you should start considering other options such as adoption, using a sperm donor or IVF," Dr Sai said, trying his best to ease the tension in the room, but Akon was not listening.

"So, doctor, you are telling us there is no way we can traditionally have another baby?" Lara broke the silence with a trembling voice.

"No, I am not saying that. There is a slight chance that you could conceive naturally, but with Akon's low sperm count, it would be a miracle."

With that, Lara and Akon walked out of the office. They did not hold hands anymore. They did not say a word. They left the hospital, got into the car, and drove home in silence. When they arrived home, Akon spent half an hour pacing around the living room while Lara headed to the bedroom, mumbling to herself.

My enemies have pursued me to the UK, Akon thought. "Where are you going?" he called out to his wife.

"I need to rest," she answered without looking back.

Akon fell into a soft armchair and put his head between his palms. He did not know if he should cry or scream. He did not know if he was angry with the universe or himself. The culture he was familiar with never suggested that men could be the source of infertility. Only now did Akon realise how stupid and false this point of view was. However, he was also worried that Lara would tell others and it would become a gossip subject. He trusted his wife but was still concerned.

Suddenly, Akon heard a sound. He looked towards the bedroom and saw Lara leaning against the wall, crying, her body trembling. Akon knew how hurt she was and wanted to say something to his wife, but words vanished from his mind. He looked up and whispered, "God, please, help me find a solution to this problem." Almost as soon as he had said it, he had an idea.

My friend, Kay.

The idea consumed him. He felt joy blended with pain and preliminary regret.

*   *   *

Akon drove Lara to the shops to pick up groceries. On their way home, Lara said, "Dear, the doctor said it could be over ten years before we can have another child. We both know that we cannot wait that long."

"You are right. Time is not on our side," Akon agreed.

"I am overwhelmed with boredom," Lara added.

"Why don't you concentrate on reading for your law exams?" Akon suggested.

"That gives me a headache."

"We should try to get you a night job, or any job," Akon added. "We could do with the extra money."

*   *   *

Akon had trouble falling asleep at night, but this was unknown to his wife who felt lonely and neglected.

One day, he snapped at Lara and told her to do some charity work instead of pestering him unnecessarily. Lara had been hurt by his harsh words. She did not understand why he spoke to her that way. He hardly slept in the bedroom anymore. He would sleep in the living room and join his wife in bed later.

Lara was anxious and afraid that Akon might be cheating. As she lay in bed alone every night, a million thoughts ran through her mind. She concluded he was either seeing someone else or was into something shady that he did not want to expose.

Thinking of how to ease her boredom and loneliness, Lara remembered her old friend, Iyabo, who lived in Manchester with her family. She called her, and they made plans to see each other the following weekend.

"Do you remember our friend, Iyabo?" she asked Akon when she went to tell him of her plans.

"Yes, I do. How is she?" Charles, Iyabo's husband, was also their friend. The couple had married a few months before Akon and Lara, and they had since moved to England.

"The last time I saw them was when they attended our wedding," Akon said. "Oh, how time flies!"

"Yes, that's true," Lara replied. "Well, Iyabo is coming over next weekend, and I would like it if she could stay over for the night."

Akon, sensing trouble, inhaled deeply and said, "Lara, I don't think that would be possible. You know the house is crowded. You always complain that I do not spend enough time with you. So, we need to have our weekends to ourselves. Darling, why didn't you say anything to me before now? I assume Iyabo is coming by train, so it would be better for her to spend the night in London. I just had an idea; why don't you book her a room at a hotel?"

Akon paused to adjust his tie. He sighed and said, "Look, Lara, can we talk about it later? I must dash off to work. I am running late."

Lara sighed and looked through the curtains. She had expected a different response from Akon. Exasperated, a tear rolled down her cheek. Her husband was dumping all the responsibilities on her. She had to pick Jabez from school in a few hours, take care of the house, and use what little savings she had to pay for a hotel room for her friend, Iyabo.

Her husband's reaction was quite suspicious. *Was he hiding something?* She shrugged it off *Akon might act strange at times, but he has nothing to hide.* She wanted Iyabo to come over though. So, she called her to know her plans. After the second ring, Iyabo picked and said, "Lara, how are you, girlfriend?"

"I am cool," Lara replied. She felt nostalgic as she heard her friend's voice over the phone. It had been a long time since she heard someone speak her native language to her. She did not know how much she had missed it until now. Not wanting to waste time with pleasantries, Lara went straight to the point. "We did not finalise the day or time you'd be arriving."

"I am coming on Saturday. I will be on the first train and should arrive at the Euston station by 11 am. I purchased an open ticket and depending on how the day goes, I will spend the night in London. My sister lives in the Elephant and Castle area. I can stay the night at her place, which helps anyway. She had a baby two months ago. We can meet up at a restaurant or hotel, and we can spend a few hours talking."

Lara felt a huge weight lifted off her chest. "That sounds good; I can't wait to see you."

Iyabo met up with Lara the following Saturday at the Busway Café for coffee and muffins. "I booked a place for two in a Chinese restaurant on Old Kent road for 2.00 pm," Lara told her friend.

"That's so sweet." Iyabo was excited to hear this. They hugged each other. The two friends had not seen each other for many years.

At the restaurant, they were ushered to their table. She had paid for four hours so they would have enough time to catch up. Before the main meal, they had some hot mint tea and prawn crackers. They later looked through the menu and made a choice, including drinks and dessert.

After discussing general things, Iyabo shot Lara a question, "How is your husband?"

"He is fine. I am shocked he agreed to stay at home

with our son. I am glad he did, sha. At least we can have enough time to gist."

"Good!" Iyabo replied dryly.

"Let us leave men and their wahala jare. It is good to see you, my friend. You have not changed much, but I can see you are eating well. See how chubby your cheeks have become!" They both laughed at this.

Noticing their conversation was dying down, Lara continued, "So, I've been here for more than a month now. I think it should be around five weeks, and girl, I am bored already. How is Oga Charles? I hope he is fine."

"Yes o," Iyabo replied with a note of sadness. "We have three children, all girls. One is sixteen years old; the second is fifteen while the last is twelve." After mentioning the ages of her daughters, her mood lightened a little, and she said, giggling, "Three gals on my makeup, clothes, and shoes. I know girls are usually daddy's girls, but in my case, Charles wants a boy, and I am not ready to get pregnant or have any other child at forty-two. I have chromosome abnormalities, and my last girl was born through a Caesarean section at seven months."

Lara nodded as Iyabo continued, "Besides, I am the one that has a stable job; he has been in and out of jobs. I work full time as a pharmacist. Looking after children in this country and jostling work takes its toll. Sometimes, I work for twelve hours, including drive time. My husband struggles to get it. Charles studied Architecture in Nigeria, but he could not work in that field here. It seems there is a subtle ceiling that makes it difficult for those that are foreign born to get into high-paid positions. Charles went to do an MBA, can you imagine? Yet, he could not get a job with that. Potential employers turned him down because of a lack of experience. He went to do IT, got a contract job for three years, and the market crashed. So, he is back to square one.

"When we had children, it was easy for me to return to work after maternity leave. Charles opted to stay at home during the day and work at night. He was a chauffeur for one of the premier hotels for almost five years. This affected him because he could not transfer his education into work. Charles sank into depression and resorted to alcohol as a coping mechanism. The humour was lost from his voice, and he isolated himself from his family and friends. I try not to say anything that would upset him; if not, his next statement would be, 'Is it because you earn more than I do?' My sister, this country is not like Africa. It has a way of dulling your sparkle, especially when your expectations are not met. In addition to these struggles, we fell into debt. I was tired of working seven days a week. Can you believe, Charles and I have considered divorcing two times? The first time because he made bad decisions with money, and we almost lost our house. The second was when he committed adultery. We only stayed together because of two things—the mortgage, which is in our joint names, and the children, because they are still under sixteen."

Lara stared in shock. "What? You guys have been dating since secondary school. This is terrible to hear."

"Yes, we have," answered Iyabo. "I heard rumours that my husband was cheating on me with a girl in Nigeria. He lied to me, saying his mum was sick, but it did not occur to me to ask his mum if she was sick. I just greeted her as normal because I knew she suffers from arthritis. Unknown to me, he went for an introduction with the family of this lady. You know how social media easily spreads gossip. Well, it was a friend of his friend that posted the introduction pictures on Facebook. He came back two weeks after complaining of malaria. In my mind, I could not be bothered. I slaved for Charles, girlfriend. I have obtained over £50,000 in loans for him twice. So, you can imagine how upset I was. I became the breadwinner in the house, and I covered his back. When I confronted him, he first denied it. Then I showed him the evidence I had gathered, the pictures of them wearing the same outfit."

At this, Iyabo sounded broken. "Instead of apologising, he tried to justify it, saying he was an African man, and it was his right to marry more than one wife. He made it look like I was making a fuss about nothing. When he said this, I felt like I was talking to a stranger or, better still, a monster. I did not recognise him anymore, and I wished the earth would open up and swallow me at that very moment."

Hearing this made Lara speechless. Not knowing what to say, she said, "I am listening."

Iyabo continued, her voice regaining some strength. "I told him I would report him to the authorities for bigamy; then it dawned on him that he was in trouble. He pleaded and asked his relatives to speak to me. I did not report him but guess what; the girl was already pregnant for him. She had a boy who is now three years old. Of course, Charles said he had an affair with the girl who was an old workmate when they were in Nigeria, but because she was pregnant, he had to pretend he would marry her. To cut the long story short, I stopped being the breadwinner o. I moved some of the bills to his bank account to let him pay. I also started paying for childcare so he cannot use it as an excuse anymore. Thank God, our last born is now 11 years old. Soon, I will be free from these excesses."

"So, tell me, what became of the £50,000 you loaned him? Did he return it?" Lara asked.

Iyabo laughed. "He did not return anything. He told me he had started some businesses in Nigeria—a water packaging business and an internet café. He also told me he had purchased a piece of land in Nigeria, but I did not see or receive any gains."

"Oga Charles has shocked me o," Lara said. "If this was coming from someone other than you, I would have said it was a big fat lie, but coming from you, I just have to accept it as the truth."

"Abeg, which kind Oga be dat one?" Iyabo laughed. "He has lost that respect."

"So, what's happening to him now?" asked Lara. "Is he working?"

"Yes, he is. In fact, he is working round the clock. It is not for his children here; he has a responsibility to his son in Nigeria. He thought he could cherry-pick jobs in the UK, but Naija people don't understand that nonsense!"

Deciding to switch the topic, Iyabo asked, "How is Uncle Akon?"

It was Lara's turn to feel down. "He is trying, but I am surprised the time is not there. He works round the clock, and by the time he comes home, he is tired. Also, he is becoming a full Britico."

On noticing Lara's sad tone, Iyabo replied, "Really, you had better be happy you have a husband that is becoming a Britico rather than a Nigerian o. As a Nigerian, they can rubbish you, but as a Britico, they know the rules, and they will be more careful. How is Ranti?"

"She is fine. She is working now," Lara replied.

"Are you planning to send for her now that you are in the UK?" Iyabo asked.

"I haven't thought about it, but hush, please. My husband does not know about Ranti. It's a secret," Lara said, lowering her voice.

"What?" replied Iyabo. "That's bad. If a man will marry you, he would."

Lara tried to defend herself. "Well, I was told to keep it a secret. But it is haunting me now. We are struggling to have a second child and I am already a mother of two. I know I should not be this unfair to Akon, but what can I do? And besides, Ranti is no longer a child. If I disclose who I am to her, she may not accept me."

"How long can you hide a child for?" Iyabo replied. Lara looked away, avoiding her friend's probing question. "Remember," Iyabo added, "we have known each other for a long time. We grew up in the same compound. If there is anyone that would tell you the truth, it is me. I had my reasons for asking us to meet at a restaurant instead of your home. I wanted us to catch up on some of our girly stuff!" They both giggled.

Iyabo called for the waiter and asked for more ice cubes. "So, any job interviews or offers yet?" Iyabo asked.

"Yes, I have had two job interviews, but no offers at all," Lara replied. "I am bored at home."

"Enjoy the freedom while it lasts. You will need it in the future."

"Thanks, my dear friend," Lara responded, seeing some truth in Iyabo's counsel.

"You will be fine," assured Iyabo. She tipped the waiters as they stood up to leave.

Just before they left, Iyabo turned and said, "It'll take me six minutes to get to the station from here. So, I do not need to take a bus. Your train goes in the opposite direction, underground; mine is going north. My sister will be expecting me. Lovely girl, she has even cooked for me—pounded yam and efo."

On hearing this, Lara salivated. "Wow! That dish makes me really miss home. I wish I could follow you to your sister's place."

"Come now, no big deal," Iyabo said.

Lara politely declined the offer. "My husband will be upset. He had to change plans so I could come and see you. One more thing, please do not ever discuss Ranti with Akon. I will talk to him when it's time."

Iyabo nodded. "I completely understand, my dear." They hugged each other and went their separate ways. This time, the hug felt like they were signing a pact and taking an oath of secrecy.

*   *   *

Lara returned home, determined to show appreciation to Akon and let him be, rather than complain.

Akon had spent the evening thinking. The urologist had given them options. Adoption was out of the question. IVF was costly, and Lara, being over forty, would not get it for free. He dismissed the idea of visiting a sperm bank. Another idea was growing in his mind, but it was absurd. He needed to mull over it and get used to it. He thought of involving Lara, but decided against it. Due to her personality, behaviour, and strong Christian roots, she would never agree to it.

Akon had hatched a plan, but he required his closest friend for the scheme to work. He decided to invite Kay for a drink so they could discuss his plan. It was almost a week before he gained the courage to talk to Kay.

22

During the following week, Akon met with Joro, his Kenyan friend. Joro had called him at work, and Akon was eager to see how he was doing. They met at Roasty and sat at an outdoor table as they liked to do on a warm London night.

"How are you doing, my friend? Has London been good to you?" Akon asked with a laugh.

Joko also laughed. "It has been a rough ride, but I am getting by, my friend. I was able to bring my wife to join me in London. She is a nurse. I finally got a teaching job at a private college. I would say I am doing well. It took me a while to learn the ropes—the most appropriate residential area for me, my way around the city, how the system works, and things like that. I once had problems with documentation when my papers expired and was almost deported. I spent three nights in a junkyard."

"Why a junkyard?"

"I was afraid to go to a hotel, and during that time, I lost my phone. Someone must have reported me to the authorities when I could not produce my papers. I was afraid they would notice they had expired. So, I ran away. But I left a letter with my address and everything. I lost my phone while running away and could not call anyone. There was a junkyard near where I lived. The next day, a neighbour told me two men from immigration knocked on my door and they would return the next morning. I spent the night in the junkyard and did not go back home until my papers were processed three days later. I nearly got shot by some thugs."

"Really?"

"Yes. I will never forget it. By the way, I invited another old friend of ours."

"Who?" Akon asked eagerly.

"Wa gwaan! What's up?" a familiar voice hailed them. It was good old Greg, smiling as always. He shook their hands warmly and sat down. "Good to see you again, man. And you too, Akon, my brother. Big up yourself, respect. Mi good, mi good. Hard living, but Greg prevailed. I always prevail. Caribbean man always prevails."

They learnt that Greg was now a delivery driver. He seemed proud of himself, and they were glad that he was happy.

"We are all doing okay, man. Just tribulations here and there. Bless up. Bless up."

"I still want to hear your story, Joro," Akon urged. "Do you see how delicate it can be for an immigrant without proper papers? All you wanted to do was renew your papers, but you almost got deported before you did."

"That's right. What's more? I missed an amazing job opportunity when they realised that the papers had expired," Joro sighed. "I also learnt how dangerous it is to spend the night outdoors in London. Not to mention the cold."

Joro shared a scary experience he had one of the nights he spent at the junkyard. He was asleep inside a car when he was woken by voices. A dim light from a nearby building helped him see two men standing close to where he was. He dared not breathe.

"What you're telling me," said the man in a green t-shirt, "is that Jaymo sent you this message from jail?"

"That's right, mate," said the second man, who was dressed in blue jacket and brown trousers. Joro, listening as keenly as his curious nature allowed, could hear every word. "It makes perfect sense, doesn't it, mate? He already had his share of the money, but he was arrested before he could give us our share. You know he's a loyal bloke."

"It makes no sense to me," the man in green growled. "If I were in jail and would stay there for eight years, I would send messages to my gang who are breathing the fresh air while I'm locked up inside. Eight years means Jaymo will be in jail for three more years. It's fishy business."

"That's why I think you are a pig, Tero," said the jacket guy in disgust. "Just because you have no loyalty and no love for your gang doesn't mean Jaymo is like that too. By the way, that is why I chose Jaymo to hide the money. I knew I could trust him. Unfortunately, the Asian guy at Unlimited Jewelry swears he can recognise him, and in fact, he did. Just as I thought, old Jaymo did not tell on his gang. He kept his mouth shut."

"Okay, Jaymo is great, and I'm a pig," Tero snapped. "This message sounds like a foxy bloke trying to make his partners believe he has good intentions when he's actually hiding something from them. Why would he make the message so complicated?"

While Joro found the conversation interesting, he was wary that these two men, who sounded like robbers and discussing hidden loot, might discover him. If they saw him, they would think he had overheard things he should not have, and they may decide to end his life.

"We'll have to think hard," Blue Jacket said. "Common sense tells me the message had to be complicated so that others may not comprehend what it means—including Jeff, the messenger."

Blue Jacket drew a small piece of paper out of his pocket. "I wrote it down," he said, "but I do hope this is exactly what Jaymo said and not what Jeff imagined or hoped he said or meant to say." Joro smiled at this because that thought had occurred to him too. Messages passed from a person to another often get twisted.

"In the backpack of the red patient at the car's hospital near the wine house," read Tero loudly as Blue Jacket held the paper. He continued reading and Joro memorised the short message, word for word.

"This is rubbish!" Tero growled. "Backpack, what backpack?"

"Maybe the one with the money," Blue Jacket replied. "I know I'm brainy, but you are acting so stupid, my dear man."

Tero ignored this remark as he glared at the paper. Joro was not afraid of being spotted now and was glad he was not wearing a bright coloured shirt.

"Red patient at the car's hospital," Tero said in disgust. "Maybe Jaymo is crazy; maybe somebody knocked his head too hard."

"Why don't we have a drink and discuss it," Blue Jacket suggested. "I admit it sounds like a foolish man's message."

Joro was glad to see the two men walk away. He was getting cramps in his legs for being in the same spot for so long; besides, he had heard all he wanted to hear. Two minutes after the men left, he dragged himself cautiously out of the car and darted through the filling station to the road. He slowed to walking pace, trying to think as he headed home. This was the third night he had slept in that car, but he had no intention of sleeping there anymore, especially with a jailbird's accomplices popping up in the middle of the night. "Red patient, car's hospital, wine house, backpack," he mused. "Very puzzling. Maybe Jaymo is playing games with his accomplices."

Did backpack really mean a bag full of money as Blue-jacket thought? Perhaps it did. Joro stopped suddenly when a car blew its horn, and the driver yelled at him. "Look out!" Joro jumped in terror, narrowly missing the car. He could not wait for the situation with his papers to get sorted. He hoped they would be ready the next day. Of course, he did not dare report the matter to the police because they would ask him to identify himself.

"Blackheart men," Greg shook his head as he listened to the story. "I had some tribulations too, my brother. Greg on the run. Greg avoiding the Babylon man. Greg cannot bunks me res."

"What is *bunks me res*?" Joro asked impatiently. Sometimes he got lost in Greg's patois lingo.

"Bredren! Greg can't find no sleep, man. Immigration problem," he said in his undying accent. "But I'm fine now. I live like a meticulous man. No wild living for me. What sweet nanny goat a go run him belly."

"What does that mean?" Akon smiled. He enjoyed Greg's way of talking.

"Jamaican patois proverb, man. Whatever tastes good to a goat might also ruin his belly. If you only want to have fun and run amok in London, you may end up in tears and regret."

"Oh," Joro said, nodding in agreement. "You did not come to London just to run around with women, spend your time and money partying. If you did, you would end up in tears and regret, and perhaps with nothing to show for it.

"Yes," Akon said. "Well-spoken, friend. We must work harder than everyone else. We must work harder than the native people. It's a sink or swim situation."

They promised to keep in touch as they parted. "We need to look out for each other. Black people should stick together," Joro had said. "One might have a problem the other has experienced before. Or you might have information that would benefit someone else."

When Akon got home that night, he informed Lara he met up with some old friends. "Our stories are almost similar. We had to learn how to survive in London the hard way," he told her. "You are lucky you are not experiencing much of that."

*   *   *

Kay had not yet moved out of Akon's house yet. He had asked to stay for at least two more months. Akon invited him to Roasty Restaurant the following Thursday. He had mulled over his plan for a week. How could he tell his friend about this sensitive issue? He felt Kay would have no problem with his proposition, but Akon felt he might find it easier to broach the subject over a bottle of wine or two.

"I have two matters to discuss with you, my friend. Both are serious."

"I see," Kay said. "Well, I am curious."

"One is a matter we have discussed before," Akon continued. "You know we have talked about starting a business together. I have been doing some research. You would be shocked to learn that seventy percent of new businesses in the UK fail. Reliable studies have shown that an estimated thirty percent of new businesses fail within two years. Half of all new businesses do not make it beyond the fifth year. To make matters worse, an estimated two-thirds do not make it beyond ten years. Sobering but true."

Kay raised his eyebrows. "I didn't know it was that bad."

"When people understand why most start-ups fail, they will avoid the pitfalls," Akon said. He was still trying to gather the courage to discuss his main agenda.

"Do you want to know why they fail? Many entrepreneurs do not take the time to plan. A plan outlines the necessary steps to success. Also, many business owners do not prepare enough for a new business. Lack of adequate funding is another reason start-ups fail. Even established businesses fail a few months or years down the line for this reason. As one person said, 'You have to feed the business until it begins to feed you.' Are you with me?"

"Yes, yes. Capital. Poor planning." Kay was doing his best to concentrate but his mind kept trying to figure out what the second issue Akon wanted to discuss.

"Another reason for business failure is the issue of location. Just because your business is in a densely populated area does not mean you will succeed. You should ask the following questions: Are there similar businesses in the neighbourhood? Are the people living in the neighbourhood the type of customers you want to target? Starting an expensive restaurant in a middle or low-income neighbourhood, for instance, may not be a good idea. Some businesses do better in residential areas while others do better in busy business districts."

"I have a suggestion, my brother," Kay interjected. "Why don't we discuss this business issue over the weekend when we are sober and can take down some notes? I am curious about the second matter you want to discuss. It seems like a serious matter by your expression and caution."

Akon ordered the third round. They were both getting a bit tipsy, and the matter did not seem so elephantine.

"Now, my friend," Akon spoke, lowering his voice even though the tables were well-spaced. "If two friends go hunting and one exhausts his arrows before his friend, what should they do?"

Kay frowned. "That's deep. I didn't know you were a man of proverbs, Akon."

"What should they do, my friend?"

"Of course, the friend with arrows can help the other friend out."

"Good, good. What if two friends are driving in their separate cars and a friend's car breaks down?"

"The other friend could help by towing his friend's

car," Kay said. "I still do not understand. Do you need some help? You know you can always count on me, Akon."

"I have a third one for you," Akon said. "What if..."

"Abeg, no more proverbs. Have you become Solomon? Just get to the point, my brother."

Akon sighed. "I would never discuss this with any other man," he said. "I have run out of arrows. My car is broken, my friend."

"Man mi, we have been sitting here for several minutes now. Won't you tell me why you asked us to meet today? You want to ask me to leave your house, right? I knew it," Kay said, and he stood up from the table. "Be a man; talk to me."

"Relax, mate. I know you are man enough to leave when you have found a place, but that is not it. Not every problem involves money, my friend," Akon replied. He did not know how Kay would react to his request.

"Then what is the problem? If you do not tell me, how will I know what I can do to help?" Kay asked, curious about what could be bothering Akon so much.

"I would like you to *shag* my wife. Yes, my wife. Impregnate her." Akon finally dropped the bomb.

Perhaps it was the serious expression on Akon's face or the impact of his words, but Kay burst out laughing.

"It's obvious you are drunk. We should go home."

"I am serious," Akon said, "and I am not drunk."

Kay stared at him, still laughing.

Akon remained serious. "I mean it," he said.

Kay stopped laughing and stared at him incredulously. "You can't be serious," he said, lowering his voice and looking around to see if anyone in the bar was listening to them.

Akon nodded slowly. "I am serious, my friend."

Kay was lost in thought for a minute. Then he narrowed his eyes and said, "It just occurred to me that you might be testing me, Akon. You want to know what kind of a friend I am."

Akon shook his head. "For goodness' sake, Kay! I am serious. And to prove that I am serious, I will pay you three thousand pounds. Not because I am rich, in fact, I intend to take out a loan to pay you. The matter is that important to me."

Kay realised Akon was serious. Akon further confided in his friend. "My wife and I have been trying to conceive for the past few years. About three doctors have confirmed that my wife is fertile, but I have a low sperm count, and it could take me years to father another child. It is a hit and miss game, mehn! And you know my family, my mother especially, has been putting pressure on us. While I was away, my mum and sisters developed an attitude and would often spite my wife. This distressed her because she knew she was not the problem, yet she couldn't speak out."

Kay took a deep breath. "Does your wife know you are the problem?" he asked.

Akon became agitated. "What do you mean? You want to use the information I gave you against me, abi?" he asked.

"Grow up, man!" Kay said. "I only asked a simple question. I cannot just accept to do what you require of me if I don't have the details. So, talk to me, brother."

Akon sighed. "It took almost three years before we had our first son. And since then, we have tried and tried again, but my wife has not conceived. We never intended to have a huge gap between children; we wanted one every other year. We visited a urologist and did some tests. The results revealed I have a low sperm count."

"Well, that was in Nigeria, I guess. But have you visited one in the UK to confirm?" Kay asked.

"Yes," Akon said, "It's the same report. The readings bordered on what is medically termed *azoospermia*."

"Say what?" Kay asked.

"It means I have low sperm count," Akon replied, feeling embarrassed.

"So, why didn't you do something about it?" Kay asked.

"Like what?" Akon said.

"Ha! Are you not a Yoruba man again? Take it to the native doctors," Kay said.

"Come off it!" Akon said sternly. "How could you suggest such a barbaric method of solving a problem?"

"Whoa calm down. I was only trying to give a suggestion. Anyway, my apologies."

"Apology accepted."

"So, what is the deal?" Kay asked.

"I want you to impregnate my wife," Akon said.

"How in the world do you expect me to do that?"

"Help a brother," Akon pleaded. "I am at my wits end and cannot think of any other way out of this problem."

"Hmmm." Kay was deep in thoughts. "I need to remind you about something."

"What?" Akon asked.

"Your wife is a spiri-koko, an ardent believer. Do you want her to turn me into a demon and start the binding and losing game on me? Besides, your wife is a lawyer. What if she sues me in court? Then it would be all over the place. The tabloids and bloggers would make money off my shame, and then my estranged family back home would have a mouth to talk and disgrace me. Mba, tufiakwa!" Kay snapped his fingers to emphasise his point.

"You think I'm stupid? Nawa ooo. You need to trust me. Of course, I have it all planned out. Don't worry," Akon assured him.

Kay leaned forward and whispered, "So, what's this failproof plan of yours?"

"I have identified a drug you can use to knock her out. It is called Rohypnol, a form of tranquillizer. I obtained it through an old contact in China because it is not available on prescription. It makes users fall asleep, and it dulls their memories. It is ten times stronger than Valium. She will not remember a thing before and after the act. So, you are safe," Akon explained.

"Have you forgotten she's a lawyer? If this goes wrong, I will be facing rape charges," Kay said worriedly.

"It would only go wrong if she woke up in the middle of the act. But I can assure you she would not. This drug is that strong," Akon exaggerated. "She would also lose her memories, and even if she remembers anything, she will think it was me. My wife will not sue, not in this country anyway. She is more interested in preserving her marriage. She wouldn't want to destroy it."

Kay nodded slowly. "If you say so, but I am scared o. Should we do a memorandum of agreement?"

Akon was furious. "Put yourself in my shoes. This is

hard enough for me also. How many men can stand to watch their wives having an affair with another man, or worse, being raped and would not fight the intruder? Listen, we do not need an MOA. Trust is enough. Or would you use this against me in the future if it goes the other way?"

"Can you hear yourself? I thought you said your plan was failproof!" Kay snapped. He was getting irritated.

"In life, we have to be ready to take risks. Think about how I feel about doing this," Akon said.

Kay took a deep sigh. "So, how much are we talking about here?"

"Three thousand pounds. I will pay you half in advance. After the deed, I will send you the other half, just a simple bank transfer."

"What? That is too small for the trouble abeg. Do you know that sperm donors make as much as ten thousand pounds in the US?" Kay said, wanting better compensation.

"Well, this is not a formal arrangement. It is just a bond between two friends. Here is what else I can do; I will pay the deposit for a one-bedroom flat for you anywhere between Zone 2 and 3. I want you to search for a flat around that area."

Kay remained deep in thought.

"Excuse me for a minute. I need to use the restroom," Akon said, getting up.

Many thoughts ran through Kay's mind as he waited for Akon. *"The one with a head has no cap, and the one who has a cap has no head." Lara is a virtuous woman, every man's dream, but look at what her husband is doing to her. She is a respectable and decent woman. If only...* Kay was so immersed in his thoughts and was not aware Akon had returned from the toilet.

Akon tapped him on the shoulder. "What do you say? Are you in?" he asked.

"Yes," Kay replied.

"Thanks, man. Give me your account details."

"Sure," Kay said, taking out a note pad and a pen. "And your wife won't know you are moving money from your account?"

"Of course not. I have another account she is not aware of. I will leave no traces. Remember, she is yet to understand how the monetary system works in this country."

"We have a deal. But make sure you stay away during that time. I don't want to carry out such a plan with you hanging around the house," Kay said.

"Sure, I will work out something, my guy," Akon replied.

They laughed and ordered a box of takeaway pizza.

23

Lara and Akon were in bed after a long day. They had a habit of chatting before going to sleep. While they talked about how the day had gone, Akon thought about his plan with Kay and felt guilty all over again.

"Babe, I'll be travelling to Leeds for that work conference this weekend. Do you remember?" Akon said.

"Oh, yes. Everything is packed already. But you should be back the same day, right?" Lara asked, unaware of what was going on in Akon's mind.

"Sure, but I will have to go to the coach station late on Friday night. By the way, Kay will be back on Friday evening and will be with us over the weekend. He will stay in the guest room. The roof of his house is leaking, and the landlord cannot arrange for repairs until next

Saturday. I thought instead of paying for a hotel, he could spend the weekend with us." Akon gritted his teeth silently as he thought of how Kay would get intimate with his wife. For the hundredth time, he wished things were different and he did not have to ask his friend to impregnate his wife. He felt like his life was messed up.

Lara paused then said, "Why not? He is not a stranger. He only moved out two weeks ago, and Jabez seems to get on well with him. He loves children; I can see. Sure, he will keep us company."

"Thank you for understanding, sweetheart. Alright, goodnight babe," Akon said, turning off the bedside lamp before pulling Lara close. About thirty minutes later, Lara was asleep. Akon, however, could not sleep; different thoughts were running through his mind.

The first part of the plan was in motion. He would, supposedly, be at a conference in Leeds, while Kay did his part of the plan. If all went well, Lara would conceive, and only Akon and Kay would know how the pregnancy came about. Akon felt horrible for lying to his wife. He would hang around at Kay's apartment, probably watching movies. He planned to use public transport.

*   *   *

Kay arrived at Akon's place at about 6.00 pm.

"Uncle Kay!" Jabez shouted. "What is your favourite video game? I have a new game but need a second player. It is boring playing alone. I want someone I can beat, not a robot," Jabez said to Kay.

Akon and Lara laughed. A three-course meal was laid out at the dining table later that night—starters, main meal, and desserts. At the table, Akon praised Lara's cooking.

"Darling, how did you make all of this all by yourself? The sweet potatoes and carrots are simply perfect," Akon said to his wife.

"Aww babe, thanks." Lara smiled.

"It is unbelievably delicious. Thanks, Madam," Kay said.

"Thank you, Kay," Lara replied.

Akon could not help feeling angry at Kay for complimenting his wife. *I am sure he cannot wait to sleep with her*. He knew he was being paranoid, but he could not help it.

"Mum, I want more nuggets," Jabez said.

"I think it's time for bed, Jabez. You've had enough," Lara replied.

Jabez laughed. "I usually sleep by ten on weekends, Mum. Please, just a few nuggets and extra time. We are having fun. I know you and Uncle Kay want to discuss stuff that happened before I was born."

Kay laughed. "You should consult me for history lessons, Jabez, not video games."

Jabez had his nuggets and went upstairs to bed.

Akon got three glasses and stood up. "I'll get more ice and straw."

"Let me do it, darling so you can leave for the coach station," Lara said.

"Nah, its fine, babe. Let me serve you," Akon kissed her forehead while Lara blushed, and Kay pretended to look away.

Akon was in the kitchen alone to administer the drug powder to Lara's drink. He shook it and put in a slice of lemon. He sighed and closed his eyes. *Lara, please forgive me. It is for the best.* The guilt weighed heavily on him. He walked back to the dining area with the tray of glasses and served each of them.

"A slice of lemon, Lara, just the way you like it," he said with a forced smile.

"Aww, thank you, my love," Lara said as she sipped on her tropical fruit juice. She did not notice Akon's nervousness. Akon hurriedly cleared the dining table and put the plates into the dishwasher.

"Come over, dear." Akon ushered his wife to the living room. "You look tired."

"I think I ate too much. Have you fixed Kay's room so he can go to sleep?" she asked.

"Yes, I have."

"Don't worry. I will be okay on the sofa. I want to watch some sports tonight," Kay said.

Ten minutes later, Akon took Lara to their bedroom and came downstairs to speak with Kay. He then left the house as his taxi was waiting.

Kay was left at home with Lara who was fast asleep. He wondered how and at what time would be the best time to strike. He thought about Lara. She is disciplined. Her strong Christian beliefs does not condone what they planned to do. Even though Kay was not religious, he did not see any moral justification for violating someone else's wife.

But he needed the money. Besides, he did not want to let Akon down. And it was not like he was being asked to do something dangerous anyway. Akon had said the drug would knock Lara out for six hours, at least. It should come into effect within half an hour.

He waited for about thirty minutes and tiptoed into the bedroom. A million thoughts ran through his mind. What if she woke up suddenly and found him in the room? Kay considered feigning an asthma attack. He would tell her he had come to the room to seek help instead of calling 999. What if she was not asleep? How would he explain being in the bedroom she shared with Akon? He hesitated for another two to three minutes and then tried to shake her awake, but she did not move her eyelids.

He hurriedly undressed her and inserted himself into her. She was completely out.

After ejaculating, he stood up, cleaned her up and put her clothes back on. She was like a zombie throughout the ordeal.

Kay went to the guest bedroom but could not sleep. The horror of what he had just done kept him awake. He did not fall asleep until after midnight. Before he slept, he received a text from Akon that read, "How far, my guy?" Kay did not reply.

By 5.00 a.m., he had received over fifteen texts from Akon, which annoyed him. The next morning, Akon called him.

"Friend, how far?" Akon asked.

"I still dey sleep. I'll call you back later," Kay replied and ended the call.

Akon felt uneasy; he did not know what to think. He could not sleep, neither could he focus on the TV he was watching. He felt guilty and ashamed of himself. He wished he could just come home and hold his wife.

In the morning, Kay left the guest room and had his bath. He found Lara and Jabez having breakfast.

"Hello, Kay. Did you sleep well?" Lara asked. "I don't know what came over me. I felt very drowsy. The next thing I recall is waking up at 7 this morning because of the alarm clock. I still feel tired, but I have to get Jabez to his Saturday lessons," Lara said.

Kay could not look at her as she spoke. He felt guilty about the previous night, but he could see that she did not have the slightest idea of what transpired.

"How are you getting there?" he asked.

"We'll get a bus," Lara replied.

"Bus? Let me drive you. I'll go home afterwards and check what is happening with the repairs," Kay said.

On their way, Kay was still feeling guilty, and he offered to drive her to the mall if she had any shopping to do.

"Ah, thank you very much," Lara replied.

"It's the least I can do. You and your husband have been kind to me. I am indebted to you."

Kay dropped Lara at home after the shopping, and then called Akon. "Oh boy, I don leave your house o," he said.

Akon jumped up. "So, what happened? Did you?" he asked.

Kay understood and replied, "Of course! It is done."

"I see. I will pay when I'm sure the mission was successful," Akon said.

"Don't you dare play games with me. You agreed pay me after the act. Please, transfer the £1,500 to me latest by six in the evening or else..."

Akon knew he was in trouble. "Na you sabi. Calm down. Your money will be in your account."

When Kay ended the call, Akon closed his eyes and hoped it was all worth it. It was late in the evening, but the rays of the setting sun still managed to sneak into the living room through the window. Another warm day had passed by.

Meanwhile, four weeks later, Lara felt heavy.

"This must be the blues," she whispered to herself.

Even though she was happy and grateful for everything, the fact that she had not yet gotten pregnant made her melancholic. She approached the window and opened it. Leaning on the windowsill with her eyes closed, she inhaled the coolness of the quiet evening breeze. In that welcome amber glow, Lara's brain became a perfect empty horizon, not seeing, yet content to sit. Lara felt the gentle energy of nature wash over her as the last rays of the magical sun mixed with the music of nearby crickets. This moment of bliss helped Lara's bad feelings disappear. As she opened her eyes and looked down, Lara saw her husband, Akon, hurrying into the building.

"Hey, honey!" Lara called him.

Akon looked up and smiled at his wife.

"Dinner is ready!" Lara said with her sparkling voice.

Akon was only a couple of stairs away from his house, but his heart could not stop beating crazily. Akon wanted to open the door of his beautiful, cosy nest as quickly as possible, eat his amazing wife's food, and hug his son. Akon rushed upon the stairs.

"Honey, I'm home!" Akon announced as soon as he stepped inside and hung his jacket.

"Hey, Dad!" Jabez ran towards Akon and hugged him.

Akon kissed his son on the forehead. They walked into the kitchen together. The heavenly smell of Nigerian food swirled around Akon's head.

"Wash your hands," Lara said and touched her son's nose.

The boy turned around, running to the bathroom.

"Let me get you a bowl of water and soap so you too can wash your hands." Lara smiled at Akon.

Akon scoffed and followed his son instead.

The three of them sat around the table. The dinner looked appetising. The hot and spicy egusi soup with pounded yam was the best food one could ever wish for that evening. After serving her husband and son, Lara took a seat as well.

"I have not eaten anything today," Lara said.

"Why?" asked her husband.

"I have no appetite, my dear," she replied as she took an orange from the fruit bowl.

Akon and the boy had started eating. Lara knew she should be hungry, but instead of wanting to eat this delicious dish, her stomach was grumbling again. The feeling of heaviness rose in her body once more. She closed her eyes for a second, wanting to forget about this strange sensation, but the more she tried to get over it, the stronger it got. Lara slid her chair back and stood up.

"Are you okay?" a confused Akon asked when he saw Lara barely standing on her feet.

"Yes, yes. I just need to lay down for a bit. Please, enjoy your dinner," Lara said and smiled, but her pale skin and trembling fingers said the opposite. She turned around and walked slowly upstairs. After each step, Lara felt her heart turning over, and her gag reflex appeared from time to time. She managed to walk to the bathroom and knelt.

"What is happening?" she whispered though she had an idea of what might be going on. A mother's heart cannot lie. Lara felt a little bean moving around in her body, making her feel nauseous.

"Am I pregnant?" Lara smiled, but this beautiful

thought got mixed up by the feeling of her temperature rising drastically.

A couple of minutes went by. Akon lost his appetite as well. He peeked at the clock every second, waiting for his wife to return to the table. But Lara did not show up. Akon closed his eyes and felt cold sweat sliding down his forehead.

"Finish your food," Akon said lovingly to his son and ran upstairs.

As he got closer to Lara's bathroom, the more nervous he felt. "Lara?" Akon froze when he saw Lara lying on the cold floor.

"I feel feverish," Lara said.

24

Akon grabbed his wife in his strong arms and took her to the bed. Even though Lara could not stop trembling, she still smiled. Akon did not understand why Lara had such a happy face, but he did not ask any questions. He laid Lara on the bed and wrapped her up in blankets.

"Here, have some Paracetamol." Akon brought a glass of water close to her parched lips.

Akon slid his finger over Lara's forehead and smiled at her. "What did you eat that messed up your tummy this much?" Akon asked.

"Honey," Lara mumbled.

Does she have the flu, gastric issues or could she be pregnant? Akon tried to get her to rest and gave her some warm water. After a while, she no longer felt feverish.

A week after, Lara became sick. "This is strange. I do not usually throw up. I think I should book an appointment with the GP," Lara said.

Luckily, Lara was able to secure an early appointment. The GP ran a blood test. They also tested her urine for infection. The GP said he could not find any infection in the urine and suggested it could be a viral infection. He told Lara to take things easy and rest at home, and the infection would disappear with time.

They left the doctor's office, but Lara still felt weak and nauseous, although she was no longer throwing up. Three days later, Lara still had the same symptoms.

"Babe, what if I'm pregnant? Can we get a test kit?" she said to Akon.

"Sure," Akon said. He stopped by at the pharmacy on his way from work and bought a pregnancy kit. He could not wait for Lara to do the test. He also ordered pizza as his wife was too weak to make dinner. *I hope she is pregnant.*

Lara felt Akon was acting unusually strange. They tested it twice just to be sure, and both came out positive. Lara was pregnant.

"Alleluia! Thank God it was not a disease or infection. I was scared at first," Lara said with excitement.

Akon held his wife close to him and kissed her until

she became queasy.

"Babe, you are going to squish me." Lara laughed as she struggled to pull out of his hug. She could tell that Akon was happy.

"You are having my baby. This calls for celebration," Akon said with a wide smile. Deep inside, Akon was uneasy, but he tried to hide it. He knew that Lara's pregnancy was the result of the scheme he arranged with Kay four weeks ago.

Two weeks after confirming the pregnancy, Akon informed Kay that his wife was pregnant.

Akon and Lara agreed they would not inform their relatives back in Nigeria until the baby was born.

Lara could not cope with work, so she resigned from her job and stayed at home. Jabez was now thirteen years old and was in Year Eight going to Nine.

*   *   *

It was a Thursday evening, and Lara was set to watch the news and cook dinner at the same time. She was all on her own. Akon had not returned home; he and some friends were meeting on the high street to help raise funds for the people at the *Help First* charity.

The shrill noise of the phone broke the evenings calm. Frowning, Lara picked up the phone, wishing it had not disturbed her peace. It was her Ugandan friend,

Urumba, whom she had met at Jabez's playground. Urumba had handed her a pamphlet about a charity fund they were raising for children who had been displaced by war. It had interested Lara. They took to each other as if they had been childhood friends.

"Hi, Lara. All alone?"

"Yes, Urumba. How are you?"

Lâra had changed her church, but due to the nightmares she had been having, she had to confide in her Ugandan friend. Urumba worked as a social worker and was committed to working for many charities. She was a professed Christian and was married to a man called Sanyu, a musician and an actor.

Lara and Urumba became close because Urumba introduced her to their current church, a multi-ethnic church whose focus was more on reaching out to the vulnerable and overseas missions. Lara felt more at ease there than she did at her former church. When she became pregnant, Akon started following her to church, mainly because it was a diverse church. Akon felt easy there but was not committed to any church group, not even the men's fellowship.

Lara was happy because she had found a gathering that was not obsessed with cars, clothes, or other material items, but more interested in helping the needy, accountability, and practical love. All of these were done through what was called *cell groups*.

Initially, Akon did not want Lara to hold cell groups in their house, but after much talking back and forth, he allowed it on the condition that he would not have to be present during these meetings. This embarrassed Lara, but she accepted it even though she had many unanswered questions. Indeed, many things had been bothering her.

Lately, she had been having terrible nightmares. One of her dreams felt so real. She did not know why though. At first, she attributed it to the stress she had been going through with the pregnancy and work. Stress can cause nightmares, right? But after a while, she did not know what to think. This recurring dream was disturbing. Her baby was in some sort of a glass box, surrounded by alien creatures with disc heads and six feet. They were prodding, measuring, and doing all kinds of things to her child, and she could only watch and scream, although no sound escaped her mouth.

Other dreams were equally strange. Her bump becoming a balloon and floating away. Kay coming to take her baby, appearing like a genie from a golden glowing lamp. "Blood of Jesus!" she had screamed. The last one seemed the strangest. Why was Kay even in her nightmares? Akon came into the room and saw her covered in sweat.

"Another nightmare?" he asked her. She nodded.

Akon understood. He had been having nightmares too, although he had never admitted them to Lara. Since that awful weekend, he had dreamt of shiny steel robots in luxurious cars chasing him. He had been hearing voices too. Just last week, while at work, the walls of his office seemed like they were covered in blood. He froze as small images of genies appeared on the walls, but they all disappeared suddenly. He could have sworn he was not asleep. It was a trance.

Lara could not sleep properly anymore, and it was taking its toll on her. She needed someone to talk to.

Lara and Urumba agreed to meet up for a chat. She was close by and wanted to be sure Lara was home.

"You didn't attend church on Sunday. Is everything okay? It's been a busy week, and I didn't have time to ask you about it," Urumba said.

"My sister, I have been feeling tired since Saturday evening, but not the usual kind of fatigue. You know I love our church. I prefer this church to a certain church I belonged to in Nigeria. I was a firm and committed believer back home in Nigeria. But, due to the pressure of always raising money and trying to outsmart one another in church, I became weary. I heard there was a group of women gossiping about me, saying I had only had one son. Since my husband did not follow me to church, they said I must be wearing a wedding ring for a ghost husband."

Lara did not reveal the gossip was from someone who knew her in secondary school and was aware that she took a break from school because she had gotten pregnant. The person was saying that Jabez was not her first child. Lara could not afford to let Akon know about it; that was why she never persuaded him to come along, but it was different now as they were in a new church.

"I didn't like the attitude of the sisters in this church. It was all about the latest bags, their children's schools, etc. They never talked about the kingdom of God or helping the poor, which I am passionate about. The pastor treated us coldly when he noticed Akon did not attend church. He never called or visited to find out what was going on in our lives. The pastor was not approachable. He only made himself available to people who gave the most and were regular church attendants. Finally, I gave up on that church. But I am happy with our church," Lara continued.

"I am glad about that," Urumba smiled.

Lara was reluctant telling Urumba about her nightmares and how they scared her. She recalled they started after she found out she was pregnant. In some of them, Kay seemed to be raping her right there in the bedroom she shared with Akon, while Akon watched. In others, she had a baby, and Kay was trying to steal him as he lay in his cot. She found these dreams disturbing because Kay was a good family friend. She could not imagine him hurting her or her unborn child. When she mentioned it to Akon, his response was beyond shocking.

"Eeeeh! So, now you are fantasising about my friend, Kay! Do you know that sometimes people dream about the things that occupy their minds during the day? Have you forgotten that out of the abundance of the heart? Is that not in your Bible?" Akon snapped. "So, you want to sleep with Kay?"

"How can you say such a thing? You know I am faithful to you!" Lara said, almost in tears.

Akon had refused to understand how she was feeling. From then on, she decided she would keep these things to herself. She had been plagued by the same dreams since Sunday night. She now decided to share them with her friend, Urumba.

Urumba was silent for a moment, and then she said, "I think you should pray about it. Let us hope it is nothing serious. But as Christians, we should never take things for granted because we are in spiritual warfare. If it gets out of hand, you should talk to the pastor. I will be praying with you. Did your husband stop imagining a Benz was chasing him?"

Lara laughed. "While I see Kay in my dreams, my husband sees a Benz chasing him. I also made fun of that Benz story. Maybe he's getting revenge by mocking my bad dreams."

*   *   *

Lara recalled her first job as a waitress. Even though her employers were nice, the customers treated her differently, especially when they heard her accent and did not seem familiar with some menu items. She was still learning about English cuisine. Besides, she felt uncomfortable. Suppose somebody who knew her as a lawyer back in Lagos showed up and saw her waiting on tables? Suppose they went back and told her friends at home? "You know Lara? Akon's wife? The one who left for London to join her husband? She is waiting on tables in a small restaurant in London! Abeg! Were there no restaurants in Lagos to wait on? Lawyer indeed! Solicitor-cum-waitress. I can wait on tables, and I do not have a law degree. People will come back to boast that they work in London when they have transformed from lawyers to waitresses!"

Lara was in a reflective mood. She remembered how paranoid she was about anyone finding out that she worked as a waitress. The job was a bitter-sweet experience for her; some customers were hostile, while some were warm and friendly. Some even left tips. She also had an opportunity to support one of her colleagues at work who was going through a distressing time.

Tanya was normally friendly and talkative, but that afternoon, she had been reclusive, and did not speak to anyone.

"Tanya."

"Hi, Lara," she replied.

"Hey, are you okay? You are not looking yourself today." Lara sat down and placed her tray on the table.

"I'm fine actually. Just thinking about my cousin, Ama. I've mentioned her to you before, remember?" Tanya said, finally picking up her sandwich and taking a bite.

Lara nodded. "I think I remember her. She is the one you said got engaged to a guy living here, right? Then he sponsored her so she could apply for a visa as his fiancée."

"Yes, that's Ama." Tanya sighed heavily before she spoke again. "I'm really worried about her. She stays with me sometimes, you know. Especially when Lucas, her fiancé, goes out of the country on business or something. Last night, she stayed over. Around midnight, I went to the kitchen to get water. That was when I saw Ama slumped in a chair in the living room, staring at nothing."

Lara waited for Tanya to gather her thoughts. "So, I went to meet her. She was looking gloomy, and her eyes were red like she had been crying. I had noticed she had become withdrawn for some weeks now, but I thought it was her job situation - she just lost her job.

"I tried to console her by saying another job will come up soon, that she would be fine. It was then that she told me it was not the job that was making her sad. I asked her what the problem was, but she didn't want to say at first."

"Did she tell you eventually?" Lara asked.

"Not before I begged her and told her that I would not allow her to sleep if she did not tell me," Tanya said.

Lara leaned forward and gave Tanya full attention.

"Why are men like this?" Tanya asked. "You would not believe what Ama said. In fact, if I did not see the evidence with my own eyes, I would not even have believed it."

"What happened?" Lara asked, feeling anxious.

"She told me Lucas said he was not interested in her anymore. She said when they met back home and she later came to London, he was so nice to her. But now, he has become ruthless, talking to her anyhow and threatening to leave her. In fact, his attitude is now bizarre. Then she pulled off her blouse. Lara, if you see my cousin's body, you will wonder if it is a human being or an animal that beat her like that."

Tanya wiped the tear that slipped down her face.

"When I saw it, I screamed. I told her to report him to the police, but she said that was not possible. Lucas told her she would be deported because she doesn't have the correct papers."

Lara gasped, shaking her head. "Is that not better than for her to die in his hands?"

"I asked her the same question, but she told me she cannot go back home like that."

As Lara recalled the conversation, her heart went out to the woman, but there was nothing she could do. At least, she was lucky. Akon could be difficult, but he had never raised a hand against her.

*   *   *

At work, Lara avoided eye contact with customers who appeared like fellow immigrants. When it was her turn to clean the outside of the restaurant, she would put on shades and a hood that she hoped would disguise her. *Lara, an accomplished lawyer from Lagos, mopping the pavement of a restaurant! No, that information must never reach her old acquaintances.* The new immigrant friends she had made in London might understand, but her old Lagos friends would not.

Lara recalled how an elderly lady had stared at her when she spoke in her native accent as if she were an alien. There were three elderly British ladies at the table, and she had approached them to take their order.

"Good morning. May I take your order, please?" Lara asked as politely as she could.

"Where are you from?" one of the ladies at the table asked.

Lara hesitated. "Africa."

"I recognise that accent," the lady said, and Lara smiled.

"So many of these people are coming to the UK," another lady said. "Soon, this country will be full of Africans and Asians."

"There is war and hunger in those countries. We must show kindness," the third one said.

Lara wanted to lecture them right there and then. What made them think immigrants were running away from starvation and death? How would they react if they knew she was a qualified lawyer but the systemic racism against those who did not grow up in the UK made the job market a challenge for her?

Lara knew that troubles did not just melt away if you relocate. *I hate these motivational speakers. Name it and claim it. This notion of claiming London is a fake promise. When you move from Lagos to London, you replace one set of problems with another.*

She had taken another job in London. She worked as a care worker for three months even though she was too qualified to work as one. Her accent had not helped matters. She also worked with a bogus magazine firm and left immediately when her suspicions were confirmed. People who met her now might think she merely transitioned from a law office in Lagos to another in London. She had to attend classes when she realised her previous papers required some bridging courses to have a solid footing as a solicitor in London.

Lara remembered the magazine scenario. She went there on a Saturday. She and her new friend, Cindy, stepped out of a taxi and walked to a building across the street. They were excited at the prospect of a new job. Each day, they could make eighty pounds.

"This will help me raise some money. Akon is straining to pay all the bills. Studies will have to be done through evening classes," Lara had explained. She met Cindy at a charity event and the two were now close friends.

"It's not bad at all," said Cindy, whose brother had informed her about the job.

"I'm grateful for this job," Lara said.

She and Cindy stood at the door after pressing a black switch and hearing a buzz upstairs.

"Great Life," Lara frowned. "Funny name for a company, isn't it?"

"It's actually a printing firm," Cindy responded.

"Printing. So why the name *Great Life*?"

"As long as I get a job, I don't care if they call it Great Life or Great Dive."

"Don't be so carefree, Cindy. Let us find out what it's all about. We might have a 'great life' working here."

Lara did not tell Cindy she had no intention of working there long-term. She would only work while she studied.

25

A young woman of about twenty-four appeared at the doorway. She looked at the two ladies for a long time as if trying to analyse them and make whatever conclusions she needed. "I suppose you are the new hands," she said at last. "Welcome to Great Life. I'm Suzy."

"I'm Cindy."

"I'm Lara."

"Come with me."

Cindy and Lara exchanged glances as they followed Suzy. She led them through the brown, brightly polished stairs to the first floor. She entered a well-furnished room with shiny desks, state-of-the-art computers, executive chairs, and flower vases brimming with beautiful displays. The new arrivals gaped in admiration.

Two men sat on two chairs at the end of this large office. They were casually dressed in jeans and T-shirts.

"Welcome, ladies!" One man sprang to his feet. He was heavily built, had a three-week beard, and moved with a surprising ease for a man his size.

They shook hands.

"Sit, sit, you lucky ones. Lucky indeed to be working for Great Life."

"Come on, Suzy," called the seated, clean-shaven man with a slim frame and long face. "Get them some tea and sizzling sausages!" he called towards a staff kitchen.

"Wow! I could do with that," Cindy said enthusiastically. "I had no breakfast," she explained as Lara frowned at her.

The men laughed, but Suzy only made a face.

"While your breakfast comes," the burly man said with a toothy smile, "we may as well get on. Time economy is one principle of Great Life."

"Talking of Great Life," Cindy piped in, "what does the name mean? If this is a printing firm, why such a name?"

"Very inquisitive, I see," the man nodded, amused. "Good for a worker at Great Life. Great Life has just been born, and as the company grows, you too will grow with it. By the way, excuse our shortcomings on mannerisms. We should introduce ourselves and get to know one another. I am John Pole, and I would be pleased if my staff would be so kind as to address me as *sir*."

The new employees could not help smiling. No doubt, Mr Pole was the funny one.

"Pleased to meet you, sir," Lara said, smiling. "I'm Lara."

"Cindy, here," she said and continued, "And who is the other boss?"

"The other boss?" Mr Pole seemed genuinely shocked. "I'm the only boss. This is my junior, Mr Abednego."

"You don't have to call me *sir*. He is the Manager. I'm the IT guy," Abednego said.

The ladies stared at the three computers in the room.

"Are we the only employees?" Lara asked with a frown. "What does Suzy do?"

"Suzy is my secretary," said Mr Pole. "As for the other employees, each day we have two different people in."

"Why?" Cindy asked.

"That," said Mr Pole, "is none of your business. I also insist on being addressed as *sir* while we are at it."

"Ah," Abednego said eagerly, "here comes tea, bacon, and eggs.

They had breakfast in silence as Mr Pole explained he did not believe in chatting over a meal.

Lara was trying to figure a few things out about the strange boss and strange set-up.

After breakfast, Mr Pole said he would tell them about their work and Great Life.

"At last," Cindy said. "I mean... at last, sir."

Lara could not help but laugh as Suzy gave a choke that sounded like suppressed laughter. Suzy seemed to be both amused by and wary of Mr Pole.

Mr Pole sprang to his feet in his quick style and said, "Both of you can break the sound barrier in typing. I hear. Good for you. Cindy, sit at that computer. Mr Abednego will proceed to give you some work. It will be mostly typing as this is a reporting firm. We have some hot news. This is a weekly magazine, you know."

"Alright, sir," said Mr Abednego.

"Okay, sir," Cindy said, following Abednego.

"Come with me," Mr Pole called to Lara.

There were three sharp hoots of a car's horn outside the building.

"Suzy!" called Mr Pole.

There was no answer.

"Where's this girl? Suzy!" he yelled.

Abednego looked out of the window. He turned

around and said to Mr Pole, "It's those guys, boss."

"Are you sure?"

"Of course, I'm sure!"

Mr Pole turned to Lara. "Now, have a quick mind as you work here, young lady. Run downstairs and tell the guy honking that horn we are in New York and won't be back for two weeks."

Lara gaped at him. "Tell him you are in New York?"

"Yes! Pronto! Tell him before he comes upstairs! We owe that guy enough money to sink Great Life. Rush, lady!"

"But that is a lie!"

Mr Pole looked as if he had been slapped. "What? Are you disobeying my orders?"

"Go on, Lara," Abednego said.

"I can't! I am not good at lying. I hate lying!" Lara was not ready to compromise her Christian principles.

Mr Pole angrily turned to Cindy, then seemed to change his mind. He turned to Abednego instead. "Is he still in the car?"

"Of course. He's still hooting as you can hear."

Mr Pole ran towards the kitchen. "Suzy!" he screamed.

Again, there was no answer.

He came back, fuming. "Want to keep your job,

woman?" he bawled at Lara. "I'll give you another chance. Tell the man in that car we are out until next week!"

Lara stood still with her arms crossed.

"He's leaving, sir," called Abednego with a sigh. "I hope he won't be back!"

"He still thinks we are out of town I suppose." Mr Pole ran his hand through his hair. Then he picked up a file and entered an inner room without another word.

Abednego shook his head thoughtfully. "You ladies got off to a bad start. Looks like you will need to make up your minds about what you want to do and what you must do. I'll assign Cindy her work first, then you," pointing to Lara.

Cindy was ushered to a computer. Next to the keyboard was a small file with plain white papers, handwritten and filed in.

"This is news, weekly news," Abednego said. "You had better go through each item first, and then type it. I will connect the printer to your machine in the meantime. Hold on, Lara."

After reading through the documents, Cindy said, "You mean all of these happened last week? Can you believe I didn't hear of a single thing mentioned here, not even on TV?"

Lara ran over to see. She read through some of the papers.

"Did all of this happen here in London?"

"About fifty percent of it," said Suzy as she walked into the room. "All we need is news, right?"

"Where were you?" Abednego called from where he had gone to pick up a LaserJet printer.

"Ladies," she said, ignoring him.

"Do you mean," Lara whispered to Suzy, "the other fifty percent are lies?"

"Maybe sixty percent," Suzy said, laughing quietly. "Ssshhh!" she added, a finger over her lips. "I'm not allowed to discuss this with you."

Cindy and Lara exchanged a horrified look. Then Lara shook her head at Cindy. "This is wrong," she said. "This job seems to open many doors to things I'm trying to avoid. I am leaving. What about you?"

Cindy stood up.

"Hey, wait!" called Suzy.

"What's up?" Abednego called, holding the printer in his hands.

"They are leaving!"

The man placed the printer down on the desk and glared at them. "Is this a joke?"

"No," Lara said firmly. "I have made a resolution to do the right things every day, and all I am getting here is a chance to do the wrong things. Say goodbye to Mr Pole for me."

As Abednego called out to Mr Pole, they left.

It was a good thing they left the job when they did. Mr Pole ran an illegal, unregistered tabloid business, which published advertisements for visas and jobs to developing countries. They had collected thousands of pounds from unsuspecting, innocent migrants who wanted to come to Europe, Germany, France, and the UK. The ladies were barely across the street when they spotted law enforcement authorities entering the premises. Lara and Cindy realised how close they had come to getting in trouble with the law for working for an unscrupulous company. The experience made them wiser.

As soon as they walked out of the building, Mr Pole had received a call. "Who is this? Why are you using a private number?"

"Never mind that. I do not want you calling me back. I want to be the one making them, Pole. I want you to call the police right away and report yourself and your business for lying to the public."

"Who is this? Stop playing mind games with me. Do you know who you are talking to?"

"I thought I used your surname."

Mr Pole walked over to the window. "Listen to me, mister. You'd better hang up this phone right now or I will find you. And when I do, you'll be very, very sorry."

Abednego and Suzy exchanged a knowing look. Pole thought himself a tough guy who could handle any situation.

The man at the other end spoke again. "I suppose you are trying to impress your staff. I have records to show you create fake news to sell your magazine. I wish I were there to see how tough you would act when the two police detectives, who should be there any minute, interrogate you. They want to interview the subjects of your news stories – if they even exist. Last week, you printed a defamatory story about our company. Instead of suing you for that story, I have decided to put you out of business. The police are on their way."

As he spoke, a police car pulled up outside the building. Mr Pole sprang from the window and hung up the phone. "Some police detectives are here. It seems that psycho on the phone called them. Come on, we must get rid of all the information on the computers. He said they are likely to start investigating the credibility of our news, sources, and contacts. You all know most of the news is hogwash. We must do something. Come on, move!"

Suzy walked towards the door. "There's no way I'm getting involved in this. I'm out of here!" she cried.

"What? How dare you walk out on us?"

"I wouldn't handle the situation like that, boss," Abednego advised.

"Shut up and start deleting every file in that computer, you fool!" Mr Pole screamed. He turned to the door and realised Suzy had gone.

"Suzy!"

Pole ran out the door, hoping to get to Suzy before she opened the front door. But she had just opened the main gate for the two detectives when he saw her. He retreated and ran back to his office, cursing.

"Set the office on fire," he said to Abednego, who gaped at his boss.

"But why? We may sell fake news, but we can always say we were just writing a story, boss. We haven't turned it into a magazine yet."

Pole slapped Abednego on the back. "You are a genius, Abednego. But what about the magazine cover and company logos on my machine? I'll hide the CPU or throw it out the window."

He switched off his computer at the mains. He ripped the CPU off the cords, rushed to the window, and threw it down onto the pavement, where it smashed into pieces just as the detectives came in.

"Excuse me, gentlemen," he said as he tried to brush past them.

The two detectives could not establish any convincing

or concrete evidence, but they placed Mr Pole and Abednego on the police watch list. Mr Pole eventually dropped his magazine idea.

Suzy found Lara and Cindy standing across the street. "I guess it's all over," she said.

"It was only a matter of time," Lara responded, shaking her head.

26

Lara sighed and leaned on the kitchen counter. She had had the same dream again. It did not make sense to her. Why did she keep having this troubling dream? What could it possibly mean? Kay was a good family friend, and her dream of him violating her and claiming her baby did not make sense. He always checked up on her to know how she was doing. He cared about her and her family.

Lara looked down at her protruding belly and caressed it gently. She was in her fourth month. After trying for a long time to conceive, she was happy that her prayers had finally been answered. Akon had been supportive and caring, always eager to meet her needs. He had also started planning for when the baby would be born.

Lara heard the front door open and close. It was Akon returning with the goat meat pepper soup she craved that morning. The pregnancy had her longing for different types of food she would not normally eat.

"Babe," he called out.

"In here. I am in the kitchen," she called back to him.

"How is my *sunshine* doing?" He pecked her on the cheek and put his ear on her stomach. He liked doing that, to keep track of the baby's development.

"We are doing great, darling. I only wish these dreams would stop. I'm getting more confused every day," Lara said, her forehead creasing.

"The same one again?" Akon asked, not looking at her. He was nervous but tried not to let her notice.

"Yes. It does not make sense that I am having dreams about Kay taking my baby from me. It just doesn't make sense," she said.

"Stop worrying your pretty head over it. Remember what the doctor said?" Akon said, trying to soothe her. He wished the dreams would stop. *What if she remembered?* He shook his head. *No, she could never remember.*

Lara nodded. She recollected her conversation with Doctor Boxbe at the hospital for her antenatal appointment. "Doctor, I keep having these strange dreams. I cannot sleep properly due to the nightmares. They keep replaying," she had complained to the doctor.

"It is not uncommon to have nightmares or dreams during pregnancy," Doctor Boxbe had replied. "Your oestrogen levels are high around this time, and these hormones can impact your emotions. It is natural to feel irritated and experience anxiety and stress. There is nothing to worry about. I do not want to give you sleeping pills for now because you are in your fourth month, and we do not want anything to affect the pregnancy."

"Doctor, but I need to sleep soundly." Lara had pleaded. "Don't you understand? I am a career lady and cannot afford to make mistakes."

"I understand, but it's only in serious cases that we prescribe sedating tablets or tranquillizers. I will book you to see the antenatal nurse who would go through some therapy with you."

* * *

Akon was sitting in his office cubicle, lost in thought. He could not get over what he had done to his wife. On that unfortunate day, he thought he was doing the right thing. But, with the passing of time, he is realising he might have made a colossal mistake.

The lights started flickering until they blinked off, leaving him in darkness for about thirty seconds. When they came back on, everyone around him was gone, and the walls around him were covered in blood which oozed from the cracks in the plaster. He could feel his heart hammering within his chest. His breathing quickened as if he was running a marathon. He felt petrified. He could not move due to shock. Dark images of dead, rotting foetuses appeared on the wall.

Akon felt a hand on his shoulder, which startled him. Just then, everything went back to normal. "You alright, mate?" his work colleague asked. Without saying a word, Akon grabbed his jacket and walked out.

Meanwhile, Lara was at home, trying to get some sleep before Akon arrived. She was all alone in bed. After several attempts, she finally nodded off. Almost immediately, a bright light shone on her face, burning her eyeballs. All around her was white, and when she tried to get up, she discovered she had been chained to her bed. Her belly bump was missing. Her baby was in a transparent glass jar, floating in formalin with the umbilical cord still attached. Surrounding the baby were strange beings with disc-shaped heads and six feet, doing all sorts of measurements to her child as if it were a guinea pig in a lab. Lara tried to scream, but no sound came out of her mouth. She pushed harder, but still could not make a sound. Not even the creatures could hear her. Akon had returned only to find Lara tossing and turning violently on the bed.

"Lara, Lara!" Akon shook her vigorously.

Lara woke up sweating and screaming. "It's okay. It's just a nightmare," Akon consoled her, holding her in his arms. Akon checked up on Jabez, but he was still asleep. Lara's scream did not wake him.

27

The nightmares were getting worse. Lara insisted they visit Prophet Dan, but Akon was hesitant. He preferred a psychiatrist to a prophet. But seeing that the nightmares had not reduced, he decided to give it a try.

On a Wednesday, they visited a Pentecostal church on the outskirts of East London called *The Sweet Waters.* It was established in the 1990s by a man named Daniel Nkosi, offering salvation and healing to his congregants, mainly of African descent. The church was empty, and the prophet was alone in his office. "Please sit, my children." Lara and Akon sat facing him in his office.

"How are you, children of God?" he shook hands with them.

"Not doing great. I have been having nightmares which are getting worse each day," Lara said, holding Akon's hand.

"When did it start?"

"Right around the time, I got pregnant."

"What about you?" the prophet asked Akon.

"I... I am fine."

"Fine?"

"Yes."

"Give me your hands," the prophet requested, and the two did as he asked.

He closed his eyes and prayed, squeezing their hands as he spoke. Throughout the prayer, Akon kept staring at the prophet until he was done.

"I can sense some dark energy, a secret between you two," the Prophet said, looking pointedly at Akon. "Something is not right. Your hands are not clean, sir. Confess to her and end this suffering."

"I have nothing to confess," Akon answered.

"Are you sure?" Prophet Dan asked.

"Yes, I swear."

I cannot help you if you do not tell me what is going on in your lives. For us to find a solution, we need to come out clean and confess," Prophet Dan urged.

Akon got up. "Meet me outside in three minutes, or

find your way home," he told Lara. Akon could not take it anymore.

Lara followed him outside and found him waiting in the car. She got in. "What are you hiding from me? What did you do?"

"I told you it was a terrible idea coming here."

"He is a man of God and the only one who can help us right now," Lara argued.

"Help us? What do you mean? He cannot help us. We need a professional therapist."

"We did see a therapist, and it didn't work out, remember?"

"I cannot keep doing this. I am sorry, but I just do not see how he could have helped us."

"If you are hiding anything, please tell me. I need to know," Lara said, tears rolling down her cheeks.

Akon strapped in his seatbelt and drove home without saying a word.

*   *   *

Akon could not look at Lara in the eyes. These days, he found it hard to discuss the pregnancy with her knowing the part he played in making it happen. Kay's attitude towards him was also worrisome. Akon resorted to using sleeping pills, and they worked.

As for Lara, she turned to prayer and fasting to curb

the nightmares, which Akon always frowned upon. According to him, it was bad for the baby and her health. But she carried on fasting. It seemed the only way she found peace and comfort from her nightmares.

During the fifth month of her pregnancy, things got even worse. The sleeping pills were not helping as before. Lara was nagging him more than ever.

"I can feel it. You are hiding something from me," Lara said to Akon one day as he got ready for work.

"I can't do this right now, Lara," he answered indignantly, putting on his shoes.

"Did you talk to an herbalist to get me pregnant?" she asked.

"Are you out of your mind or something?" Akon snapped, putting on his jacket?

"Akon, why are you on the defensive? I need to know if you are involved in some sort of cult, voodoo or something!"

"This is getting out of hand; do you know that? Do not listen to everything the Prophet tells you. He is a charlatan and nothing else. This has nothing to do with the supernatural. This is us, and God gave us this child just as he gave us Jabez."

"Whatever you did, God is punishing us right now. You need to come clean. I know something isn't right," Lara insisted.

"I am sorry," Akon replied and walked out, slamming the door behind him.

*   *   *

"Kay is such a nice man, and he seems to care about the baby. He's always calling to check on me," Lara announced one day, a few months later.

Akon stiffened and scowled. "Who? Kay?" *What the hell is wrong with him?* He hoped Kay would not get attached to the baby. Akon had paid him three thousand pounds for the job to keep his mouth shut.

Lara nodded. "Yes, maybe he misses his own kid. He calls me almost every week to check if I am feeling okay. And he bought a car seat and rattle for the baby when he visited last week. He is really sweet."

Akon was not pleased to hear this. What was Kay trying to do? He decided to talk to Kay about this. He did not want Kay hanging around, trying to bond with the child after it arrives.

The next day, Akon met with Kay at a café to warn him to stay away from his wife.

"I don't understand. Am I not allowed to see how she is doing? When did that become a crime?" Kay asked.

"I already told you. Stop calling her or buying any stupid gifts for the baby. We had an agreement, and I have paid you. So, stay away," Akon said. "Sperm donors just do the job they are paid to do. They don't loiter around fertility clinics the way you are hanging around my wife."

Kay gritted his teeth. Akon was oblivious to the feelings Kay had towards his wife, even before their secret plan. Kay knew he had agreed to keep his mouth shut, but he was finding it difficult to detach himself from his child.

"You are overreacting," Kay said. "I have been a friend to your family for years. Don't you think it would be strange if I suddenly start keeping my distance?"

Akon grabbed Kay by his collar and whispered menacingly. "This is my baby, and I don't want the baby to have two fathers. So, as I said before, stay the hell away!"

Akon stamped his feet on the floor and stormed out of the cafe. As he drove home, he tried to erase the memory of that fateful night. He had convinced himself it was for the best, but he was now scared Kay would try and lay claim on the baby. Besides, the nightmares that Lara kept having made him afraid she would one day remember what happened. That would be the end of his marriage. He could not afford to lose his family.

Akon arrived home, and as he entered, he saw a quick movement to his right. He turned sharply, but nothing was there.

*   *   *

Lara bit into her apple as she packed Jabez's lunch. She closed her eyes as a splitting pain shot through her head. The headaches had worsened. She wondered if they were due to a lack of sleep. She made a mental note to see her doctor, removed her glasses and rubbed her eyes.

These days she was easily exhausted, all thanks to the baby. She smiled as she placed a hand on her belly. She and Akon had agreed they were not going to find out the gender of the baby. They wanted it to be a surprise.

Akon and Lara had started making a list of names they would choose from. Lara knew their baby would receive so much love from Akon. She smiled but soon after felt the pain shooting through her skull again. Her vision went black as she stumbled backwards.

When Akon arrived home, he found her lying on the kitchen floor, unconscious.

"Lara! Lara! Oh, my goodness. Lara!" he yelled.

There was no response. She lay still on the floor. Akon's heart thudded as he lifted her in his arms and carried her to the car. *What is happening? Is she in premature labour?* But going into labour does not make women unconscious. He fumbled with his car keys before finally inserting it into the ignition. He hurriedly started the car and raced to the hospital.

One hour later, the doctor called Akon to the office and asked him to sit down.

"Doctor, what is it? Is she alright? What happened to her? Is the baby okay?" he asked desperately.

"Calm down, Mr Akete, we have everything under control. There is a little complication with the baby. It is a sporadic one that happens in some pregnancies. We would need a blood transfusion from the baby's father as soon as possible. I understand you are Lara's partner, right?" the doctor said.

"Ye– Yes I am her husband," Akon said uneasily.

"Well, we have no time to waste. We must carry out the operation quickly. If not, both the baby's and mother's life could be at risk. I'll send one of our nurses to prepare you for the procedure."

Akon's heart was beating rapidly as he thought of what to do. He had warned Kay to stay away from his wife. How would it look if he went back to him, begging to save his child? He could not lose his baby, and certainly could not lose his wife. So, he swallowed his pride and called Kay. As soon as he told Kay what was happening, he rushed down to the hospital. The doctor was confused.

"I thought you were the patient's husband," he asked, frowning at Akon.

"Yes, I am, but there's a little issue with my blood

genotype. Please, let him do the transfusion now. As you said, there is no time."

The doctor, a Somali man, just shook his head and muttered to himself. He brought out the consent papers and Akon signed them. Several hours later, the doctor came out of the operating room and was accosted by Akon and Kay, who had been pacing restlessly.

"Doctor, how was it? Are they okay?" they asked breathlessly.

The doctor smiled. "Yes, it was successful. Both mother and baby are fine. In a few minutes, you would be able to see them. The baby is lucky to have two fathers who care so much."

When the doctor left, Akon turned to Kay. "Thank you very much for your help, but you are no longer needed here. You can leave. I'll send you another £1,000 for the cover-up," he said coldly.

"I don't need your money!" Kay spat.

"Well then, I guess we have nothing to say to each other again," Akon said and turned to leave.

Kay stood there, shaking with anger. He gritted his teeth and walked out of the hospital.

One week later, Lara was at home recuperating from the surgery. Akon was making her lunch when they heard a knock at the door.

"I'll get it," Lara said.

Lara looked through the peephole and saw Kay standing at the entrance.

"Kay! Long time," she said, opening the door to let him in.

"How are you doing, my dear?" he asked her with a smile.

"You did not visit me at the hospital. Are we quarrelling?"

"I'm sorry, Lara. I have been swamped with work."

"Too busy to come and see me? It's okay sha," she said, leading him to the living room.

"Babe, Kay is here," she called out to Akon in the kitchen.

When Akon heard Kay's name, he froze and dropped the plate in his hand. *How come he's here? Unannounced?* He took a deep breath and plastered a smile on his face as he stepped out of the kitchen.

"Hey guy, what's up?" he said, coming to shake his hand.

Kay smiled at him with an equally fake smile.

"Let me get you something to drink, while you guys catch up," Lara said and went to the kitchen to get Kay a glass of juice.

As soon as Lara left the room, Akon turned to Kay with rage. "What the hell do you think–"

"Please, spare me the empty threats. I can come and

go as I please. You have no right to ask me to stay away from my child!"

"We had an agreement! You were to stay away forever. You have no right to the child. The child is mine now."

"Well, I changed my mind. I put that baby in Lara's womb, and I am the father!"

Akon wanted to grab him, but Lara returned with drinks, smiling. There was nothing he could do.

28

"Hello? Is anybody home?" Aderonke called as she knocked on the door. It was half open.

"Yes, sister. Come in." Lara said in a loud voice and continued singing to herself.

"Ah, Lara! Do not leave the door open when you are home alone. You are a pregnant woman!" Aderonke walked inside bustling.

"Good evening," Lara smiled at her, and the friends hugged each other. "As always, you brought something," Lara said, pointing at the pot Aderonke was holding.

"I made pounded yam for you." She put the pot on the table and took a seat.

"You should not have."

"Yes, I should. I am like your sister. The relationship between your husband's family and mine go way back. I need to take care of you, my precious girl." Aderonke, also known as Rosemary, was like family friend to both Akon and Lara's families.

"Thank you," Lara said as she took off the cover. "These look delicious!"

"Just put them in the microwave, and they would be ready to eat in a few minutes."

"Thank you. I am grateful for everything you do for us."

"I want to help out the best I can. You are seven months pregnant, and you need support."

"Akon tries to be home as much as possible, but his work schedule is crazy. He explained to his boss that I am heavily pregnant," Lara said as she caressed her belly. "So, the boss lets him work fewer hours."

"Having a supportive husband is the best present a pregnant woman could ever wish for."

"Yes, and he also helped to decorate the baby's room. We turned the guestroom into another bedroom, and it looks lovely. Do you want to see it?" Lara asked with sparkling eyes.

"Of course, I do!" Aderonke followed Lara to the baby's room. "Wow! This looks enchanting."

"I already imagine my baby boy sleeping here."

"What did you just say?" Aderonke clapped her hands in excitement.

"What?"

"A baby boy? Do you know the sex of the baby?"

"Yes. We could no longer wait. Yesterday, we broke our promise to keep the gender of the baby a secret. I was so curious; the suspense was becoming unbearable! " Lara laughed out loud.

"Another boy! That is amazing! Congratulations, darling!"

"We are so happy. Akon was full of joy. Although I wanted a daughter this time, it does not matter now. I love my son with all of my heart!"

"Yes, and Jabez will have a little friend as well."

"That is another reason I am glad we are having a boy. Even though there will be twelve years between them, I still believe that my sons will become best friends."

"Of course, they will!"

"Sometimes, I feel like Jabez is jealous of the baby." Lara touched her belly gently as if to keep the baby from hearing the sad truth. "Jabez was angry the other day when we bought toys for the baby. He claimed that when he asked his dad for a PlayStation, Akon said he had no money." Lara walked gingerly as they both headed back to the kitchen.

"Oh, that would have broken Akon's heart."

"Akon reassured him and explained how much happiness a new baby would bring, but it didn't work."

"Don't worry. Jabez will fall in love with his little brother the moment he is born."

"I hope so. I am concerned about Jabez's jealousy. Hopefully, it will fade away."

"My dear, you have to be careful with these children. You might not realise it, but they are watching every step you take, and they might interpret your actions the wrong way," Aderonke said.

"I learnt my lesson the hard way when my kids were taken from me by social workers. They accused me of neglect. I kicked against my family living separately, but my husband, Dele, did not want to live here in the UK. I argued with him, telling him that children need their father. Unfortunately, he preferred to build his business empire instead of listening to the voice of reason. You could imagine how I felt. I called my husband and informed him that the social services had taken our children. Instead of been sympathetic, he was livid. He blamed me for being irresponsible.

"Later on, family members prevailed on him, and he decided to join me in the UK. I was shocked when he arrived in London as he had not spoken to me for two weeks since the incident. In fact, he attended the family court and joined me in attending the parenting classes. Luckily for us, the children were placed in my sister-in-law's custody. Dele realised he needed to be there for his kids. Within one year, we adjusted our schedule to rebuild our family again. We worked so hard, Lara. I missed my children so much. I almost went crazy. However, the children were returned to us within twelve months. Since then, Dele has been an upright father, spending time with the children. Having their dad in their lives has stabilised them. Now they are in college."

"Wow! I did not know you went through all that. I am sorry, Ronke. I will hold on tight to Jabez."

"My dear, be careful with Jabez. He is of legal age now."

Lara sighed softly.

"Honey, I am home!" Aderonke and Lara heard Akon's voice.

"We are in the kitchen!" Lara responded as she took the pounded yam out of the microwave.

"Good afternoon, sister Aderonke!" Akon greeted Aderonke and kissed Lara.

"Look, sister Aderonke brought food for us."

"This smells amazing." Akon could not wait to have dinner. "We had been relying on readymade food from Iceland. I am not a good cook, and Lara is too pregnant to cook nowadays."

"In Nigeria, we had a lot of extra help. Now, we must jostle many activities to take care of Jabez and a new baby as well," Lara explained.

"By the way, where is Jabez?" Aderonke looked around.

"He is a big boy already," Akon said proudly. "He goes and arrives from school independently."

"Jabez is doing great," Lara agreed. "And in other good news, I am sleeping better every day."

"That's good. You are nine months' pregnant, nine and you deserve a good sleep," Akon said as he kissed Lara on the forehead. "By the way, how about the naming ceremony?"

"What about it?" Lara answered, caressing her belly.

"In the UK, we need to provide the baby's name after he is born and tie it around his wrists."

"Okay. We should agree on the name. It's time."

"Well, well, let's see what we have in the diary." Akon opened his dairy and looked at the list of five names. "What if we added Samuel, John, Omotanwa Ayomikun, and Iretioluwa?"

"I like them," an excited Lara suggested.

"You are going to confuse a child if we call him all of these five names!" Aderonke laughed.

"We can have a name for different days of the week," Akon added.

"We still need a formal name for the baby at least in the African way. We should do the child dedication in church," Lara said.

"Honey, don't rush. Let us do one thing at a time. My only wish is for you and the baby to be healthy and happy," Akon said and kissed her forehead once again, holding her hands in his.

* * *

That night, Akon was woken up by Lara's shouts.

"Akon! Akon! Wake up!" Lara shook his arm.

"What is it?" Akon jumped up when he saw Lara's startled face.

"I think it has started! My water is about to break!" Lara screamed in pain.

"I have everything in the car. I packed you a bag three days ago in case of an emergency. Do not worry about anything. I'll take you to the hospital right now." He leapt up and helped Lara down the stairs.

"It hurts!" Lara breathed in and out.

Akon took Lara in his arms and gently helped her into the car.

"We will be in the Hebrew maternity ward of The Amazon Hospital in fifteen minutes. Don't worry about anything." Akon kept calm because he knew Lara needed his help more than ever before.

When they arrived at the hospital, Lara was rushed off, and Akon sat anxiously in the reception, waiting for good news. Suddenly, a doctor came into the waiting area and called out for him.

"Akon? Can I speak to Mr Akon?" The doctor was looking around the reception for him.

"I'm here!" Akon rushed to hear the news.

"So, a natural birth will not be possible. Your wife cannot push because the baby's head is stuck," the consultant gynaecologist explained.

"What should we do?" Akon asked.

"Caesarean section is the only option."

"Will Lara be okay?" a petrified Akon could not stop asking questions.

"Everything will be alright. We don't want any complications, so we need to act soon."

Akon could not sit down. He paced up and down, waiting for any kind of news. But for two hours, nobody walked out from the operating room. After what felt like an eternity, a nurse came out with a smile on her face. "Mr Akon," she said, "the CS was successful. Congratulations! It's a boy."

"Oh, thank you so much!" Akon sighed in relief.

"You can now visit your wife and the baby."

Akon could not contain himself. He ran to the room. Lara was holding their baby in her arms.

"He is here," Lara said with a trembling voice. She had eyes full of tears.

"He is beautiful" Akon could not stop his emotions as well. The man was full of joy. He held the baby's hand and kissed him repeatedly.

"Bless him," one of the nurses said to her colleague. They could not stop watching the touching scene.

"He is cute," the colleague agreed.

Lara and Akon caressed their baby. "Which of the names should we choose for the baby?" Lara asked.

"What about Ephraim?" Akon asked.

"Ephraim was not even on our list, but it is perfect." A tear rolled down her cheek.

"We are going to take the baby for a minute," said a midwife. "We will clean him up so the mother can rest."

"Excuse me," Akon apologised and left the room. He took his phone and called his mother.

"Mama! Our new son is born!" he announced to his family with vibrancy in his voice.

29

Two weeks after the birth of the baby, Akon was back at work. He loved spending time in the coffee shop during lunch breaks. After a busy morning at work, Akon would visit the one in the corner of the street, the coffee shop of white cups, black coffee and small jugs filled with cream. It had that ambience of friendly chatter. Here, Akon could take a seat, feel caught up in other people's social lives, and have time to contemplate. On the street outside were food vendors, giving the centre of the colossal city a sort of market atmosphere.

Akon sat at the window. It was a cold day in November. He wrapped his fingers around a warm mug of coffee and smiled as he watched people outside, running up and down, trying to avoid one another. Everybody seemed busy. They were always heading somewhere, constantly checking the time, and dreaming of a couple of hours of leisure. This had become the pattern of Akon's life as well. Life was so busy that he could hardly meet up with his closest friends or travel back home to visit family. But at this moment, Akon did not care. He did not miss anybody because the people he cared about—Lara and the children—were always by his side.

However, he worried about Kay and his attitude towards the baby. He could still make a claim for the child because it was biologically his. Akon was afraid Kay might let out the secret, and it would become a scandal. Deep inside, Akon had not been a happy man since his baby scheme. Neither the baby's arrival nor the money he had borrowed from the bank to keep Kay silent gave him any relief.

Akon was eager to support Kay in his decision to move out of the UK. It would keep him away from his family forever. He recalled Ephraim's naming ceremony in anger. It was a low-key occasion with just twenty-five people. Akon had invited a few people as he did not want to make it a typical Nigerian party. He had been lying low since he relocated to the UK. Lara's pastor, Alfie Royce, a white man, was present with his wife, Mace, to name the baby.

"Children are a gift from God. It is my pleasure to name this blessed child. I have been given a list of names; however, I can't pronounce most of them," the Pastor had joked, and the guests burst into laughter.

He glanced at the paper in his hand. "I have ten names here. This is what I like about the Nigerian community. They still practice the old saying that it takes a village to raise a child. The Nigerian community is such a supportive one." Akon watched in confusion as he spotted Kay slipping a paper into the hands of the Pastor. Pastor Alfie opened it and laughed.

"I'll hand this over to the MC to help me pronounce it." Akon and Lara had invited their old friend, Mr Dele, Aderonke's husband, to act as the MC.

Akon was shocked that Kay could even think of giving the boy a name, but he held his cool. A couple of years ago, Kay had told him he wanted to start a new life elsewhere, but he was still struggling to put the money together. Akon considered getting another loan to help Kay move out of the UK. Akon remembered when he was the one in Kay's shoes, looking for a job and a house to stay in. Even though Kay frustrated him out of his house, he had forgiven Kay and moved on. *Life happened to Kay*. He knew he was not supposed to be happy over someone else's misfortune, but he was happy, nonetheless. Kay had become distraught and cranky as he had lost all his earnings in the UK, and he could no longer get a decent job.

Kay had reflected upon his life that day. He had

never been one to maintain relationships, and the longest he had held a job was three years. He wanted to get out of the UK as fast as he could. He had so many debts to individuals and companies. He owed a lot because he often lived above his means. He was nearly forty-six years old and had been in the UK since he was twenty-three. Yet he had nothing to show for all the years of struggle. Kay had no wife or child he could proudly call his own. He had asked Akon to loan him £8,000 for his relocation, promising to pay the money back. This loan made it possible for him to save up some money. He was able to go to Canada as an international student. The deal was for him to shut up about the baby as Akon did not want Lara to discover the truth. Eventually, Kay moved out of the UK. Akon was relieved as if a heavy burden was finally lifted from his shoulders.

*   *   *

On an early Saturday morning, the sun struggled to get past the grime of the window blinds in Akon and Lara's bedroom. Akon liked how the sun rays caressed his cold skin. So, he did not turn around. The outside world was still silent. Only the irrigation system's low voice is slowly getting to work, mixed with the birds' lazy cooing and Lara's favourite song. Akon smiled when he realised there were no concrete plans for the weekend. He had not written anything on his to-do list.

After working hard for the whole year, he truly deserved a good summer holiday. Akon wanted to continue playing with the sunshine that slowly got hotter. He also wanted to listen to some soft music.

Akon wrapped up in his blankets as he heard tender footsteps reaching upstairs. Lara opened the bedroom door slightly and chuckled.

"Get up, honey! It's already 9 o'clock," she said.

Akon sighed. He did not want to leave the bed, but he knew a working family man never sleeps this much.

"I deserve a day in bed," Akon complained while sliding out of bed.

"I know, honey. You deserve a good rest." Lara approached and kissed him. "But Aunty Eli and Anton are visiting today. So, I want to get ready for them."

Akon lightened up as soon as he heard that Mr and Mrs Emilio were visiting for the weekend. He had never met Lara's late mother's elder sister's daughter, Elizabeth, but he heard her and Lara talking on the phone from time to time.

"That's amazing!" Akon said with excitement.

Before the guests came, Akon and Lara cleaned the whole house so well that the kitchen counters almost sparkled. The delicious smell of Lara's creations mixed with the freshness of the house. Lara did not just feel the need to clean up because it was a simple rule when one is expecting guests, she also wanted to show off whatever they had. Lara was proud of Akon and even though their house was not a mansion with marble stairs, Lara wanted to make sure that people saw how hard Akon worked to get to where they were.

"I hope they will not be late," Lara said. "Rice and peas will be ready soon. I am also making jerk chicken and goat curry as I want to please my Caribbean uncle."

Akon realised that Lara was nervous. She paced up and down, clearing her throat from time to time.

"Hey, honey. Everything will be alright. She will not judge you. And what is there to judge? The house sparkles!" Akon wrapped his arms around Lara.

"As you know, this is the first time that Aunty Eli is coming and, of course, with her husband, who is from the Caribbean. I have not seen Aunty Eli since she moved to America, and I do not even know Uncle Anton. I want to make sure everything goes smoothly," Lara answered.

"It will be alright," Akon touched Lara's nose with his nose. They both laughed, and the stress momentarily faded away. Lara realised that no matter what happened this weekend, Akon was in love with her.

Suddenly there was a knock on the door.

"They are here," Akon said, and they both went to the door.

Outside, Elizabeth and Anton stood with wide smiles on their faces. Elizabeth was as fit as always. Her skin glowed, and her black hair dropped down to her waist. Behind her stood tall, athletic Anton, holding bags in both of his hands.

"Hello, darling!" Elizabeth said and spread her hands to greet Lara, "I could never imagine you'd grow into such an amazing and gorgeous lady!"

"Hello, aunty!" Lara answered in a loving voice and hugged her.

"Wow, congrats about your new baby."

"Thank you," Akon and Lara echoed. "He is presently sleeping while his big brother had gone out for music lessons," Lara added.

Akon, Lara, and the Emilios sat around the dining table, which was filled with different dishes.

Aunty Eli looked around. "You have a beautiful home," she said in astonishment. Anton agreed.

"Thank you. We worked hard for everything you see here," Akon said, holding Lara's hand under the table.

"Please, have jerk chicken," Lara said, passing the chicken to Anton.

"This dinner looks amazing. I see you have done some Caribbean food. Mmmm… the food touched up with fried yam and fried rice is delicious!" Anton said with amazement.

"Lara is the great cook," Akon said.

"And you are a great husband for noticing," Anton answered, and had the first bite with satisfaction.

Elizabeth sighed with a smile on her face. "Oh, honey, we know a lot about working hard to get even a small thing. We have been living in America for years now, and we still struggle daily."

"But you guys look like you've got everything one could wish for. As I know, Uncle Anton is successful in his career as a psychologist. You have lots of customers because you are known as a great physiotherapist," Lara said with a little bit of confusion because she did not get why the couple might be struggling.

Anton and Eli looked at each other and smiled.

"Honey, I am scared for my son when he goes out for a simple walk. He is twenty-one years old, a great student and a good citizen. You might ask why? Because he is not white," Aunty Eli said.

Lara's brows creased as she listened to Elizabeth.

"Till this day, the police still kill black people in the street based on mistaken identity, and sometimes for no reason at all. There is a general assumption that all black males do drugs. Sadly, they are easy targets," Elizabeth said with a trembling voice.

Anton tapped his wife's shoulder. "There are places we cannot go at night. I took my office and moved to the city centre just because the neighbourhood was full of police at night. Some people would think the presence of police while walking on a dark narrow street means safety, but no, not in a black man's case—it spells danger.

"One time, I was about to lock my office. It was around midnight. I had had a long day and was looking forward to seeing my wife and children at home. All I could think about was the hug of my twin daughters, my wife's kiss, and a nice dinner with my sweet family. I only needed to get home and all the stress of the day would fade away," Anton said, smiling.

But his smile soon disappeared. He looked down and continued, "As I headed towards my car, I saw a black man walking down the street, singing to himself. He smoked a cigarette and threw it close to the bin. And from nowhere, a couple of white men jumped out and pinned him against the wall, yelling at him. I wanted to help the poor black guy, but then I saw the police, holding bats in their hands. I thought they would be on the black man's side, but I was wrong. In front of me, two policemen beat up the poor man while shouting: 'Who gave you the right to throw the cigarette and sing while walking on white people's land?'"

Lara felt her eyes watering up while listening to the tragic story. Anton looked up, and with a lower voice, he continued, "I had to go back to my office and spend the night there because if I walked that street, anything could happen to me. Maybe a beautiful family was waiting for that man who was beaten up and left in the streets. I do not know if he survived. I called the ambulance and headed back to my office, thinking I should not be another victim. My family needs me." Anton's voice got hoarse when he said, "Because of this, I moved my office to another street."

Everybody sat quietly. Lara did not know what to say, but she thought this silence made everything even more painful.

"But some good things still happen in America," Aunty Eli said, with a more cheerful voice.

"Please, tell us," Akon almost begged.

"When I started going to people's houses as a physiotherapist, many of them slammed their doors to my face because they did not want my black hands to touch their patients," Eli said with laughter.

Lara soon realised that this couple coped with the unfairness with humour and a strong spirit, and she liked Mr and Mrs Emilio's endurance.

"But a group of student activists protested against racism. Their purpose was to help black professionals to be recognised as professionals, not just black people. That helped me, my husband, and thousands more. My patients began to accept me for who I am. Some might not have liked me at first, but doors are no longer slammed in my face. People try to be more tolerant, and overtime my patients get attached to me that they don't want me to leave." Elizabeth smiled and raised her glass.

"To tolerance!" she said loudly.

"To tolerance!" everybody cheered.

Akon and Lara looked at each other, and Akon said, "This is going to be a weekend full of sad and beautiful stories."

Lara agreed and put her head on Akon's shoulder.

30

A week later, a friend of Lara, Urumba, visited on her way from work. After sharing a few pleasantries, Lara related a nasty experience she had just before she went on maternity leave. As part of her intern work in the law firm, she conducted a telephone interview with a client called Angelina Thomas.

Angelina had gotten married to Seth Jones twelve years ago, but after eleven years of marriage, the perfect union turned into a nightmare. Her body wanted to let go but her mind would not. Her love for Seth was like the raging sea. She thought she could ride the pain but did not know there was a limit to the hurt a heart can contain.

Her bedroom, which had been her love haven for eleven years, had a luxurious bed, double-hung windows, and a door – the door to the bathroom, her only safe space. These two rooms can tell their stories.

Was Angelina in a dream world when she married Seth? The dream had suddenly become a horror show, featuring Seth's baptism of beatings, an unyielding lump of inhumanity.

Angelina was constantly scared of what could happen next. She often thought about taking her husband's life but could not get herself to do it. What was the point of killing Seth? If she ended up serving time in the state prison, what would become of their daughter, Claire? She had also contemplated running away but wondered how Claire would deal with her absence.

Angelina had not always been submissive, though. One night, Seth came home late. Angelina heard the front door open and then close. Seconds later, the door to Seth's bedroom creaked as he went in to hang his signature black leather jacket. Angelina knew the routine. Seth would make his way to the kitchen and get wasted in shots of vodka. He had been wrapping himself in that vicious cycle for the last eleven years. At one point, it damaged his health, but he continued anyway.

An hour or so after he got hammered, Angelina could hear his footsteps approaching. Seth kicked the door to her room and leaned against the doorway. She stood and stared hopefully at his pierced nostrils, which looked eerie as ever.

"Where is Claire? I looked everywhere but couldn't find my pretty daughter," he asked, slurring as he attempted to enter the room.

Angelina pushed him before speaking. "What could you possibly want to talk about with Claire? You, ridiculous Mafia and drunken idiot!" Angelina's heart was pounding.

Seth inched closer and Angelina's uneasiness became obvious. She tried to step back, but Seth was way faster. In a split second, Seth wrapped his hand on the sides of Angelina's face and pulled her closer.

"You sure you won't regret calling me a Mafia? Is that what you have been telling Claire about her father? That girl loves me more than you because I am more credible." Seth gritted his teeth.

Seth threw a hot slap on Angelina's face. "Right now, you look like a nutjob! Even if you ask for help, no one will ever believe you."

"That's a big lie! You are worse than a worm!"

"You, ugly beefy!" Seth yelled as he pulled away from Angelina.

Quick on his feet, Seth darted out of the room, closing the door behind him. Angelina dropped to the floor and heaved a sigh of frustration. The need to get out of the nightmare pressed down on her as she hugged her chest.

Lara read the statement she had written from the

interview to Angelina to confirm that she had a full report. She then handed it to the senior partner.

Lara was so exhausted and could not wait to return home. As she entered the gates of her house, the lights in the living room suddenly went out. It had been a tiring day in which she had followed her senior colleague to court to watch the proceedings. The previous day had been spent marking bundles and it was a busy day at the office.

When the case got to court, she was the assigned legal assistant for Mr Thomas. Lara edged closer to the scruffy-looking defendant who had a weird tattoo design on the side of his neck. As her eyes swept over him, she dipped into her pocket and pulled out a black and white business card.

"I am Lara Akete," Lara said, extending the business card to Seth Thomas.

Mr. Thomas gripped the edge of the card and nodded.

"Do you have any other documents you want to file?" Lara asked Mr. Thomas.

"No," Mr. Thomas said, looking straight at Lara as if he was imprinting her features to memory.

Lara had read the case and knew the story. Mr. Thomas was an undocumented immigrant, who had used different names to bypass the system. The neighbours had heard Mr. Thomas's partner, Angelina Thomas, screaming, and had called the police, who visited the property and arrested Mr. Thomas.

It was obvious that Angelina had endured several months of domestic violence from her husband, but she was too scared to ask for help. Angelina was so relieved when she and her ten-year-old daughter, Claire, were taken away to an undisclosed refuge away from Mr. Thomas. She had to undergo a body-resetting treatment at the hospital because Mr. Thomas had scalded her face with hot water during one of the mind-numbing incidences.

Mr. Thomas wept like a baby when the security officers took him out of the courtroom to the immigration removal van.

"You cannot send me out of the country," he screamed. "My life-line, my daughter, is in this country. No one can take Claire from me. I would do anything, and my men would do anything to get Claire back!" Mr. Thomas struggled with the cops as they led him out of the courtroom.

A few days after Mr. Thomas was sentenced, Lara was home alone, enjoying the cold, weekend breeze blowing through the living room. The room was dark, with just enough light through the windows from the setting sun. *The bulb had blown out anyway. Akon will fix it when he comes back home later,* Lara had thought.

Lara's mind drifted to the just-concluded Angelina case. She had learnt from the reports that Mr. Thomas was a member of a dangerous Mafia organisation. She let out a sigh, not wanting those rigmaroles to spoil her quiet evening.

Although the room was dark, Lara's senses were on alert. *Why is the refrigerator not humming?* From where she was lying, Lara could see the streetlights fifty yards away. They were on. Lara focused her senses on the quietness in the house.

Without warning, Lara's stomach rumbled. She rushed to the kitchen to grab some of the take-away pizza she had previously ordered. She took a bite of one of the pieces and placed another on a plate. Before heading back to the living room, she opened the refrigerator. It was pitch black. *There must be a blackout,* she thought.

A few moments after finishing the first slice of pizza, Lara heard the kitchen door open. In an instant, a cold breeze wafted through the door. Her brain stuttered for a moment as she froze. She wanted to ask who was there, but her throat felt dry as sawdust.

The hairs on the back of her neck rose. She began to creep towards her phone but paused when she heard the shattering of a glass cup on her kitchen floor.

"Oh God," she whispered, before mustering the courage to call in a shaky voice: "Who's there?"

The response she got was the sound of something falling to the floor, followed by footsteps, and the sound of water beginning to run from the kitchen tap.

As the filtered streetlights around the neighbourhood outlined an individual, Lara stumbled over a seat and crashed to the floor. It sent a pile of CDs stacked on that sofa crashing to the floor with a racket that sounded like a gunshot in her ears.

From the passageway that led to the kitchen, a light shone on where she fell, making her heart pounded. She identified the intruder and fear gripped her heart.

"Please..." Lara pleaded, with trembling lips. "Please, take whatever you want and go."

"I want nothing," the rough, deep voice echoed through the room.

"What... what do you want," Lara stammered.

The intruder fixed the torch light on her face and Lara shielded the light from her eyes with her arm.

The man, attired in black outfits, took a step toward her, and pointed a small 9mm gun at her. "Where is Claire Thomas?" He demanded in an icy tone.

"Excuse me?"

"You heard me. Where is Claire Thomas?"

After a moment of silence, his fingers tightened on the trigger. "Anyone that messes around with Thomas messes with us all," the man smirked.

Lara glanced at the man and watched him fish out a pack of cigarettes from his pocket. He lighted a stick and released the smoke into Lara's face.

Choking on the smoke, Lara's nose wrinkled as the name rang a bell.

"I don't know who Claire…"

"Don't play games with me!" the man in the shadows growled.

Lara seemed to have a problem getting air into her lungs.

"I am giving you seven days," the man got to the point.

Sweat poured down Lara's body as the man gripped her by the throat. "Listen to me," he said. "Do not do anything silly. Do not go to the authorities, or you would regret it. I disconnected your power, and you will need to have it reconnected. I will get in touch after seven days. When I do, I expect you to tell me where Claire is. If you play games with me, somebody will die."

In a twinkle of an eye, the man turned and walked back to the kitchen. The back door opened, and the man's heavy footsteps tailed off as he got away through the backyard. Moments later, the throaty groan of a motorcycle near the rear gate could be heard.

Lara stood shell shocked for a couple of seconds. She had not realised how scared she was until then.

Lara found her phone and frantically began to dial.

"Akon!" Lara gasped. "Where are you? Please come home! You will not believe what just happened!"

Akon got home in eight minutes. The electricity had now been reconnected.

Akon was visibly worried when he heard about Lara's ordeal. They both wondered how the man found their house. Akon felt that it was better they reported the break-in to the police and ask them how they could secure the neighbourhood.

Lara was scared. She had watched films about the mafia, but her encounter with that intruder made the movies look so real.

* * *

"Don't tell me you experienced all this?" Urumba said, shocked at Lara's story. "This is quite strange. How did they know your address?"

"Sincerely, I have no clue," Lara shrugged. "I guess the mafia must have been trawling all the professionals involved in the case."

"But did they visit the senior partner or any of the court officials?" Urumba asked as she picked some of the groundnut Lara had offered her.

"Not to the best of my knowledge," Lara said with a face that showed no emotion.

"So, what did the police do? Was he arrested?" Urumba asked, sitting on the edge of her seat.

Sighing deeply, Lara responded. "When Akon called the police, they logged the call, visited the house, and interviewed me. They checked the entire house, took fingerprints, and collected statements." Lara then added, with disgust all over her face, "Can you imagine that one of the police officers asked if I knew the intruder? He even suggested that the intruder may have been drunk and entered the house by mistake. Can you believe that?" Lara asked with a slightly raised voice.

Urumba's eyes widened in disbelief.

"Akon tried to control his temper as I said 'no' to most of the questions."

Urumba could feel Lara's fury in every word she uttered. "So, what happened?" she asked eagerly.

"The case was closed for insufficient evidence after three months," Lara said as she fought back the tears.

"That could have left you devastated," Urumba commented as she extended her hands to pat Lara on her back.

"Sure… I was so traumatised! I did not expect that experience in the UK," Lara looked down in embarrassment, hiding her tears.

Just then, Urumba's phone rang. It was her husband calling to remind her of their outing later that night.

"Sorry my dear, I have to leave now." Urumba said apologetically as she stood to leave.

Lara followed Urumba to the front door, but Urumba insisted she would not need to follow her out of the apartment. Urumba could see that Lara was visibly shaken by recounting her experience and did not want to put her under more stress.

*   *   *

"Mum, I'm hungry," Ephraim said, with eyes fixed on the TV.

"Sorry dear," Lara responded as she placed his nuggets and chips in the microwave.

Taking a quick glance at the time, Lara realised that Akon would soon be back and would be needing his food as soon as he entered. She used that opportunity to set the dining table and place his favourite cranberry juice in the fridge.

Lara carried Ephraim, wanting to settle him into to the highchair near the dining table.

"No!" Ephraim screamed. He wanted to sit next to the TV to watch his favourite CBeebies programme. With his hands on the nuggets and his glance on the TV, Ephraim also had one eye on Lara's iPad tablet.

"I have told you not to eat and watch TV at the same time," Lara cautioned.

Soon afterwards, Ephraim spilled his drink and stained the carpet, causing Lara to rush to the kitchen for a napkin. She cleaned up the mess and then changed Ephraim's clothes.

The landline phone rang just after Lara placed Ephraim in the highchair. In hurried steps, she walked to the phone and picked it up on the third ring.

"Hello, is that number 26, White road?" she heard an unfamiliar voice say over the phone.

Yes, please," Lara said, her heart beginning to race.

"Is that Mrs Akete?"

"Yes, it is. Who am I speaking with?"

"Your husband collapsed at work and has just been rushed to the Marble Way Hospital," the voice said.

Lara's heart skipped, and she almost dropped the cordless telephone. She could not believe her ears. She snapped back to life and quickly called Ephraim's nanny, Gemma, who lived down the block. Lara was relieved when the lady agreed to stay with Ephraim. She hurriedly packed some clothes and toiletries for Akon and went straight to the hospital in a taxi.

At the reception, she asked the nurses for Akon's hospital ward. They directed her to ward 15 but told her she had to see the doctor first. When she got to the doctor's office, he asked her to sit.

"You are Mrs Lara Akete, am I right?" the doctor

asked, shuffling some medical reports.

"Yes, doctor. Is my husband okay?" So many things were racing through her head.

"Calm down, ma'am. Your husband has a high heart rate and an unusually high blood pressure. He is stable now, but we need to keep him here for further tests and scans."

Lara felt a little better. It was not cancer or some terrible disease. The doctor told her she could go, and she hurried to his hospital room. She was not shocked that Akon had collapsed at work. For more than a year, he had been working for sixty hours every week, combining two jobs.

Akon's face lit up as soon as he saw his wife. "I hope I survive this," said Akon. "I promise your life will never be the same again. I just need to survive this." He was a little breathless, and Lara told him to calm down.

She brought out the food she had packed for him – grilled fish and spinach – and sat in the corner while Akon nibbled. "I have little appetite," he announced. "Please, take the rest away." Lara assured him that he would be alright and mumbled a word of prayer. After a few hours, Lara left the hospital to pick up Ephraim from the childminder.

As Akon lay on the hospital bed, his mind kept wandering despite his fluctuating blood pressure. He reflected on his life. Since Ephraim's birth, he had tried to balance his love between his two kids. But within his heart, he had to struggle to accept Ephraim as his biological son. He was such a good pretender, and his wife was not aware of his theatrics. Akon found some of Ephraim's mannerisms irritating. Ephraim struggled to express himself with words, and he resorted to crying and pointing anytime he could not.

Akon admitted shamefully that he had started comparing Jabez and Ephraim, wondering if he had not made a mistake by asking his friend to produce the sperm. He hoped Ephraim would not inherit Kay's genes, and he hoped Ephraim would not be dull. He had started developing a soft spot for Jabez, ignoring Ephraim as much as he could. He knew Jabez would get the larger portion of his assets after death. However, more intense than his fear of marginalising Ephraim, or his wife finding out what had happened, was his fear that Kay might come back to claim his son and let everything out in the open. Akon had not forgotten what had happened during Ephraim's naming ceremony.

Even though Kay had moved far away, Akon could not help but reflect on the can of worms he had piled up for himself as he lay on the hospital bed. It was only a matter of time before everything blew up in his face. He was still being closely monitored because the possibility of a relapse, which could result in total incapacitation, or even death. He decided there was no running from the truth; he feared what might happen if he died without confessing to Lara. She might never forgive him even in death, and he feared what Kay might do to her if he left her unprepared. She deserved to know the truth, and it had to come from him.

Kay's continuous monetary requests had eaten into Akon's finances and wrecked him. Akon soon became indebted. He had made some bad business choices and consequently had to take on multiple jobs to settle his debts and care for his family. Kay's trip had cost Akon £8,000, which he had willingly paid because he wanted him as far away from his family as possible.

While lost in his thoughts, Lara came into the room. She smiled as she saw her husband had opened his eyes, looking better than the last time she had seen him.

"Hey, honey," she said.

"My darling, welcome."

"Thank you, my husband. How are you feeling today?" She placed her hands on his forehead and felt his chin and neck for temperature.

"I am much better now. The pains have subsided, especially the one in my chest."

"Thank God. That is good news, dear. The kids and I cannot wait to have you back home."

Akon turned his face away when she mentioned kids.

"I brought your lunch," Lara continued.

He looked at her and was flustered with guilt. He opened his mouth and said to her, "Lara, I want to discuss something with you."

Lara paused and looked at her husband. His countenance was not pleasant at that moment, which made her a bit tense.

"Right now? Okay, honey, I am willing to listen to you. What is it about? Did the doctors tell you anything while I was gone? Are you going to be alright?"

"I am fine, darling. I will be fine. It is not about any of that. Please, promise me you won't freak out and you will forgive me after this confession."

Many negative thoughts sprang in Lara's mind, but she dismissed them. *Had he cheated on her? Did he have any sort of ailment that he did not tell her about?*

"Go on, Akon. The love we have for each other should help us weather any storm," she said. "I think I can forgive you for anything."

She made her statement in the hope that whatever he had to say would not be impossible to forgive. Akon claimed to love her after all, and she knew he did.

"I did something dreadful, but I just want you to forgive me in advance, alright? Remember one night about four years ago when I had to travel out of the city and Kay stayed at our place for the night because he was somewhat stranded?"

Lara paused for a second and cast her mind back to the night in question. Akon had suddenly come up with the news of his trip and had packed up in haste. He barely packed any extra clothes. Everything about that night had seemed suspicious even to the point when Kay had come by to spend the night.

"What about the night, honey? Did something happen? I hope you didn't…"

Tears trickled down Akon's face upon realising the magnitude of what he had done to his wife. He thought of her reaction and how she would see him after what he had to say. "I lied to you, darling. I did not go for a business trip, and Kay was not stranded. I planned everything with Kay."

"You planned what with Kay? Now I am even more confused, dear. What did you plan with Kay?"

"I paid Kay to sleep with you so you could get pregnant. We wanted another child so badly. I am sorry, Lara. Please, forgive me. If for nothing else, consider my condition right now. This might be the only time I have to make things right with you."

Lara was horrified. She could neither speak nor move. She could not even look at her husband. It was like the air around her had become toxic, and she could barely breathe. Tears rolled down her cheeks.

"A-a-k-o-n-n! Ah! Aye mi! I am finished! You paid your friend to rape your wife, Akon? What kind of a man are you?"

"I'm sorry, my love. At least, give me the credit for this confession. I have lived with this weight ever since. Consider my health. Thank God I survived this. I just want to make amends, Lara." Akon choked as he spoke.

Lara became nervous and helped him with a cup of water. "Please, Akon, let us drop the topic. The most important thing is for you to get well. You look pale, and what you are saying makes no sense."

Akon further probed, "You are not saying anything, and your silence is making me feel uncomfortable. Please, say something, Lara."

Lara took a deep breath and shook her head. Looking at the ceiling, she said, "It is a pity."

"What is that?" Akon asked.

"Where do we go from here? It is a pity since nothing is wrong with me. I am fertile; you were the problem, Akon!" she snapped before adding, "Sorry, Akon. Please just get better."

He looked away in shame and tried all he could to avoid her stare. Just then, a nurse walked in with some equipment. As soon as she came in, Lara swiftly wiped the tears from her eyes with her handkerchief and turned around to face the nurse.

"I came to check his blood pressure," the nurse said.

"Go ahead, nurse," Lara replied. "I need to use the ladies. I'll be right back," she added, speaking to no one in particular.

Inside the ladies' room, Lara fell to the floor, sobbing as silently as she could. How could her own husband do this to her? It was as if she was reliving a scene from her past, but her husband was the villain in the story this time around. What was she to do now? What would people say if they ever found out? How would she be able to look Kay in the eyes after this? She felt hurt and devalued. She knew it would be impossible to forget what had happened, but she also knew she had to forgive her husband. She had also kept a secret from him all the years they had been married. And even though she considered what he had done a much bigger ill, the truth remained that she had also not been honest with him.

When she was eighteen years old, her grandmother had sent her to one of her mother's cousins who lived in Abeokuta. Lara was to look after their new-born babies for a few months because the Aunty had become seriously ill following the birth of the babies. Aunty Gbemisoke had five children before the twins, and all of them were girls, but Uncle Tolu wanted a male child. This caused a lot of friction between them.

Uncle Tolu would physically abuse her in the presence of others and call her a witch. He accused her of hiding the destiny of male children for her selfish purpose. Aunty Gbemi only attended primary school while her husband was a teacher.

Lara's grandmother could not raise enough money for her school fees. So, the family decided she should stay with her aunt in Abeokuta. She gained admission to Ogun State Polytechnic but could not afford hostel accommodation. Aunty Gbemi had fibroid, and she bled most of the time. She was like a woman with the issue of blood. Uncle Tolu was no longer sleeping in the same room with his wife.

Their house was an uncompleted and unpainted building with about seven rooms. Only five were completed. Lara had her own bedroom, and on one occasion, after Lara had put the babies to sleep, Uncle Tolu tiptoed upstairs to Lara's room.

"I am grateful that you agreed to come and help your aunt. Just let me know if you need anything. I would give it to you," he had said, stroking her shoulder.

"Thank you, sir."

"I also understand that you want to attend school in Abeokuta. I can make arrangements for that." Then, he touched her without her permission.

"Please, don't do this to me, sir," Lara pleaded. She was a virgin, and she did not even have a boyfriend at the time. Uncle Tolu told her to keep quiet. His eyes had become red.

"Say nothing. Just lie down. You are a beautiful lady. Let me love you for the night. Please, my love. Your aunt has been unwell since the past five months. I cannot touch the housemaid. I just wanted a fresh chicken like you."

"I can't do this," Lara said, and she burst into tears.

Uncle Tolu assured her and forced himself on her. He promised to make sure she enters the university. Lara ran out of the house before five in the morning. She went to the garage and boarded a vehicle to her grandmother's place in Oyo. She broke down and narrated her story.

A month later, she missed her period. Her grandmother did not allow her to abort the pregnancy. She kept her indoors, and when the baby was born, she was adopted into the motherless babies' home. After five years, one of Lara's aunts picked up the child and took her as her own. Lara had been a part of Ranti's life, supporting her education. She kept this secret from everyone who knew her, including her husband.

Lara wiped her eyes and washed her hands and face in the washroom before heading back to her husband's ward. The nurse had left the room long before she came in. Akon turned to face her and held out his hand. She drew closer to him and took his hand while staring into his eyes.

"I am sorry, my love. I regret what I did. I was a coward, and I did not consider how you would feel. I am ashamed of my selfishness. I am so sorry, Lara. Please, I hope you can forgive me."

She stared blankly at him for a while. She tried to hold back the tears that had formed in her eyes. The tears fell anyway, and she wiped them off with a single swipe across her face.

"It is fine, Akon. Even though what you did was cruel and unreasonable, I have decided to let it go so we can be happy."

"Thank you, Lara. Thank you so much."

"I have something to tell you too, Akon."

"Okay, go on, love. You can tell me anything."

Akon had reclined against the pillow that supported his head. He was scared that Lara would explode. It was soothing to see her handle the news with maturity. Little did Akon know it was his turn to receive a bombshell.

"How would you feel if I have a child outside this marriage?"

"W-h-a-a-a-t?"

Akon jerked up from the bed and unknowingly hit the alarm. A nurse rushed in immediately.

"Do you require anything, mister?"

Akon had not yet recovered from what he heard. It took him a while to realise the nurse was speaking to him.

"Sorry, what did you say?"

"I asked if you needed anything. You pressed the alarm."

Akon looked towards his right wrist and realised it had been on the alarm button all along. "Oh no, I'm sorry. That was a mistake." He withdrew his hand promptly.

"Okay, let me check your blood pressure again," the nurse said and hastened out of the ward to grab her equipment. Lara lifted her bag from where she had kept it and took the food closer to where Akon lay.

"Please, eat your food as soon as she is done. I will come back with your dinner in the evening. Let us talk when you are much better, okay?"

She kissed him lightly on his forehead and stepped out of the room. Before she left the hospital premises, she pleaded with the nurse to make sure Akon had his lunch.

31

For the remaining days Akon stayed in the hospital, he and Lara never spoke about that day's revelations. Neither did they act like there was a problem between them. Akon had convinced himself that Lara said what she said because she was hurt. He thought she wanted him to feel what she felt for a split moment. He understood he had hurt her and was willing to do anything to make it up to her.

When Akon was discharged, Lara took him home. He was well on his feet now. Jabez ran to embrace his father, and Ephraim giggled as he lifted him up. Ephraim was a cute little boy with grey eyes almost like Akon's. Jabez had taken after Akon in every aspect—his eyes and complexion. He was fairer than his father though. None of the boys got anything from their

Mother except for her robust cheeks.

The family settled down to dinner. Akon had missed this. After dinner, Lara cleared the table, and the couple went up to their room. Lara helped Akon with his medication and helped him recline on a seat. They had just finished watching a programme on the TV when Lara brought up the topic again. She was determined to tell her husband the truth, even if it meant he would send her out of their home. She had prepared for the worst.

Akon, on his part, could not help but wonder what could be going on in Lara's head. What if she had plans to leave him?

"I have something to say," Lara began, but Akon interrupted her before she could go any further.

"Before you say anything, my dear wife, I plead guilty. I have wronged you badly, and I take all the blame. Please, don't do anything rash."

"But I also wronged you, dear. I am guilty too."

"You've been a good and faithful wife to me. I am the one who is at fault here. I know what you said to me in the hospital was just out of frustration and to make me feel your pain."

Lara sighed.

"Do you remember Ranti?" she asked.

"Ranti?"

"Yes, Ranti, the young lady that stays with my uncle

and aunt."

"Oh, that girl who is always smiling. I almost forgot that was her name. She was about to leave secondary school when we got married, right?"

"Yes."

"She is a pleasant girl. I remember I challenged her for not attending our wedding."

"She is my daughter."

Akon was confused. He could not make sense of what Lara was saying at this moment. "What do you mean? That is not possible. You are her big aunt. That's what you are to her."

Lara went to the drawer and pulled out some documents—Ranti's birth certificate and some photos—which she handed over to Akon. "I had her while I was living with my aunt long before I met you. I was raped by my uncle, and she is the result of that assault. I was told not to tell anyone or admit that Ranti was my child."

Akon had the proof staring him; he could not believe Lara had lied to him all these years.

"I have made up my mind to raise and love Ephraim irrespective of what you and your friend did," Lara said.

"Oh no! Do not bring what happened with Kay into this. This is a different story. Getting Kay to sleep with you was bad, I know. But getting pregnant through your uncle? That is a bloody abomination, Lara! What are you saying right now?"

Lara stared at Akon in disbelief, her anger rising. She opened her mouth to say something, but no words came out. Extreme anger often left her dumb. She cleared her throat and tried again.

"Did I beg to be raped?" she began in a slow, mournful voice. Her fingers shook slightly. "Did I ask to be molested? Do you know how many days of pain I endured afterwards? Do you, Akon Akete, realise that my innocence was cruelly snatched from me in a dirty, cruel manner? Is it because I am a woman? Is it because a woman cannot not have a voice in our society?" She paused to take a breath, her anger rising to boiling point. She had had enough.

"Have you thought about the psychological abuse you have inflicted on me?" she continued. "Despite that, I am still covering up your deceit." She laughed bitterly. "Where on earth do you think you would be if you had done the same to a white woman – suddenly breaking the news to her that you had paid your friend to rape her? How dare you, Akon Akete? I cannot count the number of times you have cheated on me. You made the decision to come to England alone, took our savings, sold your shares, and left us high and dry for almost six years!

"I stuck with you through thick and thin. Yes, I did. Tell anyone this story, and they will never fault me. I might have come from a poor background, but I have dignity, and I earned it. I used my brains, not my body to earn my degree. But your family treated me like trash. They trampled on my pride, yet I respected every one of them. Several times your sisters and your mother would call me names, but you failed to stand up for me.

"You knew you had a low sperm count, yet you were silent while your family mocked and ridiculed me. Think about this; what if I was your daughter? What would you have done? Would you blame her for getting raped, pinned to the bed on a cold night?"

Lara turned on her heels and proceeded to leave the room. Akon was stunned. He had never seen Lara so enraged, yet with an underlying calm. Akon had always known she was a strong woman, but she avoided confrontations as much as possible. Akon summoned the courage to reach for Lara's hand.

"I am sorry, Lara. I just feel you should have told me before now."

"So, you still have the mouth to talk," Lara scoffed. "We'll settle everything in court, Mr Akete. I am done! If my husband cannot understand me, then there is no point. How can you ask me to defend a past that I could not control? I need my life back; I need to find my dignity and worth in the eyes of a man who once loved me."

"I did this for us, don't you understand? Were you not happy that you got pregnant? I did the best for us and now you are blaming me!"

After Akon's emotional outburst, Lara darted to the spare room, bolted the lock behind her and broke down into a sob. Akon rushed after her and banged door. "Lara, please open the door."

"I am done, Mr Akete. Please take care of your health. Call your side chicks to look after you. Please leave me alone and look after your health," Lara screamed back at him between sobs.

Determined to get his wife's audience, Akon kept on knocking.

"Mr Akete, please kindly leave the door alone. Do you want to attract the children and worse still the neighbours?" Lara asked in a raised voice.

"I am not going to leave until you open the door. I would rather die here," Akon said in a low remorseful voice as he kept on knocking.

Tears continued to roll down Lara's cheeks. This was not what she wanted. Recalling Akon's reaction to Ranti, Lara shed more tears.

Why did Akon not handle this with maturity? Lara shook

her head in disappointment. *Men! They are unpredictable!*

Lara wiped her face as she stood up from the chair. She pulled herself together and reached for the door. As soon as Akon heard the door open, he held her hands and went on his knees.

"I know you must regret that you agreed to marry me. I should have been more considerate," Akon said, with teary eyes. "You have always been a victim. Your uncle abused you. Just thinking about what that useless man did makes me sick to the stomach. I am sorry this happened to you, dear. I wish I could bring him back from the dead and make him pay with a slow, painful death. Too bad that he died over twenty-five years ago. I pray he rots and suffers in the hottest part of hell!

"I am sorry, dear," Akon continued. "I want to pour out my heart about Kay. Please, forgive me. I was desperate, and I did not want to bring shame to us. I did something that eventually brought shame upon us. I am sorry. That decision has spoilt everything for me, from my health to my finances. As for Ranti, I have already accepted her as my daughter. I will take care of her, and she is now my first child."

Hearing this made Lara teary. "Really? Are you sure?" she asked. "Akon, I am sorry for keeping this from you. I am sorry for shouting at you. I had bottled up so much over the years, especially how your family treated me." Her voice was barely audible as she held back the tears.

This was the perfect time for a hug.

Akon reached out to his wife and gave her a warm and reassuring hug. "Aya mi, I told you before and let me tell you again., this time, as an oath: I will stand by you. You have covered my shame, and very few women would do that."

Akon crowned this emotional moment by singing Tosin Martin's song, *"Olo mi, onitemi, ore mi, ololufe, oju kan o sa lada ni, lola Oluwa, ko sohun ti oya wa."* Akon added its translation, "Yes dear, you are my only love, and nothing shall separate us."

Lara let go of her anger and was able to reciprocate Akon's affection.

"It is important you see Ranti as soon as possible," Akon said. "You would have to travel to Nigeria. Take a week off work; go and visit your relatives. Let them know you have come to get your daughter. We cannot keep her away from the family forever, can we?"

Lara was surprised that Akon was the one pushing for her to see Ranti.

"I will buy a ticket so you can travel in the next two weeks. Ask for a compassionate leave at work," Akon stated. "I am on sick leave for the next four weeks, so this is the best time for you to travel to Nigeria. The children's schedule will not be disrupted. We also need

to inform Jabez and Ephraim that you are travelling,"
Akon continued as he brought out his laptop to book
the tickets with his credit card.

"You just need three to four days so I will book the
ticket for Wednesday and you will be back on Sunday. I
don't want you hanging around unnecessarily," Akon
said as he typed into the laptop.

"How about checking up on mama and your
siblings," Lara asked with a raised brow. "Walls have
ears. If they know I came around and did not visit
them, that is equal to another five years of fighting. You
know how your people are..." she explained further.

"Wow, you are such a good woman! After all they
have done to you? They never even picked up the
phone to say hello to you, and you still want to visit
them?" Akon looked surprised.

"I will do all for Christ's sake," Lara said, smiling
innocently.

"Please sort out the issue with Ranti first and if there
is more time, you can call on them," Akon responded
dismissively.

"I would also like to visit my friends," Lara added
excitedly.

"This is not a holiday, my dear." Akon had a stern
look on his face. "This is an urgent housekeeping visit.
Perhaps next year, if all things work out well, we can

visit Nigeria as a family," he said.

Lara nodded her agreement.

"Your wish is my command sir," she teased as they smiled at each other.

"Oh, my dear, you haven't taken your medicine," Lara said and dashed for a glass of water and Akon's medicine box. "You must be tired now. You need to rest so your blood pressure does not rise again."

"I'll be fine, my dear." Akon's warm smile was reassuring.

32

The seven-hour flight from England to Nigeria felt endless and at the same time, not long enough.

Lara decided not to hire a taxi to Ibadan. Inside the bus Lara boarded from Lagos to Ibadan, the same feelings and memories that had been troubling her on the plane returned with a vengeance. Her anxiety about what she was about to reveal to her daughter did not help matters. What if Ranti does not believe her story even if all the evidence stared her in the face?

She shook with the effort it took to expel them, but they returned more forcefully. And like a swimmer who had swallowed too much water, she let herself sink into the memories.

Lara put the baby in the cot, petting her until she settled into sleep. Then she peeked at the other baby and smiled when she saw she was sleeping soundly. The twins were so different, she thought. One was easy to please, but the other was difficult. Still, they were both sweet babies.

"Good girl," she whispered. "Don't worry. Aunty Lara is coming back, okay? Let me check on your sisters quickly." She moved out of the room, turning off the light but leaving the door slightly open so that rays from the hallway could come in.

The other five girls slept in two different rooms. She checked on each of them, ensuring they were all asleep and would not disturb their sick mother. Then she went back to check on the babies before going to her own room.

After taking care of seven children, she was usually tired at the end of the day. Her room was messy and dirty, and she did not want to call the housemaid to help her clean. The poor girl was working too hard anyway, cleaning the seven-bedroom duplex, cooking, and doing laundry for everyone as well.

Lara quickly arranged and tidied up her room. Then she lay down on the bed. Feeling dirty, she went to take her bath. She came back into her room and closed the door. She groaned as she remembered she had not taken the clothes she would wear to sleep. So, she moved to the bag where she kept her clothes. As she searched for something light to put on, the towel kept getting in her way. Frustrated, she let it fall and continued her search.

Finally, she yanked out a tank top, raising a fist in the air in victory. Then, she felt the touch on her backside. Whirling around, she held the tank top against her chest, as if it could cover her, and backed away, tripping over her bag in the process. She fell, her legs splayed. "Uncle Tolu! Uncle Tolu, what are you doing here?" He did not answer, and when she saw the direction of his gaze, she closed her legs, placing one of her hands over herself.

"Lara, my darling," he started, kneeling before her with a small smile. "You know, your aunt has been sick for a while. Even before she gave birth, the doctor said I could not do anything with her because the pregnancy would be at risk. But I am a man, and I have needs."

Her gasp was sharp. "No! Uncle Tolu, you know this is an abomination. We can't!"

"You know that school in Abeokuta that you want to attend? I will work it out for you and pay your school fees."

"No. Please, please, Uncle. Please don't." She stopped, shocked as he yanked the tank top away from her chest. His eyes were wide with malevolence and greed as he took her in. She opened her mouth to scream, but before she could, he covered it with his big palm.

"If you shout, I will kill you." As if he sensed she would disobey him, he stuffed the tank top in her mouth and tore her legs apart. She tried to fight him off with kicks and punches, but he was a strong man, and he soon overpowered her.

Lara was jolted from her reverie when the baby of the woman sitting beside her started screaming uncontrollably. The other passengers grumbled, but she was thankful. She wiped her face with her tearstained handkerchief, feeling lucky because the passenger beside her was too preoccupied to notice someone crying beside her.

Her mind went back to the memories. It had been her grandmother's idea to assist her sick aunt with the children. Aunt Gbemi already had a housemaid, but the work was too much for her. So, seventeen-year-old Lara, who had just graduated from secondary school, would be a great help. Her grandmother was poor. She felt that Lara's aunt would help her achieve her dream of getting into the Ogun State Polytechnic, while Lara helped with the children. Everything changed that night.

After Uncle Tolu left, she sat with her back against the door, crying and shaking in fear that he would return to inflict more pain on her. As soon as it was dawn, she packed her bags, thanking God she had not spent the little sum her grandmother had given her. She did not even look back as she boarded a bus that would take her to Oyo.

When she told the story to her grandmother, she cried. Her grandmother called a family meeting. Her uncles agreed that one of them would visit Uncle Tolu at the end of the month. However, a few days before the uncle would go, they received the news that aunt Gbemi was dead. Faced with the problem of who would care for the seven children her aunt left behind, Lara's case faded into the background and was forgotten.

Then she missed her period. It was the last straw for her at that time. She did not want the baby. She went to her grandmother to get money for an abortion. The old woman sat her down and dissuaded her from terminating the pregnancy. Even though the baby had come out of painful circumstances, it did not deserve to die. Understanding the shame that she would endure if her neighbours and former classmates heard she was pregnant, coupled with the embarrassment to their family's reputation, Lara's grandmother asked Lara to live with her. This would enable her to have the baby in the house far from those who knew her.

As soon as the baby was born, Lara's grandmother took the child to an orphanage and Lara moved to Lagos. When the girl was five, another of Lara's relatives took her from the orphanage and cared for her with her husband.

It took a while before Lara managed to go back and see the baby, although she had been secretly sending money for her upkeep. She could still remember the first sight of her nine-year-old daughter. She was pretty and outgoing. Despite everything, she fell in love with the child who called her Aunt Lara. She thought her mother was dead.

Last week, the aunt who had taken Ranti in had sent Lara a message, calling Ranti her daughter and telling her she had just graduated from the University of Lagos. She received updates like that often, and usually deleted them from her phone immediately after she replied them.

Now that Akon knew the whole story and encouraged her to tell Ranti the truth, even booking her flight to Nigeria, here she was, ready for whatever could happen. She hoped for the best.

* * *

Ranti stared at the grave faces around her, wondering what was wrong. The last time they looked this sober was when one of the senior aunts had died, and no one in the family had died recently, so what was the matter? She turned when the door opened, and Aunt Lara came into the room.

"Aunty mi," she screamed, rushing over to hug Lara. "I thought you were in London."

"Ranti, please sit down," one of her oldest uncles said and waited until Lara and Ranti sat beside each other before he continued. He asked for peace and understanding during the meeting. Then, another of her older aunts prayed.

Finally, the aunt who raised Ranti as her own child took the floor and spoke directly to Ranti, praising her obedience, kindness, and submissive nature right from a young age. Her aunty commended her for not yielding to immorality. She settled for the modest life in which she was brought up. Her aunty also praised her for not being a difficult child. She was dedicated to her studies and was now a university graduate. She noted that they were growing old, and some issues needed to be discussed before it was too late.

"Ranti," she continued, "I know you have been wondering about the purpose of this meeting. I am sorry we have not told you before now. Do you remember that when you were born, you were taken to an orphanage? We reclaimed you when you were five."

Ranti nodded. She had been happy to learn she would finally have a family. How nice of her aunt and uncle to have taken care of all her needs. "Yes, mummy, I remember."

"Whenever you talked about your mother, you thought she was dead, and we all agreed it was probably the case. Ranti, please forgive me for what I am about to tell you," her aunt continued with tears in her eyes.

Ranti became afraid for some reason.

"Your mother is not dead, Ranti."

"What?" Ranti exclaimed, forgetting it was not customary to interrupt elders while they talked. "Do you know my mother?"

"Yes, Ranti. For many reasons, we did not want to tell you. But we have decided you are old enough to know." Her aunt paused to take a deep breath. "Your mother is here in this room."

"I don't understand," Ranti said, looking from her aunt to her uncle, the people who had raised her. "You mean you know my mother, and you never told me?" Then her aunt's last sentence hit her, and she froze. "My mother is here?"

She looked at all the faces until her gaze rested on Lara, who had been quiet all the while. Tears were running down her face, and she was clutching an envelope in her hand. Ranti jumped up from where she was sitting beside Lara and turned to her aunt, the woman who raised her, the only mother she knew. "You are telling me Aunty Lara is my mother?" They both nodded.

Lara looked at her and held out the envelope with trembling hands. In it was a picture of Lara with Ranti when she was a baby. Her birth certificate was also in the envelope.

"So, you are telling me that all the nights I cried myself to sleep because my classmates made fun of me were for nothing? You are my mother, and you threw me away in an orphanage?"

She started to walk out of the room, tears running down her face. But her aunt's next words halted her steps. "Ranti, your mother loves you. In her own special way, she took care of you from when you were a baby. If not for her, we wouldn't have been able to provide for you. We only had custody, but everything you had as a child was given to you by Lara. She is your mother, and it was not easy for her. She could not take care of you because of the circumstances of your birth. Please, forgive her."

Ranti leaned against her aunt, weeping. Finally, Lara spoke. "Oluwarantimi, my child, I am sorry. I never meant to lie to you or hurt you this way. Please find it in your heart to forgive me."

Ranti felt so much pain, although her aunt treated her well, she could clearly not call her mum. Ranti had been told she was an orphan, and while growing up as one, she experienced the stigma of not having a dad or mum. Why was her case different? What changed, and why does her mother want her back suddenly? Was it because she was a girl? Or did her husband refuse to accept her. These questions plagued her mind. She looked at Lara who was crying softly. Ranti remembered that Lara always bought her gifts whenever she visited. Lara used to hug her and would often check up on her when she was in school, calling her every week.

Maybe it was true, Ranti decided. Maybe her mother did love her and had been unable to care for her. Lara would have been young when she was born. She vowed to find out the full story later. Sighing, she left her aunt's embrace and stood in front of Lara.

"It is okay, *maami*," she said. Lara smiled through her tears, pulling Ranti closer for a hug.

Ranti checked her watch. *My mother...* It was somewhat strange to think of Lara as her mother, but she was getting used to it.

* * *

The next day, Ranti met Lara at a hotel. They were supposed to meet at 4.00 p.m., but out of anxiety, Ranti left home too early and got to the hotel before 3.00 p.m.

After hanging around for a while, playing games on her phone and reading a novel, the time was 3.55 p.m. She left the hotel lobby and entered one of the elevators, which took her to her mother's floor. She walked to the door and knocked, feeling a bit nervous but happy.

"Ranti, my dear," Lara exclaimed as she opened the door. "Come in, come in." She stepped aside, and then closed the door as soon as Ranti entered. "How are you?"

"Fine, ma– mummy." Lara beamed when Ranti addressed her as her mother. She went to the small fridge to bring out drinks and cups after inviting Ranti to sit.

They talked about different things. They slowly moved from being awkward around each other to easily conversing and laughing. Then Lara brought up the real reason she asked Ranti to meet her. "Ranti, I know you completed your undergraduate degree with a beautiful result. Have you thought about getting a master's degree?"

"Yes, mummy. I applied to a university in Istanbul, but I was not accepted. Besides, without a good scholarship, I wouldn't have been able to study there. I decided it was better to do it here in Nigeria. At least it would be cheaper and easier."

Lara nodded, deep in thought. Finally, she said, "What about—have you considered coming with me? I mean to the UK." At Ranti's stunned expression, she backtracked. "No, no, if you do not want to come, it's okay. I just thought—I have saved some money, and if you can get a partial scholarship or some loan, it would be easy to pay for the degree. And you are a brilliant child. So, you can get into a good school. But if you don't want to…"

Ranti embraced Lara, cutting off her ramblings. "Oh, mummy, I am grateful." Then she moved back, a bit shy and worried. "But what about, you know, getting a visa and other things? Also, Uncle Akon and the children might not like it if they find out."

Lara smiled, stroking her beautiful daughter's face. "First of all, it was my husband who encouraged me to come and talk to you." That surprised Ranti. "Secondly, I started the application process for you to get a student visa to the UK. I am sorry if I was too forward," she added anxiously, "but I really want you to come. I have some papers for you to sign with me."

"Oh, thank you ma. God bless you," Ranti said, hugging her mother again.

"I'll be leaving the country tomorrow," Lara said when Ranti was about to go. Her daughter's expression turned sad, but she hugged her. "Don't worry, if all goes well, you'll be joining me in a month's time."

Ranti nodded and hugged Lara again before she left.

33

Akon was waiting for Lara at the arrival terminal of Heathrow airport. He could not wait to hear how her journey went, especially the meeting with her family and Ranti. As they drove home, Lara told Akon everything. She had submitted Ranti's student visa application, and once it is approved, she would send for her immediately. She told them Ranti was her daughter, and that she had bought the ticket. The staff at the enforcement office seemed friendly. Since Ranti would be arriving in the country on her birthday, Lara decided to have a party to celebrate both occasions.

* * *

When Lara went to pick Ranti from the airport a month later, her daughter's wide-eyed expression reminded her of when she and Jabez first came to the UK. They had become used to the place. So, seeing someone else react that way was amusing. She chuckled, promising to take Ranti sightseeing. When Ranti and Lara came into the house, it was late in the evening, and the lights were off. Ranti was puzzled because, according to all the stories she had heard, western countries had light every time. She was about to ask Lara when the lights came on, and she was blinded for a second.

"Happy birthday to you! Happy birthday to you! Happy birthday to dear Ranti. Happy birthday to you!"

Shocked, she stared at Akon, Jabez, and Ephraim for a second. Then Lara pulled her into the kitchen, and she saw the chocolate cake on the table.

"We wanted to do something special to celebrate with you," Akon said, pulling her into a brief, casual hug.

The boys were talking a mile a minute, first welcoming her than asking her all sorts of questions about Nigeria. Lara cut the cake and served it with drinks. Ranti was overwhelmed at the warm welcome. She had been afraid they would treat her like an imposter, but everyone made her feel like she belonged.

Finally, Lara spoke up. "Ephraim, Jabez, go watch the TV. Daddy and I need to show your sister something." She froze, surprised that Lara called her their sister. Lara smiled. "We've explained to them, and they are fine. Come with us."

She followed them up the stairs as they took her to a room that had been tastefully furnished and decorated. Lara nodded at Akon to take the lead this time.

"Ranti, Lara and I are sorry about everything you went through as a child. I know you are an adult now, but we want you to stay with us for as long as you want. Your mother loves you very much, and I am sure we will become a real family as we get to know each other. This is your room. We will continue to support and stand by you, and you would never have to be alone ever again."

For a moment, Ranti could not speak. She could only sob. Then she threw herself into Lara's arms. "Oh, thank you! I never thought I would ever have a real family. I thought I would be like a stranger."

"You are not a stranger, my darling. You are part of our family now," Lara replied, though her voice was choked up.

"I am so happy. This is the best birthday I have ever had. Thank you so much."

*   *   *

Ranti woke up the next morning, feeling excited. Lara had promised to show her the sights, and she could hardly wait. The house was somewhat quiet, although she could hear the faint sound of clangs and bangs coming from the kitchen. She smiled as she thought about the whole birthday surprise of the previous night. She climbed out of bed and threw on the robe hanging on the back of the chair.

"Good morning ma– mummy," Ranti said with a smile as she entered the kitchen. Lara was preparing something that smelled heavenly, and for a second, Ranti paused to breathe in the scent.

Smiling with pleasure at the greeting, Lara replied, "Good morning, darling. Hope you slept well."

"Yes, I did. I have never slept better. Why didn't you wake me up? I could have helped." Ranti pouted a bit, feeling uncomfortable with Lara being up before her.

"Sweetheart, you needed to rest after that long flight. I couldn't have woken you up. Anyway, aren't you hungry?"

Ranti shook her head and moved towards the sink to wash the few pans and pots that Lara had used. They fell into an easy conversation, and Ranti found herself recounting some of her experiences as an undergraduate.

"I just thank God, maami," she continued, reverting to her native tongue as she remembered some of those experiences with emotion. "I don't know how I would have graduated, but for the grace of God. It started in year three. You know how many girls wear skimpy outfits to school. Anyway, I did not want to draw attention to myself. So, I always wore conservative clothes.

"I thought I was safe because of that. Also, I never went to beg for grades from lecturers. I was popular in the library because I spent most of my time there. But reasons unknown to me, one of my results was not released. Our class governor told me the lecturer wanted to see me.

"Maami, you should have seen me that day, shivering as if I were about to die. When I told my friend, she said I should not worry. Everyone knew Mr Ikofi was a flirt, but it never went beyond the classroom. He was even a senior pastor in one church. Anyway, I walked into the office and greeted him. He smiled at me, calling me dear and darling as if I were his wife or something. Then I asked what he wanted, and he said he wanted me to be his girlfriend.

"I was shocked. I just sat there, staring at him. I recovered from my initial shock when he moved closer and touched my shoulder."

Ranti laughed as she remembered how scared she had been. "I knelt down to beg him. I told him my life story. I told him I was an orphan. It was like a miracle because from what I heard, these men are persistent and can even become terrible when you refuse them. But God helped me. He released my result the next day."

"Wow, that must have been terrible," Lara said, sighing. The memories of what her uncle did forced themselves into her mind, but she pushed them away. She thanked God that her daughter did not experience a similar thing.

"That was nothing. At least that time, it was just a result. In the first semester of my final year, I had a worse experience." She could remember it like it happened yesterday.

Ranti was seated at one of the tables in the restaurant, waiting for her next class and engrossed in the textbook she was reading. When she heard someone clearing their throat, she glanced up to see a guy standing beside her.

"Hi, I'm sorry. Can I join you? The other tables are occupied."

"Of course," Ranti replied with a smile. He looked familiar, and he stared at her with recognition. She tried to remember where she had seen him before. When she asked, he laughed and said, "Digitalli."

She was puzzled. She worked in Digitalli, a store that sold electronic gadgets. She had never seen him during the employees' meeting. "You don't work there."

"No, but I go there often. I just like computers and these electronic gadgets. I would have gotten a job there; but then, I would have been working instead of enjoying that electronic goodness. I am sure I single-handedly keep the store in business though." He said it with a wink, and Ranti laughed.

"Thanks for that. Please, keep buying." They both laughed and Ranti politely asked, "What is your name?"

"Oh, I forgot we are not as popular as Ranti." Ranti rolled her eyes, and he smirked. Then, he held out his hand and said, "Hi, I'm Alex."

"Hi, Alex. Well, you already know I'm Ranti." She paused, then asked, "What would you like to order?"

A waiter appeared beside them. "You hijacked my question, Ranti." He said it with a mock glare but smiled to show he was teasing. The waiter turned to Alex and asked what he would like to order.

"I'll have a fruit cocktail, thanks."

The waiter nodded and said, "You must be a pretty lucky guy to be on a date with Ranti. I'd give my best shirt to be where you are right now."

"Of course, I am a lucky guy," Alex grinned.

As soon as the waiter moved away, Ranti frowned at

Alex. "We only just met. Who told you we are on a date? This was just a chance meeting. Don't read any meaning into this."

"Fine, fine," Alex said, holding up his hands in surrender. "But don't rule out the possibility of us dating. One of these days…"

"Don't hold your breath," she said.

"So how are the campus and the project work going?"

Ranti froze. He could have guessed she was a student because of the textbook, but how did he know about her project? Recalling stories of girls who had been stalked by dangerous guys, she felt a shiver run through her. "How did you know about my project?"

"Aaah, I have a couple of friends in your class. You may not know them though. I'm sure you must have a million classmates."

That reply was too smooth for her to trust. Ranti decided to probe deeper. "And you have nothing else to talk about with your friends except me?"

"Actually, it was through Aku. You know my friend Aku that works in Digitalli with you, right?" Ranti nodded. "Well, I saw you once when I came to say hi to him, and I liked you. So, I asked about you and discovered you were in the final year."

Still feeling uneasy, Ranti nodded, putting her book

in her bag. "I have to get going. I have something to do."

"Okay," Alex said softly. "Can I get your number?"

"I'm sorry. I don't give out my number when I first meet someone." Besides, she was not sure about him yet. He might be a bad person, and until she confirmed from Aku, she would be cautious. Better safe than sorry.

"Well, you can have mine," he replied, holding out his card. She took it and saved the number on her phone.

*   *   *

After Ranti had narrated how she met Alex, she sighed and did not say a word for a long time. "So, what happened?" Lara prompted.

"Hmmm, maami, two days later, I spoke to Aku. He told me Alex was dead."

"What?" Lara screamed.

"Yes, he had been killed by cultists. It was after he died that his secrets came out. From what Aku told me, he had been working with a cult for a long time. He used to stalk girls and kidnap them so the cult could use them for rituals. I was to be his next victim. He recorded everything in a book. He had been *shadowing* me for days, following me everywhere, using his friends' social media profiles to check my posts. He knew something about me that I never even told many people. If he had not died, he might have gotten to me. In fact, when I found out, I did thanksgiving in church."

"He recorded everything?"

"Yes, his diary was discovered by those who packed up his things to send to his parents. They told Aku who informed me. It was a horrible period for me. I don't even know how I managed to pass my exams that semester."

"Thank God for sparing you o!"

"Yes o. It is one of the reasons I do not talk to strangers. Otherwise, once I get to know people, I am outgoing. That is why I studied something related to media arts and dancing in school."

Lara shook her head. She was not the only person with bad memories from the past. She was happy that Ranti felt close enough to her to share her experiences. "It is good to do what you love. It makes you happy. I'm glad you overcame those challenges." They smiled at each other. "Why don't you eat and dress up so we can go sightseeing?"

* * *

Years passed, and Akon got a more stable job with greater pay, which even included paid annual leave.

Things looked great for the family. Lara worked part-time with a law firm for two years before deciding to quit the job and stay at home with the boys, at least until Ephraim was about five years old. The job was strenuous and did not give her time for anything else. Also, Ephraim required more attention. When he was two years old, Lara noticed something about him. He had difficulties with his speech. He always mumbled his vowels together. She and Akon took him to a speech therapist who diagnosed him with mild *Einstein Syndrome*. Ephraim would need speech therapy to speak better. Lara was frustrated and angry, and she took it out on Akon when they got home.

"This is entirely your fault!" she poked him in the chest.

"I don't understand. How is it my fault?"

"Oh, now you ask me? I do not have this ailment in my genes, and I am almost certain you do not too! If only you had been man enough to get me pregnant yourself, we would not be here right now!"

"Oh, really? Just the same way you deceived me into this marriage. This marriage of deception! I could have divorced you!"

"Oh, really? What is stopping you then? Let us settle this in court! I was raped, and you, my husband, engineered it! What kind of a man are you?"

Akon became silent again. No matter how he chose to see things, what he did to Lara was a grievous error.

"Please, Lara, I thought we were over this already. I am sorry I lost my temper."

He watched as Lara fell to the floor and cried her eyes out. He sat beside her, kissed, and caressed her. Ephraim came in at that moment needing help with the TV. Akon lifted him up and went to assist him.

By the time Ephraim was ready to begin school at age five, he had gotten much better with his speech. He already had a wealth of knowledge at his disposal. However, in the first two terms, he was placed in a special needs class.

Lara's decision to stay back home was facilitated by the experiences and challenges of motherhood with Ephraim. This triggered her interest in children's issues. Lara knew what she needed to do. She knew it was time to consider another career path. So, Lara went to study childhood studies. She completed the degree and changed her career.

*   *   *

Akon loved spending time at the gym. Expending his physical energy surprisingly relaxed him. Whenever Akon was done with his workout and weightlifting routine, he would say goodbye to the gym instructor and enter the shower cabin. This time, Akon stood under the hot water and smiled, while thinking about his new role and the challenges ahead. He knew he was up to the task.

For ten years, Akon had dreamt of being a successful man. Finally, his family would earn British citizenship. Akon had built enough skills to start his personal project. The new job Akon had started could open fresh pathways for his career. If his boss liked him, he would have the chance of career development.

As Akon walked out of the shower, his phone vibrated. He had missed a couple of calls from his younger sister, Fola.

"Hello, brother!" Instead of hearing Fola's accusatory voice, Akon instantly felt that her tone was sad and melancholy.

"Hey," Akon answered as his heart raced.

There was a silence for a couple of seconds.

"Fola, hope all is well."

"Broda mi, ha! Erin wo! Mama is dead!"

Akon's heart dropped as he closed his eyes. He knew this would happen sometime soon. His mother had been ill for a long time now. However, no matter how many times you tell yourself that parents would die before their children, you are never ready to lose the person who raised you with all their heart and soul.

Akon stood up and left the gym without looking back. He needed fresh air to clean his mixed-up mind, but as soon as he stepped out of the gym, everything changed. Instead of mourning, Akon was faced with a dilemma. He would not be able to travel to Nigeria for the funeral because of his new job. He knew he would get into a massive argument with his siblings and relatives because of this.

As he drove back to his London home, a question wreathed his mind, *What about my new job?* When he arrived home, Lara was sitting in the dark, drinking tea.

"Hey!" Lara stood up to greet her husband, but as she walked closer to him, she realised he did not look himself. "What's wrong, honey?"

"Mama is dead," Akon said without looking at her.

Lara gasped and covered her mouth with her palm.

"I will be alright," he said.

However, Lara knew Akon was not okay. He only said these words not to make her nervous. As his wife of twenty-one years, Lara knew when melancholy crept into her husband's body.

Akon took a seat at the table and opened the laptop. "I need to call the family on Skype. I need to tell them I will not be able to travel home for the burial."

Lara tapped him on the shoulder and left him in the living room. Akon sat, waiting for the Skype call to connect. Finally, Fola answered.

"Hello," Fola said with a shaky voice.

"Hey," Akon responded. "Sorry I hung up on you this morning. I wanted to rush home so I could talk freely."

For a couple of seconds, neither of them said a word. Fola sighed from time to time.

"Look," Akon said, as he finally gained courage. "I know we need to plan fast for the burial, but I would not be able to attend."

Fola did not seem surprised. She scoffed and answered, "I knew it. You became a real robot. You only do whatever your wife says!"

"Lara has nothing to do with this. I just got a job at a new company. I have not even been there a week and cannot ask for days off. My boss is hard on us, and if I miss even one hour of work, I will lose it. I cannot leave it now. I am sorry," Akon said.

"You know, the whole family will fight you because of this. You are losing the family who stood by you. All because of that woman who bosses you around!" Fola said angrily. As she was talking, Bose came on Skype.

Fola ambled in her seat, phone in hand, "What? You are not coming? But…" She was interrupted by shrill gales of mocking laughter from her younger sister, Bose. Fola's body stiffened as Bose lunged for the phone.

"I am sure your useless wife is the one stopping you from coming to your own mother's burial. Such insolence! Well, you have always been irresponsible, so there is no surprise there. That was what happened two years ago when I asked for my son's school fees."

"Abosede!" Fola's burning eyes stared.

"I'm telling the truth, and you know it. He is not the brother we remember. His wife has brainwashed him."

"Enough! Don't you dare," Akon screamed from the other side of the phone. The pattering of rain on the windowpane was the only sound he wanted to pay attention to until his wife Lara was insulted.

"Whatever. Just send us the money, useless big brother," Bose said with a devilish smirk. She slammed the phone on the table and dashed out of the house, her son on her heels.

"I'm sorry," Fola said into the phone, staring at Bose as she left.

Bose lived on the cutting edge of style. At twenty-four, she did not complete her polytechnic education and had manipulated her mother, making her lose a huge sum of money in her shop. Akon blew out air in defeat as the call ended, running his hands through his thick hair.

Jostling Mama's burial with this is almost impossible, he thought. As soon as he let himself into the house, his wife knew something was terribly wrong. In one sweeping gesture, she held his hands in hers. His eyes shone with fresh tears when he shook his head and said, "My mum is gone, Lara. And she is never coming back. She is dead. Oh God, she is dead."

At five feet, she felt like a mouse beside him. She led him to his favourite sofa and allowed him to sob.

"Mama prayed for me to succeed. She paved the way for me through prayers and hard work. And now, she is not here to enjoy it. It worked, Mum. It all worked out," he whispered.

"I'm really sorry, honey," Lara said in a low but soothing voice, her small hands rubbing his back.

Sweat and hot torrents of tears poured out from him all at once. Time stood by, watching faithfully. "I have to travel to Nigeria. I told my sisters it was impossible because of this new job."

"Baby, whatever it takes, you have to be there. I do not want them to think I made you stay back. They are in pain. So, they can think anything."

"But the job?" Akon asked.

Akon studied his wife, every inch of her petite body absorbed in thoughts. He loved how her forehead creased with worry lines at the slightest problem. She was his rock now and forever. Her sing-song accent cut through his mind, and he heard her say, "I've got an idea."

His raised eyebrow was an indication that he was listening. "How about you report to your job?"

"But—"

"Akon, I'm not done. Listen to me."

"Yes, ma'am."

So, with a smirk, he watched her carefully put the plan together. "Call your siblings and tell them you are coming home in three months' time. No plans must be made without you. As the eldest, you make plans and send it to them. Immediately you resume work, ask for compassionate leave, but first ask your sister to obtain the death certificate. Show this to your boss and negotiate the number of days. Of course, you would take care of the expenses as your mother remains in the morgue. I'm sure no one is cruel enough to deny you of saying your final goodbye to your mother," Lara said in one breath.

"Wow! That is one heck of a plan. Thank you. You are so smart."

"Oh, please! Let us not speculate about the obvious," Lara said, a smile tugged at the corner of her mouth.

34

Akon was giddy with excitement as he flagged down a taxi at the international airport in Nigeria. Settled in the backseat, he allowed his mind to race. Lara's suggestion had worked, and his boss had granted him compassionate leave.

How long has it been since he left Nigeria? His excitement congealed into nervousness as the taxi roared to a screeching stop in front of the family house in Ikorodu.

Akon fiddled through the contents of his bag and paid the driver. As expected, his relatives welcomed him warmly. His sisters, however, were not pleased to see him. As time flew by, arguments broke out among his siblings and their father's relatives who claimed their mother had nothing. Of course, that was far from the truth. Mama Akete was an enterprising trader and earned her own money. She was a firm believer in the dreams of many.

His father's house was more like a museum of disappointment and fury. So, he linked up with friends after he came home. There were traditional rites that he did not want to be involved with. He stayed at a hotel, many thoughts rummaging through his head. It seemed as if he had never lived in Nigeria or grew up there. The behaviour of the people was strange to him. There was no respect for the dead.

As the hazy sunlight tinged the family house, the noise from well-wishers increased. By noon, Akon and the family lawyer arrived. Akon's trust for his relatives depreciated every second, but he maintained a firm demeanour.

"Mama Akete made no will, but Chief Akete's will was yet to be disbursed due to family friction among the three wives he left behind when he died fifteen years ago," the Lawyer said, his red-rimmed glasses on his large nose.

On the day of the burial, friends, well-wishers, and family members filled the family compound. After laying her remains in the ground, the reception kicked in fully. It was a huge ceremony because mama Akete was loved and appreciated by many. Akon sat among friends as love bathed the surrounding. Staying over with friends after the burial ceremony was a steep price to pay for not reaching out to them all these years.

A few days after the burial, Akon was at the airport, his friend, Seyibo beside him. His heart swelled up with gratitude as he hugged him one last time. Stepping into the Virgin Atlantic, he prayed silently, "Please God, journey mercies."

During the flight, he made small conversations with the man beside him. He did not know why, but the man looked familiar. As he chewed on the fried chicken, he laughed at the jokes the man was trying to make. Then it hit him!

"Mr Bradley?"

As the man looked closer, his eyes widened in surprise.

"Akon?"

Bradley Leo was one of the CASS summer school directors he attended a couple of years back.

"Oh, how do you do?" he said in his Liverpudlian accent.

"I'm good, sir. Thank you." Akon made a mental note to give Brad his business card. "It's been what, twenty years?"

"I believe so. Oh, how time flies!"

Unknown to both men, they tossed out honorifics and talked about everything and anything. Brad Leo's

"C'mon, mum! Why don't you drop me at Magan's first after church? There will be food at theirs."

"I will drop you after lunch," Lara replied firmly.

"Oh, mum!"

"Enough is enough! Family comes first, my dear."

Without saying anything, Jabez returned to his room and began the countdown till Sunday.

Akon eventually persuaded Lara. They would drop Jabez at Magan's place after church. When they arrived at the address, Magan's mum greeted them with a smile.

"Welcome, ma'am! Thank you for bringing Jabez over," she said.

"Not a problem at all," replied Lara. "I am sure the boys will have fun."

"Let me show you where the boys will be sleeping," Magan's mum said, ushering Lara into the house. She noticed her empty hands. "Oh, did you forget his backpack? It is no problem. We have spare pyjamas and a sleeping bag."

"Pyjamas?" Lara asked.

"Yes, it's a sleepover. Didn't you know?"

"Silly me. I forgot," Lara replied, pretending to have forgotten. She was fuming but could not reveal her displeasure. Her son omitted this information on purpose to embarrass her and make it seem like it was unplanned. She could not say no to this woman otherwise she would think that Jabez and her were not communicating.

"Jabez? Can you come over for a second?" she called. "I think we left something in the car."

Left alone with him, she grabbed his arm. "Listen carefully; I will not say this twice. I see what you did here, and it was dishonest. How dare you lie to me and embarrass me in front of another parent? You should have never hidden this from me. I did not want you to come in the first place. You will stay here tonight, and I will pick you up tomorrow. When you get back home, you would be grounded. You're lucky that I'm not making a scene here, do you understand?"

"Yes, mum. I am sorry. Can I go?" he said weakly.

"Your father will hear about this. We are not done. Hope you're happy with it."

Although his mother was visibly upset, seeing her drive off was a relief. Jabez finally had a moment to himself to be young and free. He could not wait to be with his friends, to listen to music, dance, and chat away. Hours flew by before he knew it, and he was standing in the living room with Ben and Magan sipping soft drinks. Dinner was delicious. The three boys gossiped about other classmates.

"Do you know Zahra? The girl that calls herself ND, Nile daughter? Her big sister is throwing a party next week. Her parents are out of town, and she has the house to herself. Are you coming?" Ben asked him.

"I do not know. It was hard enough to convince my mum to let me stay here. I had to lie and say it was just for a couple of hours. If it were not for your mum, I would not be here," Jabez asked.

"What's up with your parents? They seem strict. Aren't they, Ben?" asked Magan.

"Yeah, they are calling you all the time. You can't even come out with us to the movies after 7 o'clock in the evening," agreed Ben.

"It's the culture. Nigerian parents are so strict compared to yours. I feel trapped. I cannot do anything. And it is not like home is so much better," sighed Jabez.

"What do you mean?"

"My mum never has time for me. If she is not studying for her online courses, she is either working or taking care of my brother. We do not talk, and when we do, she is always screaming at me. I cannot tell her anything about my passions or interests. She disagrees with everything."

"What about your dad?" Ben asked.

"He's not home much either. He works extra hours

to support the family, I understand. But I cannot remember the last time we had a good chat. When he comes home from work, he's always exhausted. That man can take a kip anywhere and call it a day."

"That's such a shame. Have you tried telling them?"

"It's impossible. All our discussions end up in arguments. My mum calls me names or yells without reason even if I explain things to her. She was not always like that. I spent my early childhood in Nigeria, and it was blissful. Something shifted as soon as my brother was born."

"My parents never scream at me to be honest," Magan said. "They are Somalians, but they grew up here. They understand British culture and find it easy to integrate while keeping their culture."

"Neither do mine. They get disappointed though, especially when it comes to school. Other than that, they're pretty cool," added Ben.

"I wish I had your parents," said Jabez.

"C'mon, it's not that bad," reassured Ben.

"It really is. I can't wait to be free, to have my own place, my liberty, and the power to decide what I want to do and when."

"You don't want to do something stupid like run away from home, do you?" asked Magan.

"Absolutely not, where would I even go? I just want a little bit of attention. My brother gets everything, and they do not even care about me. They want me to clean the house, shop, go to school, and never complain. Anything else, they do not care about. It would be nice if they listened to me. I want to tell them things."

"Like what?"

"I wanna be a music artist one day. When I am home alone, I sing and write songs. It is my passion. If my parents knew about it, they would go mad, saying it is not a decent profession. They would ask me what people would say and so on."

"I'm sorry to hear that. Maybe it will get better eventually."

"Maybe…"

"What are you going to do?"

"My dad wants me to study Maths and become an accountant. My mum wants me to study law. I want to study something creative like music or fashion. But there's no way they would allow that."

"Do they check your room or anything? Your phone?"

"I think so. Probably when I'm not home."

While the boys chatted, Magan's mum came in and beckoned to Magan, "Casho waa diyaar wiilashana waa inay yimaadaan miiska cuntada…" She spoke to Magan in Somali for a few moments.

Not bothering that his friends would hear him speak

in his native language, Magan responded, "Haa hooyo, si fiican ayaanu ahaanaynaa waad mahadsantahay."

"Boys," Magan's mum said, turning her attention to the friends, "do you love rice and lamb?"

"Yes, yummy!" they said in unison, and made their way to the dining table.

Magan helped his mum to set the table, decorating it with a lot of vegetables, pastries, and lemonade.

"I love sambusa," Magan said as he looked longingly at the table and licked his lips.

"This is meat pie," Jabez interrupted.

"No, it is sambusa," Magan replied.

"In Nigeria, pastries that look like this are called meat pie. My mum makes them sometimes," Jabez explained.

Magan's mum overheard what the boys were arguing about. She walked up to them and offered to settle the matter.

"Sambusa is a triangular-shaped, fried pastry. You can fill it up with spicy minced meat or vegetables. I will pack some for you to take home to your mum."

"Thank you ma," Jabez replied, Magan and Ben staring at him in disbelief when they heard him say 'ma'.

As the boys ate, Jabez continued his story. "As I was saying, my mum once checked my phone, and she saw a text 'IDEK' on my phone. She seized the phone and did not allow me to take it to school. So, when I returned home, she asked me who IDEK was. I tried to explain that there was no one named IDEK, but she would not believe me. It took my dad to weigh into the matter before I could get my phone. I explained that IDEK was short for 'I don't even know."

The boys bursted into laughter.

Magan laughed nervously. He seemed irritated. "My mum would never do that," he said. "She says I own my personal space. She would not even touch my belongings without permission."

"Ha, I wish," snorted Jabez. "Can you imagine my mum asked me to get her iPad, which I did. She had the laptop on her lap at the time. When I brought the iPad to her, I asked her where she wanted me to put it. She became angry and said, 'Put it on my head.'"

Jabez's friends echoed "put it on my head" and started to laugh hysterically.

"You must be kidding me," Ben said. "It seems no matter what you do, your mum cannot be happy."

"I think she is struggling to accept that I am becoming my own person, and she just freaking wants to control everything I do." Jabez was visibly downcast. "I'm not a bad boy and they know it. She just wants me around doing one domestic chore or the other, and I have to take permission for everything!" he exclaimed.

"It cannot be that bad," Magan said. "At least they look after you well," he continued, pointing to his top-of-the-range sweatshirt and his designer trainers. "I just think your parents are being protective. My parents are strict too, but they do not impose their standards on me. I think it is because I am the last born. My older siblings were not that lucky. Even then, my parents are not too bad," he stated.

"I remember one time," Magan continued, "when I was out with my cousin, Assad. He had given me a polythene bag to hold as he was carrying a lot of shopping. I placed the bag in my rucksack, and I forgot to hand it over to him. I should be fourteen at that time. My mum checked my room and found the polythene bag with a cigarette lighter and two cans of Stella Artois in it. My dear Lord! You should have seen how she yelled at me. I tried to explain it was not mine, but she was having none of it. My mobile phone was taken away, and I was grounded for a month. I could not even play video games for weeks."

"That's messed up," Ben said.

"You can say that again," Magan replied.

"My parents have so much love for my little brother," Jabez said. "I wish I could have some of their time and respect. They refuse to believe I am growing up. It is embarrassing. Do your parents have huge expectations for you?" Jabez asked, looking at each of his friends.

"They want what's best for me, but they are not controlling," Ben said. "I do not ask my mum for permission to go out. I just tell her where I am going."

"Same here," Magan said.

"You are lucky. My mum is strange; she wants to control everything I do."

"I know you're stressed," Ben said, putting a hand on Jabez's shoulder. "We are going to the bowling teen tournament tomorrow. Join us. It will help you take your mind off things. What do you say?"

"If I can convince my mum, why not?" Jabez said with a smile.

* * *

The next day, Lara pretended Jabez did not spend the night away from home without her permission. She was willing to overlook it. In a way, she and Akon understood he was growing up although they were not prepared to fully embrace the idea. They were happy he was safe, spending time with his friends, not doing anything out of the ordinary or being disobedient. The atmosphere was calm, and they had lunch together.

"How was last evening? Did you have fun?" Akon inquired in a friendly tone.

"Lovely. We stayed up late playing video games," said Jabez.

"Were there any girls over?"

"Besides his mom and sister, no."

"Good. I want you to focus on your studies. You have your entire life to find a girlfriend. School is more important now."

"Dad, I'm not seeing anyone."

"Just making sure. We are your parents; we should know."

"If you find a lovely Nigerian girl, you will tell us, right?" added Lara.

"Mum!"

"What?"

"I don't fancy anyone," Jabez said with a red face. However, the question seemed to have brought up other possible issues.

"A mum should know where her son is," Lara said. "Plus, I want nothing but the best for you."

"What if I fall in love with an English girl?" Jabez asked.

"Well, I just thought someone that shares the same values as yours might be a better fit for you," Lara replied.

"I don't mind the English ones. You are raising me here."

"You don't want to upset your father."

"We shall see."

"So, what's the plan for today?"

"Can I see my friends later?"

"Sure. Be home early."

Jabez was surprised he was not punished for his cheeky attempt at escape and was shocked to hear that his parents would let him out again. He just had to promise he would be home by 8.30 pm. With that, Jabez rushed to see his friends.

Although he promised to be home just after eight, Jabez lost track of time. He and his friends were enjoying bowling, doing one set after another. Jabez also forgot that his phone was on silent. When he got home, it was a little past ten. Lara was livid. Akon had tried calling him countless times, but he had not picked up. The storm was about to be unleashed.

"Where were you all this time, and why didn't you pick up your phone?" shouted Lara.

"I was out with Ben and Magan," Jabez explained. "We went to the cinema, so I put my phone on silent. I forgot to turn it back on. I didn't hear the phone ring."

"Am I supposed to believe that? I told you to be home early. Do you know what time it is?"

"Sorry. I lost track."

"Jabez, I know you are sixteen now, but I don't expect you to disobey me when I tell you to do something. Do you want me to ban you from going out with your friends?" Lara snapped "Oh, I wish I could slap you. I told you to come home early as I was supposed to attend a church meeting and needed some help around the house. I missed church because of you. Look at the laundry! Do you want me to come over and teach you a lesson?"

"You can't hit me, Mum," Jabez said confidently. "I am sixteen. This is ridiculous."

"Eeei! What do you mean I cannot hit you? How dare you? Am I not your mother? I am an African mother, and whatever I say goes. I brought you into the world, and I can take you out of it! And what happened to Mama? Now, it's Mum."

"What's wrong with me coming home after 8.30 pm? This is summer; it is bright at night. I am home safe and did not do anything wrong. Anyways, the school says we should report if we are mistreated at home, and we should not encourage an environment of violence. This is London, Mum, not Nigeria, where parents flog their kids. Children are protected by the law here. Social services will come and take me away, and you would be charged in court. So, you should not be talking about flogging me. That is child abuse, Mum, child abuse! You should be asking to speak to me, not threaten me!"

Lara was appalled. "How can you talk to me like that? This is all your friends' fault. They are teaching you the worst things. You do not have a say so long as you live under my roof. You are going to do exactly as I tell you! You are not allowed to see those friends of yours anymore."

"If you dare touch me, I will tell the school counsellor about it, and he will call the police."

"How dare you!"

"Lara, stop," Akon interrupted. "Let me have a word," he said, beckoning to his wife.

Akon took Lara into their room. This situation was about to escalate, and it was not something he was prepared to see. Jabez might have been late, but he was a teenager, and they could not risk his future because of it.

"We can't go on like this, Lara. Jabez is growing up. We need to give him some freedom. We moved to this country to provide him a better future, a new purpose. It is only natural that he sees things other kids are doing and wants them too.

"Parents here are more relaxed, and while we cannot be like them, let us try to understand and support him. Jabez is a good kid. We need to trust him. Let us meet him halfway, otherwise, we will lose our boy. He would not tell us what he is going through if we go on like this. Or worse, he will say we are abusing him, and they will take him away from us. He would be placed in a hostel with kids from all sorts of backgrounds, and that would not help him. He may even decide not to go to university because his mind would be messed up. I am not saying we should let him do anything he wants, but we should let him have friends. He can have sleepovers and go out without us breathing down his neck. What do you think?"

"You are right. I was worried, and I thought something bad had happened to my boy. I just want us to be part of his life, to know what he's doing."

"I understand. We need to be gentler. He's not a little boy anymore."

"I will try."

"I have an idea. Let us have a barbecue. We can invite his friends over and get to know them. Don't you think he would like that?"

Lara sighed. Jabez was revolting against her, and she could not do anything about it. What went wrong? How could she fix this? Without hesitation, she nodded. Maybe if she were softer, Jabez would share more with her.

"Fine, I'll tell him about it," she replied.

Lara went upstairs and knocked at Jabez's bedroom door. She went in and found him in tears on his bed. He tried hiding it, but a mother can always sense such things.

"Are you okay?" she asked, caressing his hair.

"Yeah. Why? Did you come here to threaten me again?"

"No, dear. I have come to say I am sorry for yelling at you. I have talked to your father, and I think it is time we give you some independence. We just want to know where you are and what you are doing. Can you give us that reassurance?"

Jabez was taken aback. "It is not as simple as that, Mum," he said. "You have changed. You no longer joke with me, tell me stories, or carry me along. This changed when... all because of Ephraim."

Lara was surprised. "Nothing changed, my dear," she insisted. "Let us talk about this. What exactly do you want?" Lara wiped a tear away from her eye. The pressure of adjusting to a new life in London and all that had happened in her marriage had taken a toll on her emotionally. She realised she had indirectly taken this out on her son. "Again, I am sorry. That is why I am here to make amends. Is that understood?"

"I just want parents that understand me and let me be myself. I am not a bad child, but at the same time, I am no longer a baby," sniffed Jabez.

"I have just been protective. Maybe my methods are not working. I now realise that and want to correct them."

Jabez paused before saying, "I would like to do DJ work at weekends. I want DJ equipment."

"Okay," Lara said with a slow nod, "your dad will get the equipment as long as we know the specifications."

"Promise?" said Jabez. His face brightened up, and he hugged his mum,

"I'll try if you will too."

"Promise."

"We are also planning a barbecue for the end of the month, just for a few people," his mother added. "We'd like to meet your friends. Can you invite them over? We will invite some friends from the Nigerian community, our neighbours, and one other friend from church. There shouldn't be more than fifteen people."

"That would be amazing," Jabez smiled. "Can I choose the music?"

"If that's what you like. But remember to have diverse music too, to reflect the audience."

"Sure, Mum."

35

It was a bright day with no clouds. Akon managed the barbecue while the boys chatted away, snacking on all the hotdogs and other small chops Lara prepared. Jabez's friends were excited to see his house and family. They brought gifts for Lara, a beautiful bouquet of flowers that she displayed on the table.

Jabez could not believe how tolerant his parents could be when they wanted to. Even the neighbours had fun. Jabez was the DJ. The future seemed bright, and nothing could have spoilt it.

*   *   *

Jabez got a summer holiday job while waiting for his A-level results. He took the tray he held to a table in his section and then leaned against the wall to catch his breath. From the corner of his eye, he spied two men walking into the restaurant. There was something weird about them, but just as Jabez moved closer to get a good look, a customer yelled.

"I said I wanted a muffin and a latte, not a cappuccino!" Jabez turned at the roar, searching for the customer. It was from the other side of the room, and he saw Rehaan scurrying to the counter with a tray. He did not have to search long for the source of the bellow. The man had continued his rant in a lower tone, though it was still audible above the voices of other customers.

"These immigrants are a pain in the neck. He probably doesn't understand the language we speak." Jabez winced at the man's contemptuous tone, anger welling up within him when he saw Rehaan's unhappy expression.

"It's alright, George, dear," the woman seated opposite him said. "The poor things would starve if they stayed in their countries. At least, they have a fighting chance here."

The man muttered under his breath, and Jabez shook his head. When he first came to the UK, he was shocked at the animosity and hatred with which the blacks were treated. Now, he had become used to it. Though he sometimes wished things would change.

He was lucky enough to have come here when he was younger because it had been easier for him to pick up English mannerisms and a British accent. He did not face as much prejudice like his mum who still spoke with a hint of Yoruba accent.

A customer signalled to him, and he headed off at once. Just as he moved past the window after getting the customer what he wanted, he saw a vehicle with an insignia he recognised as that of the immigration officials and remembered the two men who had walked in earlier. With a shrug, he continued walking towards the staff break room to rest for a moment. Rehaan and Dakarai, his two closest friends amongst the staff, were in the middle of a deep conversation.

"So, don't worry about customers like that, okay?" Dakarai said supportively. "You must have a thick skin because people like that will always be there. Some are even worse."

Getting the gist of the conversation, Jabez joined them, nodding. "I have seen worse since I started working here. You will get used to it."

They continued to encourage Rehaan before the conversation shifted. "I can't believe today was so busy," Rehaan groaned, sinking into one of the chairs. "I am exhausted."

"I know, right? My legs feel like they would fall off,"

Dakarai added.

"Did you guys see those immigration officers when they came in?" Jabez asked, also sitting down while he massaged one of his calves. He was looking down, so he did not notice the look of shock across his friends' faces.

"What immigration officers?" Rehaan asked. It was his panicked tone that made Jabez look up.

"The ones that came in about fifteen minutes ago." Rehaan sprang up from his chair, as did Dakarai. Surprised, Jabez stood and followed them as they moved towards the front door, ignoring the customers trying to gain their attention. However, they stopped short when they saw a couple of policemen standing outside the door.

"Jabez, do you know where the key to the back door is kept?" Dakarai asked, since Jabez had been working there before them. "Please, you need to help me. I do not have proper papers. I came here with a visitor's visa, and it has expired. The man who promised to help me secure a permanent residence went underground as soon as I paid him the six hundred pounds he asked for. Please, Jabez."

"That's horrible," Jabez said, his surprise changed to understanding and pity. He had heard of stories like this before, and human wickedness never ceased to amaze him. "But I don't know where the key is. Mr Ajah started keeping the key when he discovered that staff used the door to steal things out of the restaurant and come in late to work."

"What am I going to do now?" Rehaan asked. "I have been using my cousin's papers since he went back home to Bangladesh. The officers will realise I'm not the one if they see the documents."

Jabez had always thought it was only the dodgy ones who had false papers, but he knew better from what his friends had gone through before coming to the UK. He could not blame them for doing what they did to escape their previous situations. "I wish I could help. I'm sorry."

"Well, there's nothing I can do," Rehaan said "I have to get past those officers at the door before the immigration guys come out."

Rehaan tried to escape, but the officers stopped him from leaving until the immigration officers came out. The workers were told to gather in the break room.

Just as they expected, Mr Ajah told them the officers wanted to see their papers. It soon became apparent that Rehaan and Dakarai did not have proper documentation, so they were taken out forcefully. The dissatisfied customers left without paying when it became clear no one was paying them any attention. When Mr Ajah told

Olivia Olajide Aluko

the staff to go home because the restaurant's license had been suspended indefinitely, Jabez felt sad for the man. He was a nice man. It was an oversight for him not to ensure his employees' papers were up to date.

Later that evening, Jabez recounted the story to his parents. "Don't be too bothered about them. The worst that can happen is deportation. It's not a death sentence," his mother had said.

"But it is not fair. I know they did not have the right papers, but that does not mean they are bad people. They are not here to steal. They just want to work and survive."

"Jabez," his father said unsympathetically, "proper procedure should always be followed. If the country allows people who do not have their papers to come in, it could lead to something else. I know it is not easy. You were young when we came here, so you might not remember all we had to do. At some point, we had to sell all our properties back in Nigeria. We were almost homeless, but thanks for some friends who helped. You have to man up and face challenges, son."

They talked for a while, and Jabez could not help but notice that his parents were acting agitated even though they sympathised with his friends and boss. "What is the problem with you guys anyway?" he asked. "Why are you jittery?"

His mother had been waiting for him to ask this all along. She flung her arms around him immediately. "Oh, Jabez, you have made us proud." His father was smiling at him.

Confused, he let his mum hug him before gently withdrawing from her arms. "What happened? What did I do?"

"Son," his father said when Lara burst into tears. "Your A-Level results came in. You smashed all your papers."

"Yes!" he screamed, pumping his fist in the air.

They spent the rest of the night celebrating, and Jabez later got admitted into the prestigious Durham University to study Music and Philosophy.

* * *

Lara was preparing to attend an award night where her NGO was nominated for an award.

"Honey, I am happy my NGO was chosen," she said to Akon. "I didn't know that my work was being noticed."

Adjusting his bowtie, Akon replied, "You are not the only excited one here. I cannot hold back my delight! You know I do not normally attend these things. But since my queen is the one being celebrated, where else would I rather be?"

Jabez, who had come back from the university, was elated at the joyous atmosphere. Ranti and Ephraim were not left out. Lara had decided it should be a family outing. She bought tickets for everyone.

The night was filled with entertainment, music, heartfelt speeches, and sumptuous food. It was a night to remember. The very thought of the nomination was enough cause for celebration.

Akon, bubbling with pride and laughter, lifted his wine glass and toasted his wife, Lara. "Cheers to the best decision I have ever made in life." In response, Lara grabbed his arm lovingly and thought of how far they had come. If someone had told her earlier that they would come this far, she would have laughed in mockery.

She reminisced on the things she and Akon had achieved. Their level of success in the community was nearly unrivalled. They were known in diverse groups, and for this award, she was nominated under the category of Creative Arts. Lara did clay work; she was versatile with modelling clay, plasticine. She could create anything from animals, clothes to human pieces. Also, she had recently been given a contract to supply KYZ Toy Shops with some modelling toys. This was a big deal for Lara and Akon. A lot of good things were happening to them. In the school where Lara taught storytelling using plasticine, which was also Ephraim's school, she had become the school governor. This new position gave Lara the much-needed connection to get big contracts for her art.

On Akon's part, he was not doing badly at all. He had started a novel coaching programme called "Soaring Heights." He was invited to speak at top financial institutions and universities in the UK within the first two years of the project. Akon had begun expanding his business in Africa—Kenya, Uganda, and his homeland, Nigeria.

On the evening before the award night, they had hosted the third day of the exhibition night. Lara had been working intensely to meet up with the demands of her new clients. Ranti also stopped by to help her, while Akon covered the technicalities. Lara took two days off work. She was exhausted and felt queasy. She assumed she had the flu or had just overworked.

"I am not feeling well, I guess it is time for that much-needed vacation," Lara said to Ranti.

"I couldn't agree more. Once these events are over, I am booking an all-expenses-paid vacation for you," Ranti replied.

To this, Lara laughed and said, "So, who will run my NGO? I will be fine, my dear."

Apart from her art, she also had an NGO for women migrants and refugees who had experienced violence. This was a passion she had always nursed, and she was happy she could now bring it to fruition. Part of her responsibilities involved linking these women with qualified human right lawyers. She also had a bundle of clothes and shoes specifically for the immigrants. She even turned her garage into a collection hub.

One day, after all the work on the collection, she slept on the sofa. She did not want to go through the stress of going up and down the stairs when the delivery came to pick up the shoebox collection. Suddenly, she felt nauseous and used the toilet downstairs instead of going upstairs.

Although the vomiting stopped, she still had symptoms of tiredness and nausea. The next day, she stopped at the pharmacy to pick up a vitamin B complex. She instinctively picked up a clear blue pregnancy toolkit. *There is no harm in checking.* This time she did not want to involve Akon.

Lara got home a few minutes later, and she prepared the dinner table. She had already picked up Ephraim from the after-school club which closed at 6.00 pm. She hummed to herself, thinking of how much she enjoyed the flexible nature of her work. Following this, she went to the bathroom and conducted the pregnancy test, her heart thumping as it read positive. She had bought two kits and decided to repeat the test the following day.

It read positive again.

She planned to see her GP and requested that a test be conducted. She was booked with an immediate appointment to see the nurse who conducted the right tests and blood samples. The results showed she had mild anaemia and was pregnant. Lara did not know whether to be happy or sad; she was in shock and unsure how Akon would take the news. Ephraim's pregnancy had been full of stress, which she did not want to experience again.

When Akon returned home, Lara requested that they talk after dinner, even though Akon's favourite team, Chelsea, was playing. She said, "Baby, we need to talk."

Akon, surprised that she called him baby, decided to act like one. "Oh no, can't it wait?" Then, noticing the serious look on his wife's face, he gently asked, "What is up?"

Akon loved his Sports Channel and did not like being distracted when football matches were on. So, he told his wife, "The match starts at 8.00 pm and the time is 7.15 pm. I would appreciate it if you can be quick with it."

Lara, not noticing the haste in Akon's voice, decided to start by dropping hints. "I have picked up another bunch of flowers."

"And what does that mean?" asked her husband.

"A new shoe size," she joked, as Akon was getting irritated.

Lara said, "You are as clueless as you were when Jabez was born. Can't you just guess?"

"I am too tired to think."

Lara tried one more time. "Okay, I have bought a new puppy."

"You never had an old one!" Akon fiddled with the remote control so he could catch up with the commentary.

Lara walked close to where he was seated and whispered in his ear, barely able to hide her emotions. "I am pregnant!" she cried.

"If this is a joke, stop it now," Akon replied.

She tucked her hand into her handbag and brought out the test results she received from the GP. Akon's mouth opened in wonder. He could not say a word. He switched off the TV and asked when it happened.

"Well, I hope it is you this time," said Lara, "and not a fraudster. When the child is born, we will do a DNA test. I don't want any games."

"I would not mind too. What if it is your turn to play games?" Akon said as they hugged and kissed. "We must dance to this one. What genre of music do you fancy?" he asked Lara. "Yes, I know. I'll play Dolly Parton's *I will always love you*."

Akon looked through his record collections, but he could not find it.

"Why don't we play Whitney's instead?" Lara suggested.

Akon hummed the song as it played, holding his wife tenderly and kissing her all over.

"Look into my eyes, darling. Thanks for staying with me through thick and thin, for better and worse." Akon said in a husky voice.

A tear dropped from Lara's eyes, but he wiped it away and kissed her.

While they danced, the doorbell rang, and Ranti came in with her boyfriend. She was smiling sheepishly at her parents.

"Hello, mum, dad. What are we celebrating?" Ranti asked.

"It's a secret." Akon winked. "Who is this young man?"

"Oh, forgive my manners. Mum and dad, meet Robert, my boyfriend. Robert, meet my parents." She did the introductions shyly. Akon raised his brow at the word boyfriend.

"Hello, sir, ma'am. It's a pleasure to meet you." Robert said, extending his hand for a handshake.

"The pleasure is ours, my dear. Sit, please. Ranti, get two glasses and pour some wine." Lara smiled.

*   *   *

Lara was seven months gone. This pregnancy was not complicated like what she experienced with Jabez and Ephraim's. Everything sailed on smoothly until one day, when Akon heard his wife cry out in the kitchen. He dashed to the kitchen and bent over on the spot where his wife sat, writhing in pain.

"What is the problem, my love? It isn't time yet, is it?"

"My waist! My waist!" that was all Lara managed to say as she grabbed and pulled at Akon's shirt as if that would make her feel better.

"Don't worry, Lara. You will be fine. Can you stand? Let me take you to the hospital." Lara managed to get up tö her feet, and Akon led her to the car. Soon they were on their way. On getting to the hospital, Nurse Amy had an ultra-scan conducted on Lara, and the look on her face told Akon she did not have good news.

"The baby is in a breech position. I have spoken with the head Obstetrician, and he has instructed that Lara should be admitted for close observation."

"How long will she have to stay?"

"Well, three days, for now. Let us see how she progresses. Meanwhile, ensure you see the doctor before you leave."

Akon had gone to see the doctor and left shortly

after. On the third day, the doctor walked into the ward while Akon helped Lara get some food in her mouth.

"I'm glad you are here, Akon. We may have to conduct a Caesarean section on your wife today to get the foetus out to avoid further complications."

"A Caesarean section? Will they be safe, doctor? Is there no other option?"

"They will be fine, Mr Akon," the doctor said with a reassuring smile.

Lara held her husband, smiled and said, "I have faith."

Akon was pacing about in the reception as he prayed for his wife and child's safety.

The midwife and attending nurses had already taken Lara to the recovery room to clean her and the baby up before breaking the news to Akon. "Congratulations, Mr Akon. You have become the father to a healthy little girl."

Akon was ecstatic.

They led him to the ward to see his wife and baby. Relief washed through him as he set his eyes on them.

"Babe, are you alright?" Akon asked as he planted a kiss on his wife's cheek.

Tabitha Oluwangbotemi Akete was born in the 34th week of conception. They watched as the nurse placed the band on the baby's hand.

"We are going to have a big celebration," Akon stated as he brought out his mobile phone to capture the baby's first picture.

Acknowledgements

I have nursed the idea of writing a novel ever since I was very young, and to think that this dream is being realised decades after is amazing. The experience of turning an idea into a novel is both internally challenging and ultimately rewarding.

As a person of faith, I want to thank the Lord for sparing my life against all odds. Without His favour and love, this novel may never have come to light.

I am grateful for my parents, the late Prof Olajide Aluko, a writer in his lifetime, and Mrs Dayo Aluko, for instilling the discipline of reading and writing in me from an early age.

Special heartfelt thanks to my siblings, Sophia and her husband Sam Adesina, for timely suggestions on how I can improve the novel; Dr (Mrs) Yinka and her husband, Dr Lanre Olatunde; and Dipe Aluko, for checking up on me.

Special thanks to my accountability partners, whose positive words spurred me on to complete this work. Interestingly, they are all authors themselves: Lade Olugbemi, the Chief Executive of the Nous Charity Incorporated Organisation, for being the cheer leader on my writing journey; Temitope Olodo, President, African Security Forum, for his insightful perspectives; and Christopher Aniche, Owner/Partner, Curling Moore Solicitors, who would not allow me to put any limitation on myself.

I would like to thank Dr Remi Ajibewa, Director Political Affairs of the Economic Community of West African States (ECOWAS), for providing useful insight about the career development challenges that professionals from African background face in the UK. Thanks also to Dr Ezi Mecha for showing interest in the novel.

I nicknamed this book my "lockdown novel" because I wrote it during the 2020 pandemic lockdown, at a time of severe personal health challenges. I wrote some of the chapters lying down in bed or on the floor, with no real energy to get up. On this note, I want to appreciate the practical support of friends and comrades like Bola Oyediran, Jumoke Kukoyi, Ajoke Falase, Paul Akinbadewa, Omolola Oyewusi, Seyi

Obadare, Clive Coward, Joseph Adamson, Councillor Joanne Howcroft-Scott, and a host of others space will not allow me to mention by name.

It takes a village to write a novel too! While growing up in Nigeria, I was exposed to the literature works of African authors such as Chinua Achebe, Flora Nwakpa, Ngugi Wa Thiong, Wole Soyinka, and Helen Ovbiagele. Also, I have been challenged by the following female writers of African heritage: Chimamanda Adichie, Abi Daré, Oyinkan Braithwaite, Ukamaka Olisakwe. The authentic African flavour they added to their literary works was an encouragement to me that I was on the right path.

Finally, this work could not have been completed without the patience and professionalism of my publishing team: Mellisa, Toks, and Aisha.

Have you enjoyed reading *Life in the Abrodi*?
Kindly leave a review on Amazon—
if you purchased the book.

To contact the author:

Website: https://reinvent3r.org/

Email: olivia4changes@gmail.com

Printed in Great Britain
by Amazon